LANGUAGE AND STYLE IN
Leaves of Grass

LANGUAGE AND STYLE IN
Leaves of Grass

C. Carroll Hollis

Louisiana State University Press

Baton Rouge and London

Copyright © 1983 by Louisiana State University Press
All rights reserved
Manufactured in the United States of America

Designer: Barbara Werden
Typeface: Linotron Monticello
Typesetter: G & S Typesetters, Inc.
Printer: Thomson-Shore, Inc.

Library of Congress Cataloging in Publication Data

Hollis, C. Carroll (Charles Carroll), 1911–
Language and style in Leaves of grass.

Bibliography: p.
Includes index.
1. Whitman, Walt, 1819–1892.   Leaves of grass.
2. Whitman, Walt, 1819–1892—Style.   I. Title.
PS3244.H6   1983   811'.3   82-20881
ISBN 0-8071-1096-5

To and for A.W.H.

Contents

Preface and Acknowledgments

There have been many new discoveries, approaches, and analytic tools for examining poetry in the past few decades, but with little application to *Leaves of Grass*. The unfortunate result is that many features of Whitman's early poetry, as distinct from that written after the Civil War, have not been explained, nor has the nature of that major change in the poetry been clearly understood. I have no formal training in computer analysis, linguistics, semiotics, or structuralist criticism, but after sufficient rereading and familiarizing myself with new terms, it was possible to describe characteristics of Whitman's poetry that escaped previous commentators. I have not wanted to depart from a study of the text to the quite different task of hypothesizing the person who created that text. There are occasional guesses as to why he did this or that, but they are not to be considered with the same seriousness that I hope will be given to the stylistic examination of the poetry.

Originally I had planned to make individual studies for periodical publication, with the idea of ultimately bringing them together. But I soon found that cumulative evidence was necessary both to explain what Whitman was doing in the early editions and what stylistic changes occurred later. Thus the present book. At the time I was going through my own reeducation and was making initial discoveries about Whitman's style, a festschrift was being planned for my colleague Lewis Leary. I was most anxious to add to such a fine tribute to an old friend, but at the time that book went to press I was unable to find and then to free a chapter from the before-and-after involvement. That intended contribution for Lewis ultimately resulted in the second section of Chapter II, entitled "Oratorical Cadence." I had known about the *cursus* in a general way but had not read Morris Croll since graduate school, yet the festschrift occasioned that small but most surprising investigation. It was an enjoyable article to write, turns out to have provided independent confirmation of the oral origins of Whitman's poetry, and finds a place in this book after all—with special affection and respect to its unwitting instigator.

The rationale for the other chapters and their order will be apparent in the chapters as presented, but perhaps a few words may help. No biographer has yet explained the origins of *Leaves of Grass*, mostly because there is so little evidence to work with. But it does seem to me that we ought to work with such evidence as we do have, particularly what survives of those "barrels" of lectures written after he returned from New Orleans in 1848. Chapter I draws such stylistic inferences from those lectures and other notes to himself as seem necessary to explain the motivation and style of the first edition. Although I have great admiration for Whitman's poetic achievement, I have none at all for that self-publicity, and I hope my annoyance has not interfered with my critical evaluation of the poetry. For this chapter I expand a lecture given at the University of Tulsa symposium some ten years ago.

But Whitman did not only write and publish a new kind of poetry, he also changed as years went on. As he changed, so did the poetry. To the extent, indeed, that after reading "Song of Myself" one might think "Song of the Exposition" was written by a different person—which, in a quite real sense, it was and he was. Accordingly, the early poetry (what I call "platform poetry") ought to have oral features not found in poetry written after the Civil War. These are explored in Chapter II: first, in the contrast between the early lectures and the once popular poetry of Martin Farquhar Tupper; then, in the specifically oratorical feature, the *cursus*. But as Whitman changed in later years, he not only wrote a different sort of poetry but also tried to change the original poetry as well. There has not been a wholly satisfactory treatment of the many revisions, even though the new *Variorum* now makes it possible. The problems of organization of such a study would be enormous (for just a listing would be self-defeating), but the last part of Chapter II attempts to show why it should be done. My subjective delight in the original lines may have tempered my response to the revisions, but I trust the presentation of both the original and the changed line will support my claim of his adoption of a different poetic stance.

Chapters III and V are extensive, not because their subjects are so difficult but because I found that my colleagues knew too little about the speech-act theory or about metonymy to understand the relation to *Leaves of Grass*. That relation is, however, of major consequence. Although long, these two chapters represent the reduction and simplification of major books and articles. Since no book of the sort intended here can be read at one time, I have interposed the shorter Chapter IV, on negation, between those two long chapters to make the going a bit easier. I apologize for the use of anthologies in that chapter and elsewhere, but it seemed the only honest way to handle comparisons without computer assistance. The size of that chapter has nothing to do with the importance of its subject, for negation is not only a striking feature of the early editions but a significant stylistic feature of all literary writing, and one that merits much more attention than it has so far received.

My first intention was to put Chapter VI, on Whitman's journalistic carry-overs, right after the treatment of his oratorical concerns, but that seemed more confusing than helpfully expository on this other ignored part of Whitman's "poetic" training. I am less happy with that chapter for other reasons than just where to put it, for it opens up a problem of what we, as serious literary scholars, ought to label, to call, *Leaves of Grass*. It is proper to call it poetry, of course, but that term is not descriptive enough to suggest the illocutionary, metonymic, journalistic, and hortatory character that signifies the spirit of the early editions.

If I am least happy with the sixth chapter, most Whitman scholars will probably be disappointed with the conclusion. Poetic style is more than an accumulation or even a blending of contributing parts, and I too believe that style is the man. The trouble is that we still do not know enough about the man to be certain how the style was achieved. Just last night I was putting away some notes and came across this strange little reminder to himself that I found in the 1857 Autograph Notebook, and had forgotten to mention in this study:

> The importance of the individual —— that is
>   the greatest
> the ----------------------------------- —— that is
>   the
> the ----------------------------------- —— that is
>   the

It is only another of those many devices he used to supply order, to impose structure, on the otherwise chaotic outpouring of his imagined experience. Traditional prosody was beyond him, and when he used it what he had to say was so limited to the confines of the form that the result is ludicrous. But the traditional devices of oratory (of which the above is typical), although never applied to poetry before in the fashion he developed, did give him a language control that had no Procrustean dangers. It was, then, a discipline of sorts. Loose as that control was, it was essential, for without discipline, without order, without artistic control, no poetry is possible. The diagram, or schemata, in the concluding chapter for "Who Learns My Lesson Complete" is intended to draw attention to his skillful use of such rhetorical devices, and I hope its appearance will not give the uninitiated a structuralist shock.

As are all Whitman scholars, I am much indebted to the famous collector Charles Feinberg. But my indebtedness goes back to the centennial year of *Leaves* when he introduced me to the many discoveries of Whitman's poetic craft available through the study of the drafts, notebooks, and language notes in his Whitman collection. Charles gave me carte blanche to the many manuscript treasures in that collection, and I still remember the contagious excitement with which we first worked out Whitman's reasons for saving the only surviving page of the manuscript of the first edition. Charles Feinberg's enthusiasm, his remarkable knowledge of Whitman, his unfailing generosity and support of Whitman projects are legendary, but it is an honor to salute once more his friendly aid and encouragement. I am also much indebted, if in not quite so personal fashion, to the Rare Book Room at Duke University and to the Manuscripts Division at the Library of Congress for use of their Trent and Harned collections, respectively.

All teachers are obligated to their students, but it is good to acknowledge the patience of those in a number of Whitman seminars on whom I tested many of the ideas in this book. I am also indebted to my former colleague, the late Forrest Read, for many lively arguments that helped clarify my analysis, and to my present colleague, Louis D. Rubin, Jr., whose editorial advice has kept me from numerous blunders. My greatest indebtedness, for reasons which she best knows, is to the person to whom the book is dedicated.

Abbreviations

The following works appear frequently enough to make these abbreviations useful:

AR	*American Renaissance* (F. O. Matthiessen)
In Re	*In Re Walt Whitman*
NF	*Notes and Fragments* (R. M. Bucke, editor)
PW	*Prose Works 1892*, II (Floyd Stovall, editor)
UPP	*The Uncollected Poetry and Prose*, II (Emory Holloway, editor)
WWW	*Walt Whitman's Workshop* (Clifton Furness, editor)

Occasionally I use a shortened title for a well-known poem, particularly when the title is used many times in adjoining paragraphs. This is a common practice in the classroom and should be a convenience for the reader here. I select a key word ("Myself" for "Song of Myself," "Ferry" for "Crossing Brooklyn Ferry," etc.) but only after I have used the full title.

LANGUAGE AND STYLE IN
Leaves of Grass

❧ I ❧

THE ORATORICAL IMPULSE

There is no evidence that Walt Whitman had the personality, the temperament, the character to be an orator, a lay preacher, a lyceum lecturer, a prophet, an abolition speaker, or a public spokesman for any other cause. To the extent that teaching, even teaching at the grade-school level as he did briefly, demands oral presentation, there is no evidence of his proficiency, and the fact that he soon gave up that profession would indicate otherwise. The limited records of the Smithtown Debating Society could just as easily support the view that he joined to help himself improve his speaking ability as that he joined because he enjoyed debating and had skill at it. Nothing in the biographical record demonstrates any flair for or talent in public life, leadership roles, or even the give-and-take of group activity, whether organized or not.

Indeed, he seems to be the least activist of any of our great literary men, even Nathaniel Hawthorne. Like Hawthorne, he was an observer, and a very shrewd one, but Hawthorne, much as he dreaded it, could give a public speech once in a while—he once said, "The only way they'll get me to give a speech is when I'm cornered or when I'm cornered." The difference between them was that Hawthorne never wanted the challenges of the public arena but went along when necessary, whereas Whitman did want that challenge but could never take it. Journalism was a good career for him; he was close to public life, developed a proficiency in handling language, reported on the buzzing confusion of metropolitan life as well as on the books he read. But he would never have been a major journalist had he remained with the newspapers, for like any profession there are challenges with one's peers that successful journalists meet on their way to becoming major editors.

But it is not of major concern that Whitman did not become an orator—for my purposes it is enough to show that he wanted to be, thought he had the requisite mental qualifications (which he did) and the voice (which he did not) and the presence or character or temperament or genius. On this last, he always believed he had this potentiality, blinded himself to evidence to the contrary, invented evidence to support his belief, and welcomed interpretations of his poetry that confirmed it. It was fine when he got his friends to publish under their names his interpretation of *Leaves of Grass* as prophetic (as biographers John Burroughs and R. M. Bucke did, or the journalist Richard Hinton), but before he found such willing support he had to supply it himself in those anonymous reviews.

Three of these of the first edition are found in that catchall volume edited by his executors after his death, *In Re*. Here are some of his homemade puffs (my italics):

An American *bard* at last! One of the roughs, large, proud, affectionate, eating, drinking, and breeding, his costume manly and free, his face sunburnt and bearded, his postures strong and erect, his *voice* bringing hope and *prophecy* to the generous faces of young and old. (p. 13)

Self-reliant, with haughty eyes, assuming to himself all the attributes of his country, steps Walt Whitman into literature, *talking like a man unaware that there was ever hitherto such a production as a book*, or *such a being as a writer*. . . . Every word that *falls from his mouth* shows silent disdain and defiance of the old theories and forms. Every phrase announces new laws; not once *do his lips unclose* except in conformity with them. (p. 14)

For these ["the essences of American things"] the old usages of poets afford Walt Whitman no means sufficiently fit and free, and he rejects the old usages. *The style of the bard* that is waited for is to be transcendent and new. It is to be indirect, and not direct or descriptive or epic. (p. 16)

With *strong and steady call he addresses* men. Come, he seems to say, from the midst of all that you have been your whole life surrounding yourself with. Leave all the *preaching and teaching* of others, and mind only these words of mine. (p. 18)

The effects he produces in his poems are *no effects of artists or the arts*, but effects of the original eye or arm, or the actual atmosphere, or tree, or bird. You may feel the *unconscious teaching of a fine brute*, but will never feel the *artificial teaching of a fine writer or speaker*. (p. 24)

Such as the heavens envelop the earth, if the Americans want *a race of bards worthy of 1855*, and of the stern reality of this republic, they must cast around for men essentially *different from the old poets*, and from the modern succession of *jinglers and snivellers and fops*. (p. 28)

But having friends and followers stressing the prophetic reading of *Leaves* or advertising his own persona as in the self-reviews was nowhere near as exciting and self-confirming as the unsought-for and free praise of established critics. The farther away they might be, the better: their remarks demonstrated the independent interpretation of the work itself, freed of the presumably necessary publicity at home. A good example would be the favorable and extensive article-review by the French critic Gabriel Sarrazin. This is the essay that Whitman got so excited about that he took W. S. Kennedy's translation (without alerting Kennedy that he was doing so), had it printed, and sent it everywhere to papers, magazines, friends and acquaintants, because it said about his work what he wanted people to know and accept. Here is an example of what caught his attention:

> The man who thus announces himself—himself and his race—brings at the same time *a word absolutely new*, a form *instinctively audacious*, novel, *overstepping all literary conventions*. He creates a *rhythm of his own, less rigid than verse, more broken than prose—a rhythm adapted to the movement of his emotion*, hastened as it hastens, precipitated, abated, led into repose. At times *he will utter an almost Hebraic chant*, quitted anon as he enlarges or abandons himself to the theme. . . . *His writings come forth glowing and direct, with an immediate significance and as if spoken. As those of the ancient prophet poets his words are addressed to the assembled people.* (*In Re*: 159–60; my italics)

Sarrazin was right and Whitman knew it. In *Leaves of Grass* the words do "come forth . . . direct" and "as if spoken." It has the form of the "Hebraic chant" and of "the ancient prophet poets." Its style is that of words "addressed to the assembled people." This is no rediscovery of mine, for Jean Catel and F. O. Matthiessen stressed it, and there have been more recent articles that find the bardic or prophetic manner in the early poetry. In 1971, for instance, B. Bernard Cohen edited *Whitman in Our Season: A Symposium*, in which many of the articles referred to this prophetic strain. In particular, a fine analysis by F. DeWolfe Miller (pp. 11–17) of "Song of Myself" traces the announcement, the appearance, and the details of the function of the new and native poet-messiah. The late Bruce McElderry, in what may have been among the last of his valuable contributions to American literary scholarship, "Personae in Whitman (1855–1860)" (pp. 25–32), traced the five roles he finds in the first three editions: "the orator, the bard, the realistic observer, the personal Walt Whitman, and the lyrist." I agree with this provocative yet correct analysis of these personae and differ only in the evaluation. He thinks Whitman outgrew the "bardic inflation" of the early poems to reach the "lyric perfection" of "such a later masterpiece as 'When Lilacs Last in the Dooryard Bloom'd.'"

There seems to be, then, agreement among some Whitman critics that there is an oratorical element in Whitman's poetry. The question whether that element is in Whitman, or in the poetry, or in both has not been answered. Whitman returned from New Orleans in early summer of 1848, and it is customary to think he was a changed person, although there is little clear evidence from any objective witness. His brother George, perhaps the most ordinary, businesslike, and unflappable member of the family, does recall of this phase of Walt's activity: "I guess it was about those years he had an idea he could lecture. He wrote what mother called 'barrels' of lectures. We did not know what he was writing. He did not seem more abstracted than usual" (*In Re:* 10). What were those lectures? Most biographers have assumed that they were literally lectures, never given, and since discarded. But Whitman, as far as I can tell, never threw away anything for which he might find the remotest possible use.

Rather, it seems to me, what George and his mother called the "barrels" of lectures was that storehouse of thoughts and ideas and notes and doodling which later did get published in Bucke's *Notes and Fragments*, Clifton Furness' *Walt Whitman's Workshop*, Clarence Gohdes and Rollo Silver's *Faint Clews & Indirections*, Emory Holloway's *Uncollected Poetry and Prose*, plus the large amount of unpublished material in the Feinberg, Harned, and Trent manuscript collections. In all of this material, published and unpublished, there is not a single completed draft for a lecture, although there are an amazing number of notes relating to public speaking, sometimes opening or closing paragraphs of projected addresses, guides on oratory and elocution, hints to get this or that into some lecture, projected titles for a publication of his collected lectures (even though he had not written any), homemade advertisements for his lectures, and comments about the role of the public speaker in the middle of the nineteenth century. Indeed, they seem to be more the products of fantasy than of practical preparation for a specific talk. They do not reveal that Whitman was or could have been a famous orator, but they do show that he wanted to be.

To begin with this last, much of the reason that students of Whitman have overlooked the relationship of public speaking to *Leaves* is that the role of the orator has so diminished in our day that most of us would find it hard to give credence to the notion that a genius of Whitman's rank should be tempted by the podium. But for Whitman, as for most Americans, public speaking, oratory, was the the great art of the nineteenth century. What Ralph Waldo Emerson thought of the lyceum is certainly not so esoteric that Whitman might not have also had similar thoughts. Emerson, however, had the journal-keeping habit, and from the 1839 *Journal* Matthiessen quotes this revealing passage:

> *Eloquence. Lyceum.* Here is all the true orator will ask, for here is a convertible audience, and here are no stiff conventions that prescribe a method, a style, a limited quotation of books and an exact respect to certain books, persons, or opinions. No, here everything is admissible, philosophy, ethics, divinity, criticism, poetry, humor, fun, mimicry, anecdotes, jokes, ventriloquism, all the breadth and versatility of the most liberal conversation; highest, lowest, personal, local topics, all are permitted, and all may be combined in one speech;—it is a panharmonicon. . . . Here is a pulpit that makes other pulpits tame and ineffectual—with their cold, mechanical preparation for a delivery most decorous—fine things, pretty things, wise things, but no arrows, no axes, no nectar, no growling, no transpiercing, no loving, no enchantment. Here he may lay himself out utterly, large, enormous, prodigal, on the subject of the hour. Here he may dare to hope for ecstasy and eloquence. (AR: 23–24)

Having quoted the passage, Matthiessen cannot but note what any reader of Whitman can see: "As Emerson's enthusiasm mounts, his tone, even his words, approach Whitman's, who, even more exhilarated with the magnificent variety of the earth, wanted to bring it to unity within the measure of his songs" (p. 24). Certainly there had been enough triumphs to encourage and enough opportunity to invite anyone who wanted to begin a new career. If Emerson could believe "that the orator could speak both most directly and most deeply to men, breaking down their reserves, tugging them through the barriers of themselves, flooding them with sudden surprise that the moment of their life was so rich," so too could Whitman by thinking about the speeches he had heard, perhaps even Emerson's.

But what speakers were most effective to Whitman? Two persons, the Quaker schismatic Elias Hicks and Herman Melville's favorite preacher, Father Taylor. Preacher Hicks, Whitman recalled in later years, had a "magnetic stream of natural eloquence, before which all minds and natures, all emotions, high or low, gentle or simple, yielded entirely without exception" (*PW:* 637–38). It was his naturalness and simplicity, perfectly adjusted to an ordinary and unsophisticated audience, that Whitman praises. Hicks had no tricks of elocution but his success rested on "his passionate unstudied oratory." This was also true of Father Taylor (Melville's Father Mapple), who in Whitman's mind was the "one essentially perfect orator." Both preachers had what Whitman hoped he might have, "the same inner, apparently inexhaustible, fund of latent volcanic passion—the same tenderness, blended with a curious remorseless firmness. . . . Hearing such men sends to the winds all the books, and formulas, and polished speaking, and rules of oratory" (*PW:* 549, 551).

We have, today, not lost altogether the perception of the quality Whitman found in these men, but like him we would find it hard to name. Perhaps our overused word *charisma* is what he meant, although he seems not unwilling to find a physical basis for this influence of the orator on his audience in terms of the animal magnetism popular in his day. Edmund Reiss believes that when Whitman "writes of the 'invisible magnetism, dissolving and embracing all,' and describes the underlying vitality of the universe as 'subtle, vast, elective,' he appears to be mentioning a force close to the vital physical fluid of the animal magnetists" (1963: 81). It will be necessary to return to this point later, but for the moment it is enough to show that, for whatever reason, Whitman had thought long and deeply about the persuasive power he had responded to himself.

Whether or not we find a name for the effect Whitman is describing, it is important to see that this is no personal quirk of his own. Matthiessen says that in oratory, Emerson considered "the energy of thought and of action . . . practically indistinguishable" and that he agreed with Milton's famous statement, "True eloquence I find to be none but the serious and hearty love of truth; and that whose mind soever is fully possessed with a fervent desire to know good things, and with the deepest charity to infuse the knowledge of them into others, when such a man would speak, his words . . . trip about him at command and in well ordered files, as he would wish, fall aptly in their own places" (*AR:* 21). We will examine later the extent to which Whitman followed this transcendental belief in natural or unstructured rhetoric. What is surprising, however, is that in trying to write about the platform success of Elias Hicks and Father Taylor he unintentionally echoes the transcendental aesthetic.

Matthiessen goes on to explain that what links Emerson "most to his age is that he considered such luminous eloquence an essential property of all literature." Whitman does not, at least at first. Emerson "defined a prose writer as 'an *orator manqué*,'" as fitting a term for Whitman as for himself. "In certain moods," when Emerson was "longing for more expressive cadences than any yet found, he could say 'I think now that the very finest and sweetest closes and falls are not in our metres, but in the measures of eloquence [*i.e.*, oratory], which have greater variety and richness than verse.'" The transcendentalists' desire "to break through all restricting divisions" can be seen in Emerson's notion that "the best prose becomes poetic" and "the sublimest speech is a poem," but Matthiessen insists that Emerson's "tendency to link poets and orators whenever he listed the various arts" was a response "to a more common and widespread belief of his time" (pp. 21–22).

But Whitman would not, at first at any rate, have agreed with Emerson that oratory and poetry are not distinct. Whitman had a much more powerful response to the uttering human voice than did Emerson; the oral distinction between a speech and a poem was a real distinction to him. He did not think a sermon by Hicks was poetry, nor is there any record of his responding to any poetry then available to him as he did to Hicks. The human voice never lost its fascination for Whitman, but early in his career it was strongest in its arresting power. It is well known that he responded, and very powerfully, to music and particularly to the great singers who could bring him close to ecstasy, and it was surely the fact that he *heard* Hicks and Taylor that occasioned his response to their words.

To Emerson the change from oratory to poetry would have been one of degree, to Whitman the difference would have been one of kind, at least in the early 1850s when he was writing those "barrels" of lectures. It is important to make this point clearly and to bring in as much evidence as there is to support it, in order to show that for Whitman the origin of much of his early poetry is the impassioned prose of those lectures. What Matthiessen writes of Emerson applies far more to Whitman: "To a degree that we have lost sight of, oratory was then the basis for other forms of writing, and its modes of expression left a mark on theirs" (p. 22).

But later scholars of Whitman seem to have forgotten what earlier critics took for granted, that before Whitman was a poet—or the poet of *Leaves of Grass*—he was writing those lectures, or trying to. Furness says of this interest in public speaking, "Its importance as a key to some of the vexed problems of the genesis of Whitman's ideas about poetry has been largely overlooked in the prolonged discussion over debatable points in his personality, his main poetical themes, and his departures from accepted form. But in order to understand the fluent orotund tone of his verse, it is essential to realize that the fountain head of his poetry was in oral declamation" (*WWW: 27*). Catel writes with equal assurance, "Whitman a retrouvé, par un instinct très sûr de poète . . . la source vive du langage qui est le style oral, ce qu'il a appelé lui-même 'a vocal style.'" And he continues, on a point which also will be developed here, "Cette 'vocalisation' (il dit *vocalism*) ne l'a point empêché de s'essayer à *écrire* les premiers balbutiements de son lyrisme latent" (1930: 84).

Neither of these scholars, writing some fifty years ago, considered he was making some new discovery; rather they wished to bring back into critical attention something that had been recognized as far back as the first publication of unpublished manuscripts by the literary executors. Thus, Thomas Harned, "It is quite evident that early in life he gave much attention to the study of public speaking and had formulated a purpose to present his message in that way, before he adopted the plan of reaching the people through the medium of a printed book" (p. 245). Bucke found in 1899, when he examined his third of the literary remains, that much of what he was publishing in *Notes and Fragments* were notes for lectures. He writes in his preface, "It is made as good as certain by these notes that Whitman's original thought was to publish his ideas in the form of lectures. I believe he had formed this intention some years before such a book as *Leaves of Grass* was planned or even thought of" (p. xvi). Matthiessen had, then, some support for the position he took that "in looking now at his notebooks which, starting in 1847, belong mainly to the period between then and the first *Leaves*, it is often impossible to tell whether passages of loosely rhythmical prose were originally conceived for a speech or as a draft towards a poem" (*AR:* 550).

But here is the issue, or rather the question to be examined. Why do the "passages of loosely rhythmical prose" have to be either "for a speech" or "as a draft towards a poem"? Why not both? Let us look at some of this early notebook material in terms of its poetic uses. Bucke quotes the notebook passage, "I tell you greedy smoucher! I will have nothing which any man or woman, anywhere on the face of the earth, or any color or country cannot also have." To it he appends the note relating the line to the 1855 line, "By God! I will accept nothing which all cannot have their counterpart of on the same terms," and adds: "The above note is very early and is almost certainly a passage in a proposed lecture and belongs to the time that *Leaves of Grass* as a poem had not been planned" (*NF:* 203). But noting parallels of ideas in individual lines is not enough. Indeed Holloway (*UPP:* 63) quotes from the 1847 Notebook some notes for a lecture on the American character in which this sentence appears, "It is to accept nothing except what is equally free and eligible to anybody else," and makes the reference to the same line of the 1855 edition. Indeed in this earliest notebook in the first six pages of "notes for lectures" he himself makes reference to twenty-seven passages in the 1855 edition that treat the same idea in either the same or similar words.

In fact there never has been any question but that Whitman took ideas first noted in his lecture material for his early *Leaves*. But if this is true, what are the implications? There are really two sets of implications, those concerning his attitude to the writing that was intended for public delivery, and those concerning his writing as poetry to be read not heard. If we remember that Whitman was strongly attracted to the human voice and was strongly tempted to the platform as the highest field of human endeavor available to a citizen of a democratic nation, we will not be surprised at the seriousness and intensity of his comments about oratory. Not all of these can be dated, but all of them seem to be in the 1850s, both before and after the 1855 edition and in no case after the 1860 edition and/or the beginning of the Civil War. Much of the material used in support of the claim that Whitman had planned a career for himself as orator is found in unpublished scraps, perhaps remainders of the practical side of the "barrels" of lectures, but there are also some published but overlooked items—overlooked because they mean so little to those looking for thematic clues to the poetry, or to the poet.

Here is one page of jottings in which he reminds himself of what his style must include. "Lessons - Clear, alive, luminous,—full of facts, full of physiology—acknowledging the democracy, the people—must have an alert character, even in the reading of them. The enclosing theory of 'Lessons' to permeate All the States, answering for all (no foreign imported models), *full of hints, laws and informations*, to make a superb American Intellect and Character in any or all The States. Also the Strength, Command and Luxuriance of Oratory" (*NF: 58*). This is clearly a note only to himself. Although one may speculate as to the efficacy of telling oneself to be luminous, the rest of the note has that mixture of encouragement and direction that would identify it as Whitman's if it had been in another hand.

It is easy to overdo this presentation of manuscript notes, but since cumulative evidence is necessary, let me add a few more. These are the first two slips of some eight pages of Whitman's "Notes on Lecturing and Oratory," which Furness brought together.

"Lectures" or "Lessons"

The idea of strong live addresses directly to the people, adm. 10¢, North and South, East and West - at Washington,—at the different State Capitols—Jefferson (Mo.)—Richmond (Va.)—Albany—Washington +c - promulging the grand ideas of American ensemble liberty, concentrativeness, individuality, spirituality +c +c.

Keep steadily understood, with respect to the effects and fascinations of *Elocution* (so broad, spacious, and vital) that although the Lectures may be printed and sold at the end of every performance, nothing can make up for that *irresistible attraction and robust living* treat of the vocalization of the lecture, by me,—which must defy all competition with the printed and read repetition of the Lectures. (*WWW: 32*)

The first of these manuscript notes shows Whitman's plans to travel the country as a wander-teacher, although the comment seems to be directed only to himself. He mentions his modest admission charge and is now thinking of some sort of itinerary, but most significantly he gives the purpose of the whole adventure in his list of the "grand ideas." Now if there were *lectures* prepared to do this "promulging," either they have disappeared or they went under some other label. For clearly the whole prophetic (as distinct from lyrical) half of *Leaves of Grass* is concerned with celebrating and promoting American ensemble, liberty, individuality, spirituality, and perhaps even concentrativeness if we could only find out what it means. The 1855 Preface and more than half of the poems of the first, second, and third editions are directed to that end.

The second note brings us back to Whitman's fascination with vocal utterance that we have noted earlier, but this time it is his own voice that fascinates him. He seems here to have complete confidence in his own voice as the medium for "promulging the grand ideas." Indeed he goes further and insists that the spoken word "must defy" the written, by which he means that the oratorical inspiration of his utterance, the medium of his communication, is preeminent. He has been willing, here and in the previous advertisement, to provide a printed version (either complementary or supplementary, as the case may be) but it is never to take precedence over or substitute for the platform presentation. In Emerson's terms, he was not going to let himself become "an *orator manqué*," he was to be an orator per se.

The complete aplomb with which he not only notes but emphasizes in this letter to himself the "irresistible attraction" of his vocalization will be a surprise to anyone unaccustomed to his comments about himself. Henry Adams could adopt a third-person omniscient point of view about a first-person subject with resulting possibilities for amused detachment and subtle ironies that make the *Education* a delight to readers of even the mildest literary sophistication. *Per contra*, Whitman's first-person omniscience about a first-person subject seems to arise from his own wonder at himself. In the poetry, we do not mind, for the persona is our way of freeing the lines from egotism. But in many notes to himself about himself, he writes as if he were a split personality, the journalist half writing about the prophetic poet-orator as one Siamese twin might write about his brother. The result can be comic in effect, although always serious in intention, as here, but sometimes, as when he falsifies the record to gratify some pathological craving for praise, it can be annoying to the unprepared reader. Whitman is perhaps the

most complex and baffling poet of whom we have record, and that reputation is consequent upon the incredible naïveté which led him to pre-
serve for that record the most damaging manifestations of character.

But those notes were notes to himself and surely were not meant for
our attention (or amusement either). There are also other notes, again
not directly intended for us but apparently for some projected and contemporary audience. Here is one (from the Feinberg Collection) presented as closely as possible to the form he left:

Abrupt sentences - concise

Lectures (? Readings.)

Agonistic Arena

Short, Lapidary, and fit for an original and vital style of elocution

taking

(not ∧ more than an hour to be delivered.)

The whole presentation, from its directness to you, audience—

from the amazing and splendid athletic magnetism of its vocalization

- and from ~~its~~ the charm   and imperative

☞   - ~~and from its charm~~   of its abandon and hauteur   ∧   decision

merely

making ∧ as an entertainment-attraction, something far ~~more~~

beyond any of the

theatres

ordinary attractions of the ~~plays,~~ the minstrels, concerts, +c.-

Now what does this note signify in the words themselves and in its
form? Let us take the last question first. Is this a reminder note of Whitman to himself? Is he setting it up like a little motto to look at when,
later in the week or month, he sits down at his desk to plan and write
out his lecture? That explanation might fit the first line, for abrupt sentences are presumably valuable in a lecture, and if they are also concise,
so much the better. But from that point on, the lines seem to be more
public in intention than private. Who, in a note to himself, would insert
taking in line 5, change *its* to *the* in line 8, cross out *and* in line 9, and so
on through the rest of the page? It seems as though this slip is more
likely a draft for a poster or advertisement than a note for his perusal
alone. As such, notice what is being announced—a powerful new
speaker with an equally new style of address (directly "to *you, audience*") is ready to dominate the entertainment field. Before moving on
to the next piece of evidence, let us ask where in Whitman's writing are

there abandon, hauteur, and imperative decision? And where does he write as if talking directly to the audience? But we will answer these questions specifically and with examples later on. For the moment it is important to note that Whitman either already had or was preparing material that he considered would fit this bill we have just examined.

After 1855, of course, he did have material, and notice how specific he is in 1857 and 1858. Here are two items of those years (from the Trent Collection):

15 cents. Walt Whitman's Lectures

☞ I desire to go by degrees through all these States, especially West and South, and through Kanada: Lecturing, (my own way,) henceforth my employment, my means of earning my living—subject to the work elsewhere alluded to that takes precedence.

☞   Of this, or through the list, present and to come, (see last page of cover,) any will be recited before any society or association of friends, or at the defrayment of some special person.

The parenthetical adjuncture "see last page of cover" is explained by the literary executors: "A document indicating the seriousness of this intention to lecture was discovered at his death. It is written on both sides of a small piece of stiff paper intended as the front cover of a book which was to contain 'Walt Whitman's Lectures.'" The second item is even more specific:

AMERICA!

A PROGRAMME +c.

Some plan I seek to have the vocal delivery of my Lectures free, but at present a low price of admission, One Dime — Or my fee for reciting, here, $10, (when any distance, expenses in addition.)

Each lecture will be printed, with its recitation, needing to be carefully perused afterward to be understood. I personally sell the printed copies.

Brooklyn, New York

1858

Trade supplied by DeWitt, 162 Nassau St. New York

What are the implications here? Note how literal and factual he is. Even if one may insist that the first announcement may be the verbalizing of a daydream (Walt fulfilling some fantasy role as the wander-teacher, the prophet-poet-priest of democracy), the second is just too specific to be idle doodling. His own name, the address, date, and business firm, even the clear if comical statement that the lectures need to be studied afterward to be understood—all this is just too matter-of-fact to be fantasy stuff.

The other part of this strange, seemingly public advertisement, has this long, very curious and apparently public statement:

> Notice—Random Intentions—Two Branches
> [Henceforth two co-expressions. They expand, amicable from common sources, but each with individual stamps by itself. First POEMS, *Leaves of Grass*, as of INTUITIONS, the Soul, the Body (male or female), descending below laws, social routine, creeds, literature, to celebrate the inherent, the red blood,] one man in himself, or one woman in herself. Songs of thoughts and wants hitherto suppressed by writers. Or it may as well be avowed to give the personality of Walt Whitman, out and out, evil and good, whatever he is or thinks, that sharply set down in a book, the Spirit commanding it; if certain outsiders stop puzzled, or dispute, or laugh, very well. [Second, Lectures, or Reasoning, Reminiscences, Comparison, Politics, the Intellectual, the Esthetic, the desire for knowledge,] the sense of richness, refinement and beauty in the mind, as an act, a sensation—from an American point of view.
>
> Of the above so far both would increase the bearings upon themselves, not at any time finished any more than any live operation of nature is but unfolding, urging onward and outward, By degrees to fashion for these States (it may as well be avowed) two athletic volumes. The first to speak of the permanent soul (which speaks for all, material too, but can be understood only by the like of itself—the same being the reason that what is wisdom—music to one is gibberish to another). But the second, temporary, shall be the speech of the attempt at Statements, Argumentation, Art. Both to illustrate America—illustrate the whole, not merely sections, members, throbbing from the heart, the West around the great Lakes, or along the flowing Ohio, or Missouri or Mississippi.
>
> Curious, much advertizing his own appearance and views (it cannot be helped) offensive to many, too free, too savage and natural, candidly owning that he has neither virtue or knowledge—such, *en passant*, of Walt Whitman, going his own way to his own work—because on less terms how can he get what he is resolved to have to himself, and to America? (*WWW*: 197–98)

This Notice is one of the most puzzling of the various advertisements. How is it to be interpreted? It all depends on how one looks at the evidence, to be sure, but this three-part projected advertisement represents to me another of those musings, fantasies, daydreams, of which there are many in the notebooks, only this time with some definite signs of practicality (the address, the business firm, the date). The long three-paragraph Notice of his Random Intentions about the Two Branches is, however, one of the first indications that he recognized a difference between his programmatic or prophetic poetry and his lyric poetry. As such, it needs to be examined, although it is something less than transparent in its limpid clarity (its last paragraph I find unintentionally comic). But, to repeat, a lot depends on how one looks at the evidence—for there is a major difference in interpretation that must be presented.

My reading of the situation is that Whitman thought briefly (at least at the time he wrote this Notice) of dividing his poetry, separating the lyric poetry (the Leaves of Grass) from the programmatic poetry (something like the later Chants Democratic group). I do not know why this impulse to divide occurred, but my hunch is that by 1858 the whole venture of *Leaves of Grass* may have seemed to him to be close to failure. The initial splash of the first edition had been followed by the somewhat bigger splash of the second (bigger chiefly because of the notoriety of his unauthorized use of the Emerson letter). Since then (for two years) attention had lagged. In a bold attempt (on paper, anyway) to refocus attention on the man and his work, he was even willing to split what he had put together, give the poems separately, hand out copies at ten cents each. But he never really finished the advertisement, never published it, never gave any public readings. When the great boon came early in 1860 from the publishing firm of Thayer & Eldridge, of Boston, the idea of dividing his poetry was immediately dropped. The plan for the 1860 edition he worked out included a mixture as before, but there was a section Leaves of Grass, which began with "As I Ebb'd with the Ocean of Life" and included "There Was a Child Went Forth," and there was also a section Chants Democratic, which included "By Blue Ontario's Shore," "A Song for Occupations," "Respondez!" These two sections seem to be echoes of the two-branch idea of the advertisement.

But the whole notion of the oratorical beginnings of *Leaves of Grass* has not received much attention since Matthiessen, perhaps because of William Finkel's discovery (1950) that many of Whitman's notes on oratory were copied from Nairne and other teachers of rhetoric. The fact that he was interested enough to copy all these notes is what is important to me, and since it was not Whitman but Harned and Furness who published them as Whitman originals, there is no call for plagiarism. Be that as it may, Catel and Matthiessen have not had much impact on Whitman scholarship of the past thirty years.

There is only one scholar, but that a famous one, who rejects the oratorical-rhetorical influence completely, and since I am something of a revisionist in this whole matter, it is proper that our differences are made clear. Roger Asselineau in his valuable study *The Evolution of Walt Whitman* devotes much of his second volume to a stylistic analysis of *Leaves of Grass* to which all students of Whitman are much indebted. Yet he cannot accept the oratorical influence on the poetry at all. In rejecting that hypothesis he uses as a coup de grâce part of the statement Whitman made, the whole of which I have quoted above. Asselineau writes as follows, and I have inserted numbers in brackets in front of the points I answer below: "Some commentators, [1] impressed by the fact that there were many notes upon the art of oratory among Whitman's papers, have claimed that he wanted to apply to poetry the rules of oratory and eloquence. Nothing more false. [2] No speech has ever consisted of such enumerations and litanies as are found in *Leaves of Grass*. [3] Besides, oratory and poetry were for Whitman two separate activities which he would have liked to carry on simultaneously, [4] but which he did not confuse, as is shown by this note which he jotted down in 1858" (1962: 243).

(1) It is not the notes on oratory that "impressed" me, for they were copied mostly from Nairne and Bulwer-Lytton (whose work that Whitman copied did not appear until 1857) plus earlier writing (Day, Sheridan) that Whitman copied in 1857–1858, by which time the first two editions had been published. What "impressed" me was that (a) many lines in the early poems were found first in his lecture drafts, and (b) the syntactical rhythms of these lecture drafts are carried over into the poetry, where they are accentuated by the line division and rhetorical patterns.

(2) I think it is doubtless true that no public address in France ever had enumerations and litanies as long as those in the first two editions. But any mid-nineteenth-century collection of American orations, patriotic addresses, and memorials would put *Leaves* to shame. And what about Edward Everett's two-hour address, just ahead of Lincoln's at

Gettysburg, which treats all the battles and the officers and the war-dead with benumbing enumerations and endless litanies? And what about Lyndon Shanley's treatment of *Walden*?

(3) Oratory and poetry were separate in the sense that interest in oratory was the precursor of the poetry. But as "two separate activities," a much clearer demarcation must be made: *poetry* was Whitman's activity, *prophecy* was the role he adopted, *oratory* was only something he daydreamed about. He could never have carried on both simultaneously (that is, the creation of them), but it is quite true that he dreamed of presenting his completed poetry in oral form, as the "note" indicates.

(4) Before answering the first part of this statement, let me make a clarification about the final part of Asselineau's sentence. Whitman's statement is not really a note but much longer and more like a public pronouncement, intended as an advertisement. Part of the difficulty arises because (for reasons of space, I presume) Asselineau gives only a small section of the first paragraph. To make it clear, I have put brackets around the parts he quotes.

Now, to go back to Whitman's statement, what does he mean at the beginning when he uses the word *henceforth*? The word means "from now on," "from this time forward." He is, then, acknowledging that earlier the "two co-expressions" were combined (as they were in the first and second editions). On the matter of confusing oratory and poetry, there is certainly no question, for of course Whitman did not. But he did use oratory (or oratorical techniques) in his prophetic (or programmatic) poetry: he uses speech acts; involves "you," the audience, explicitly; employs negations, rhetorical questions, parallelism, repetitive devices, and lists and catalogs—all of these easily derived from oratory or the rhetoricians who wrote about oratory. Most of the poems of the first edition are of this sort, but there are also lyric poems, "A Child Went Forth" and "The Sleepers." These would be the co-expressions the Notice refers to and they were combined (not confused) in the first and second editions and, despite the advertisement, continued to be so.

It does not confuse oratory and poetry to use oratorical techniques for poetry. Indeed Asselineau seems to have acknowledged as much himself in his first volume, where he notes the similarity between the 1855 Preface and the poems of the first edition. In speaking of the two to four dots making caesuras, he writes: "He uses them to indicate the rhythm of the sentences and to mark the places where the reader, if he were reading aloud, would need to take a breath. This is the normal concern of a poet or an orator. He does not try to convince by argument, but rather to affect emotionally. He wants his text to be an incantation or a rhapsody. Therefore his prose is very close to his verse" (1960: 62–63). And I would add that his prose and his verse are very close to oratory. There are also a number of odd bits of evidence which any theory must encompass, such as this one: "We enter more intimately into the process by which a speech could become one of his poems, in a curious composition into which he inserted his own stage directions: 'Was it thought that all was achieved when Liberty was achieved? (Shaking the head—no—no—no.)'" (*AR*: 554). The line Matthiessen quotes is from the early version of "To a Foil'd European Revolutionaire," which was first published in the second edition (1856).

The difference between my view and that of Asselineau is, then, based on how we see the evidence, not just this projected advertisement of the co-expressions but the lecture drafts and the transfer of the oratorical elements in them to the early poetry. Bruce McElderry believed that Whitman's persona was initially that of the orator and the bard; I would only want to add another role to the persona (or another persona), that of the native prophet. If there had not been those early personae, there would not have been any *Leaves* at all. The reason *Leaves* did appear in 1855 was that Whitman found a way to overcome or to circumvent his inability to carry out a prophetic mission in the public and oral manner of traditional orators, bards, public speakers, lyceum lecturers, by finding a way of transmitting his message in print without losing the efficacy of its presumed public presentation. Every oration that he knew of, and that we know of as well, so loses its character in print that it might as well not be printed at all. What Whitman did was to rewrite, reshape, revamp his never-given speeches to gain and maintain the immediacy, the urgency, the audience involvement, the excitement, the emotional uplift of the public performance that might have been.

He once said, "I sometimes think the Leaves is only a language experiment—that it is an attempt to give the spirit, the body, the man, new words, new potentialities of speech" (*American Primer*, viii–ix). That is true, it was a new and largely successful experiment. But the question still remains, What did he do and how did he do it? That is the great and complex and as yet unanswered question. Quite aside from his notable lack of literary sophistication, his sexual and other personal problems, his perhaps intentionally false clues in regard to the shaping years 1850 to 1855, what did he actually do to language to make it work poetically? He probably could not give the answers himself, at least not in terms we can now use in our analysis (*cursus*, speech act, metonymy, negation; he did know but does not write of word choice, journalistic style, rhetorical questions, syntactical rhythms). But he knew the result, knew it was new, knew that it worked. To show how it worked is what this study is about.

But let me make my own position clear. Whitman was a poet, not a prophet, and poet he always was. After the Civil War, he became increasingly a weak (even bad) poet, and we ought to admit as much. The prophetic posture of the early poetry was just that, a posture, a stance. There is nothing wrong with that, for in art (if not in morals) the end justifies the means. Indeed every artist must assume some sort of stance (even the diarist), but Whitman did not know that. The prophetic posture, then, provided a way for him to speak, but to speak as poet. We are always interested in him, in what he reveals of himself, in his utterance. Even as we make ourselves momentarily the "you" of "Song of Myself":

> Long have *you* timidly waded, holding a plank by the shore,
> Now I will *you* to be a bold swimmer,
> To jump off in the midst of the sea, and . . . (ll. 1231–33)

we do so only in participating in the poem as a way of getting to the poet's psyche. Rhetoric, whether as a front or for real, never outlives the rhetor (and those who first heard him). If it lasts, if it means anything to later generations, it is because we are curious as to what the quality, the force, of the original statement tells us about its author. If we read and ask others to read *Areopagitica* in preparation for the coming cultural battle with the Moral Majority, we are using it not as literature but as rhetoric. As literature, we read it for what it tells us of Milton. And we read *Paradise Lost* not to know (let alone to justify) God's ways to man but to try to capture one man's (Milton's) ways to his God. The prophetic role that Whitman adopts for the three early editions, he feared would lose the affectiveness of its language, its style, if it were seen as an act, so he insisted and insisted that it was real, in his "anonymous" reviews, in his prefaces (of various kinds), in his shaping of his disciples' comments about him, and in his poetry itself.

Be that as it may, what are we to make of that statement in one of his advertisements about the "robust living treat" his audience was to get for its ten cents? Did he have a fine voice and a compelling platform manner? There is no straight answer, for as always with him he is the least trustworthy witness about himself. His disciples were not much better, although their fault was one of misplaced loyalty, not self-deception. But to the question, Was Whitman a great speaker? the answer is that he was not. He was not even a "good" speaker. Indeed it is quite possible that in asking ten cents for admission "he had his nerve," in a very different sense than Randall Jarrell used the phrase. First it is necessary to get at the truth to show *how* he falsified the facts, and then—and here is the important part of this probe—we must see *why* he lied about his platform prowess.

According to him, but indirectly, he did some speaking in Democratic party politics in the 1840s. He had Burroughs put this passage in his *Notes on Walt Whitman as Poet and Person:* "Once in a while he appears at the political mass meetings as a speaker. He is on the democratic side, at the time going for Van Buren as President, and, in due course for Polk. He speaks in New York, and down on Long Island, where he is made much of" (p. 81). Burroughs could not have "made much of" Whitman's political addresses in 1840, for he was only three years old at the time. Indeed there would be no occasion for Burroughs to put in this information at all, except that Whitman wanted it there.

As far as what actually happened, there is only one political speech in the record, the 250-word statement on July 19, 1841, in the Park, New York City. The speech is printed in Holloway (*UPP:* 51), and one must agree with that editor that the "style is amateurish, his employment of periods and vision sophomoric." Indeed the speech would have been quite forgotten were it not that Whitman himself resurrected it and published it in the Brooklyn *Daily Eagle* some six years later. The "Art and Artists" lecture at the Brooklyn Art Union in 1851 is available for examination because Whitman sent it to the Brooklyn *Daily Advertizer*, from whose columns Holloway prints it also (*UPP:* 241–

47). There is little that relates to the later Whitman in it, and were it not that he closes with a quotation from his own early free-verse poem "Resurgemus" it is doubtful that anyone could have detected it as Whitman's by internal evidence.

But for the next twenty years there is no evidence that he gave poems or lectures or lessons or political addresses from a platform or before an audience. There are other items we might examine, such as "The Eighteenth Presidency!," except that Edward Grier has already done so in his valuable edition of this strange work. Grier's important introductory essay makes the point that "although 'The Eighteenth Presidency!' is a tract, not only Whitman's use of direct and rhetorical question and reply but also his sentence rhythms suggest that he was thinking in the patterns of oratory rather than those of the essay or editorial." And further: "'The Eighteenth Presidency!' is not poetry written as prose, like the 1855 Preface; for one thing it lacks the imagery of the Preface. But the manner of the tract, and even details of style like lists of cities, the lists of occupations, and the epithets in series, which suggest the poetic catalogues, are reminiscent of *Leaves of Grass*" (1956: 12, 13). But this "Voice of Walt Whitman to each Young Man in the Nation, North, South, East, and West," which in 1856 he had encouraged rich persons everywhere to reproduce, free of charge, was not heard or printed.

Not, indeed, until September 8, 1871, did anyone have a chance to hear Whitman from the platform, and even then one would need a front-row seat to hear very much. It was the opening of the trade exhibition in New York, and Whitman did present "After All Not to Create Only" (later known as "Song of the Exposition"). As always on opening days for fairs, there was still much building, arranging, and shifting of properties; indeed there was so much racket and so little advance publicity that not many people were there in the tent to hear the poet. But a well-known "anonymous" contributor to the Washington *Chronicle*, who had got in his copy before he went to New York, thought otherwise.

> To an audience of perhaps two or three thousand people, with a fringe on the outside of five or six hundred partially-hushed workmen, carpenters, machinists, and the like, with saws, wrenches, or hammers in their hands, Walt Whitman, last Thursday, gave his already celebrated poem before the

American Institute. His manner was at first sight coldly quiet, but soon you felt a magnetism and felt stirred. His great figure was clothed in gray, with a white vest, no necktie, and his beard was unshorn as ever. His voice is magnificent, and is to be mentioned with Nature's oceans and the music for forests and hills. His gestures are few, but significant. Sometimes he stands with his hands in his breast pockets; once or twice he walked a few steps to and fro. He did not mind the distant noises and the litter and machinery, but doubtless rather enjoyed them. He was perfectly self-possessed.

One cannot but say "Amen" to that last sentence, with the application to the writer of the puff, not the poet. If the poet had been "perfectly self-possessed" there would not have been any need to concoct this before-the-event puff. All the other newspaper accounts of his performance are far from enthusiastic, as Gay Wilson Allen shows in embarrassing detail in *The Solitary Singer* (pp. 432–35), so that one is forced to ask what was behind the almost ridiculous enhancement in the *Chronicle* story.

The next year, through a prank of some Dartmouth seniors, Whitman was invited to read a poem at the June commencement. Bliss Perry gives the details of this bizarre affair in his biography, quoting from another before-the-event review Whitman wrote about himself and his Dartmouth presentation for the Washington papers. The papers did not use this already prepared story, written on Department of Justice stationery and delivered with detailed printing instructions, so Perry, finding it years later, published it. He rather grimly presents the circumstances and presumably believed that Whitman's gratuitous contribution to criticism of "the American Homer" had been circumvented. But Perry did not realize that Whitman left Hanover to go to Burlington, Vermont, where his sister was then living. Had Perry looked in the Burlington paper a few days after Whitman arrived, there he would have found these "anonymous" comments about Whitman's Dartmouth presentation:

> He was very easy in his delivery, and evinced an unusual degree of what might be called inward emphasis, but outwardly he shows perfect nonchalance. His vitality and electricity are in the voice, which, although not startling and loud is impressive and animating beyond example. . . . The lesson of Whitman's elocution is of value to our speakers and orators, who deeply need these qualities of vocal perfection—outward quiet and interior magnetism, which he possesses so abundantly. . . . Whitman uses few ges-

tures, generally speaks quietly, deliberately, only sometimes rapidly, pauses a good deal, has a way of putting his hands in his breast pockets and presents the appearance of some florid old farmer, or sea captain in a little more glow than usual; but his inherent intellectual animation is probably beyond that of any speaker of the age. (Molinoff, *Some Notes*, 28–29)

Except for the odd repetition of the mannerism of "putting his hands in his breast pockets" the two accounts are different in wording but come out of the same impulse or, better, the same conviction that the poet of *Leaves of Grass*, and of such poems as were to be included in it, must perforce be the magnetic, vital, nonchalant, self-possessed, intellectually animated speaker with electric and magnificent voice.

But actually, as Bliss Perry's friend Professor Richardson of Dartmouth recalled, "His delivery of his poem is said by those who remember it to have been monotonous and without animation, and his voice failed to fill the back part of the church. When he stepped back to his seat there was some doubt whether he had finished, so that the audience was relieved when the chairman rose and shook hands with him" (Perry, *Walt Whitman*, 204).

One wonders whether Whitman knew that he shared the platform with Edward Everett Hale, who sixteen years earlier had reviewed the 1855 edition for the *North American Review*. Hale is no shaping force in American literary criticism, and his review was not notably profound in its understanding of the literary monument he was reviewing. But he was honest in his reaction and shrewd in his perception of what Whitman was up to: "He has a horror of conventional language of any kind. His theory of expression is, that, 'to speak in literature with the perfect rectitude and *insouciance* of the movement of animals, is the flawless triumph of art' [from the 1855 Preface]. Now a great many men have said this before. But generally it is the introduction to something more artistic than ever,—more conventional and strained. Antony began by saying he was no orator, but none the less did an oration follow. In this book, however, the prophecy is fairly fulfilled in the accomplishment" ("Review," 49). Hale's friend, Charles Eliot Norton, in an earlier review (1855) was equally responsive to the new style of the new prophet. This "curious and lawless collection of poems" is "neither in rhyme nor blank verse, but in a sort of excited prose broken into lines without any attempt at measure or regularity. . . but the introduction of terms never before heard or seen, and of slang expressions, often renders an otherwise striking passage altogether laughable." The "preposterous yet somehow fascinating book" seems "a mixture of Yankee transcendentalism and New York rowdyism, and, what must be surprising to both of the elements, they seem here to fuse and combine with the most perfect harmony" ("Review," 24–25).

This is direct and intelligent criticism that could have been supported by specific examples had Hale and Norton wished to do so. And similarly "Thou Mother with Thy Equal Brood" (to use the title Whitman finally gave the Dartmouth poem) could be criticized for forgetting or rejecting the very elements these first reviewers had originally noted. The nearest parallel in the 1855 edition is "To Think of Time," the original untitled version being 135 lines to 131 for "Equal Brood." Notice the changes in Whitman's style: in 1855 *thou, thee, thy, thine,* etc., for the second-person pronoun, are not used at all, but in 1872 there are 138 uses of this "poetical" pronoun in 131 lines; in 1855 there are three inversions or other variations of standard American syntax, whereas for the 1872 poem I stopped counting after thirty-three; in 1855 American idiomatic expression (*i.e.,* words and/or phrasing which Arnold, Browning, or Tennyson would not have used) is found in well over half the lines, but in 1872, with the exception of the place names and the two French words, there is not a single word or phrase that the Victorian poets might not have used; in the 1855 poem the language, as our daily speech, is Saxon, with one word in eight being of Latin, French, or other comparable origin, but in 1872 Whitman doubles the number, one in four being a non-Teutonic word.

When Norton noted in 1855 that the "vast and vague conceptions" of transcendentalism profited poetically by being uttered in Whitman's "coarse and odd intellectual medium" with its "original perception of nature" and "epic directness" ("Review," 24–25), he sets the pattern for the honest criticism we ought to give to the 1872 poem, that its "vast and vague conceptions" remain vast and vague by the grandiose language, abstractions, repetitions, empty sonorousness, and generalized imagery, section 5 being a crushing testimony to this collapse. Hale and Norton were willing to admit that when Whitman was good he was very very good, but we have been quite unwilling to admit that when he was bad he was florid. "Equal Brood" may not be Whitman's worst poem, but it is difficult to determine why he thought so well of it.

If he ever did recognize that his voice was too weak for platform performances, it was only after the stroke of 1873, many months after the two public poems we have been examining. Indeed, even that temporary paralysis did not shatter his confidence that he might become a persuasive orator, but he tended thereafter to stress or have his friends stress the magnetism of his performance, the presence of the poet himself serving as the source of energy. One of the more bizarre efforts was his anonymous contribution to the Camden *Republican*, "Walt Whitman as a Reader of His Own Poems," for July 21, 1875, three years after the Dartmouth fiasco. It is true that he had accepted an invitation to give another commencement poem, "Song of the Universal," at Tufts College, but when the time came he was too ill to appear and the poem was read by proxy. It is not apparent that the electrical effects he writes of in the Camden *Republican* were felt at Tufts by remote control.

There is also a minor exception to the statement that he had been silent for three years after returning from Hanover. He recited his "Old Man's Thought of School" at the dedication (he calls it "Inauguration") of Cooper Public School in Camden on Saturday afternoon, October 31, 1874. The twenty-two-line poem is a mild and gently reflective application of George Fox's dictum (the church is not the building but the hearts of the faithful) to education. It is difficult to think that the fifty or so restless children and assorted members of the local PTA would tremble at the power of that particular Whitman utterance. But this is what he says of his platform performance: "His voice is firm, magnetic. . . . He uses few gestures, but those are very significant . . . the bent of his reading, in fact the whole idea of it, is evidently to first form an enormous mental fund, as it were, within the regions of the chest, and heart, and lungs—a sort of interior battery—out of which, charged to the full with such emotional impetus only . . . he launches what he has to say, free of noise or strain, yet with a power that makes one tremble." This neat physiological trick by which his "enormous mental fund" was stored in a thoracic battery "charged" with "emotional impetus" is never explained, but one can see why it might make

Whitman tremble if no one else. The Springfield *Republican* reprinted this account two days later, and in 1883 Bucke reprinted it again (pp. 53–54) in his official (and controlled) biography. It thus got in the written record and so contributed to the myth about himself that Whitman was carefully (and necessarily furtively) preparing.

But the questions remain. Why should Whitman's three weakest major poems ("Song of the Exposition," industrial fair; "Thou Mother with Thy Equal Brood," Dartmouth commencement; "Song of the Universal," Tufts commencement, by proxy) be those composed when he really knew they were to be public and oral presentations? And why did he so exaggerate the success of the two presentations he did make? Perhaps there is no simple and single answer to this second question, but let's start with it as an approach to the first. Briefly what happened was that Whitman had lost the oratorical character of his early poetry just when he was being praised and celebrated in England as the prophet of democracy. Central to what he knew about prophetic poetry was that it was oral, and when the opportunity finally came to enact that prophetic role, it had to be accepted (no matter what his inner doubts might be). Accordingly the test had to be successful, and Whitman was not one to let a few hundred surrounding, busy, noisy workmen or, later, a few score bemused and indifferent college students and their professors interfere with that.

And why, then, are these productions so ineffectual? Because, when it came right down to it, Whitman was a poet not a prophet, and he covered up his lack of prophetic inspiration by pretentious, over-"poeticalized" language of no true poetic merit that I can discover. (A personal aside: he could not but know he was, in effect, faking it, and I suspect that the worry, nervousness, and depression of those years may well have had something to do with the physical result, the stroke.) It seems cruel to state the circumstances in such blunt terms, but what other explanation is there?

Doubtless he would have rationalized these newspaper reports of his oratorical prowess to Horace Traubel and the other disciples had they discovered and questioned his flagrant doctoring of the record. Most of his self-reviews, puffs, false interviews with himself, laudatory essays that he conned his disciples into signing as theirs were always defended as necessary to counter the "enemy"—"that Boston crowd," Secretary

James Harlan and his ilk, Anthony Comstock and the prudes, William Winter and other Pfaffian apostates, and assorted agents of the literary establishment (including editors of literary magazines), all engaged in a conspiracy to keep him down. This situation of the two "anonymous" reviews of platform presentations would hardly fit any of the camps of the enemy, but I have no doubt Whitman would have found some way of doing so. He would not have had to strain himself, for his disciples were incredibly easy to convince.

But we should not be. If Whitman was so enamored of or otherwise caught up in oratorical and/or prophetic poetry that he fabricated his success to support his engagement with it, we should find out through the answers to those seven traditional investigative questions: who, whom, what, when, where, why, and how. Let me close this long introduction with brief answers. The *who* is not only Walter Whitman Junior, the sometime journalist, but also Walt Whitman the persona, the poser, the antiestablishmentarian before the Civil War and the reformed one thereafter. The *whom*, that is, the audience, is not the American worker, farmer, mechanic, soldier (they are part of his subject) but the disaffected middle-class intellectual. The *what* are the platform poems, about four-fifths of the poetry of the early editions (up to the Civil War), to be distinguished from the poems of lyrical intention and focus. The *when* (which includes the *whence*, with which this chapter is concerned), the actual creation of the first *Leaves* as close as one can date it, is the period 1851–1854, the time of this transference of his lectures to poems of the first edition. The *where* is not simply Brooklyn and Paumanok but the early manuscripts and notebooks where the experimenting was going on. The *why* is the most baffling of all these questions, essentially psychological, and rests on his inordinate craving for the regard of an audience, which he never did find (enough to satisfy the craving, anyway), and so projected his audience to the future. The *how* is the one question this book, from here on, professedly tries to answer by an explanation of his poetic language.

⧉ II ⧉
STYLISTIC INNOVATIONS AND RENOVATIONS

FROM SPEECH TO POEM

Hiram Corson, a professor of English at Cornell in the 1880s and 1890s, wrote to Whitman in April, 1886, "When I next visit the city [Philadelphia], I shall certainly arrange to have a talk with you, on certain points upon which I have long been pondering—one especially, that of language-shaping, and the tendency towards impassioned prose, which I feel will be the poetic form of the future, and of which, I think, your Leaves of Grass is the most marked prophecy." Whitman wondered whether "Corson knew how significant that . . . sentence . . . may be taken to be?—'The tendency towards impassioned prose, which I feel will be the poetic form of the future.' Do you suppose Corson advertizes that?—tells it to his classes? . . . His letter is friendly but he has the excessive caution of the university man. The scholar swells rarely—I may say never—let themselves go" (Traubel, *With Walt Whitman*, I, 286–88).

Whitman was correct about Corson's caution, for the professor never did call again and in his book *A Primer of English Verse* (1892), *Leaves of Grass* and its "impassioned prose" is never even mentioned. But Whitman too was something less than forthcoming about the poetic form or style he had started in 1855, and we never do find out from him why he thought Corson's comment "significant." Accordingly, except for a few suggestions such as the one above, any investigation of the style of *Leaves of Grass* must go first to the lines themselves and then to the man himself, through such other hints and assistance as his manuscripts may supply.

To begin boldly, why not do what Corson did not do, that is, examine *Leaves of Grass* as "impassioned prose"? If we do so, one of the most vexing and futile controversies about that work—the proper way to scan Whitman's lines—can be avoided. Looking at Whitman's pre-1848 verse will be of no help, for it was derivative, jejune, conventional, frequently sentimental—not much worse than the forgotten newspaper verse of his day, to be sure, but not notably better. It was after the return from New Orleans that he started on his new venture. He discovered a new, bold, exalted conviction about himself and American life that could not be expressed in any of the standard modes of his day except possibly that of oratory. If asked to pick a time when it dawned on him that he might—indeed, could—make the jump from journalism to oratory (a sort of "American Adam" epiphany), I would pick the spring of 1850, which would fit all the biographical, social, and cultural evidence Floyd Stovall (1974) has provided. I pick that time because Emerson gave more than a dozen lectures in greater New York City, including on March 19 "perhaps the most popular of all Emerson's lectures," that on eloquence.

In 1851 Emerson was not in New York at all, but another speaker was—the absurdly popular and grossly overrated Englishman, Martin Farquhar Tupper. William Cullen Bryant, a very good but traditional poet, was at the high point of his career as the shaping force of that great newspaper of the period, the New York *Evening Post*, and he served as Tupper's host for the spectacular, almost week-long public presentation of the best-selling (and widely pirated) *Proverbial Philosophy*. Some years later many critics, both in England and in America (including Henry James, Jr.), who felt it incumbent on them to put Whitman in his place, thought the most unanswerable and devastating judgment they could make was to compare the two, for Tupper's stupendous popularity had quickly turned to scorn.

Of all the assorted gibes at Whitman as the American Tupper, without Martin F.'s obsequious decorum that pleased Queen Victoria, none that I have examined ever document the parallels. A few lines from *Proverbial Philosophy* will show that any benefit Whitman might have got from Tupper would be external only. In the middle of a poem of some fifty lines of uneven length, entitled "Of Cruelty to Animals," Tupper has this brief catalog:

From the elephant toiling at a launch, to the shrew-mouse in the harvest-field,
From the whale which the harpooner hath stricken, to the minnow caught
    upon a pin,
From the albatross wearied in its flight, to the wren in her covered nest,
From the death-moth and lace-winged dragon fly, to the lady-bird and the
    gnat,
The verdict of all things is unanimous, finding their master cruel:
The dog, thy humbled friend, thy trusting, honest friend,
The ass, thine uncomplaining slave, drudging from morn to even;
The lamb and the timorous hare, and the laboring ox at plough;
The speckled trout, basking in the shallow, and the partridge gleaning in the
    stubble,
And the stag at bay, and the worm in thy path, and the wild bird pining in
    captivity,
And all things that minister alike to life and thy comfort and thy pride,
Testify with one sad voice that man is a cruel master.

Now catalogs are found chiefly in the early Whitman, and certainly his use of them, in much more significant and crucial fashion, is far better than anything found in Tupper. There are many of them in *Proverbial Philosophy*, more or less like the SPCA piece above. No other writer has lists and catalogs so near Whitman's in "Song of Myself," not in substance, in thought, but in external form: not only the initial reiteration (or anaphora, as Tupper or Whitman might have called it, following the terminology of the traditional rhetorics) but also the long periodic sentences (joined by a semicolon) with the multiple and parallel descriptive phrases and clauses, and even the syntactical organization of the phrases themselves. Whitman is by no means indebted to Tupper for the catalog idea, for manuscript evidence in the early notebooks indicates that Whitman was already working in that direction. And as Lawrence Buell has shown (1973), Whitman's catalogs are far more than a listing of samples, which is all that Tupper's amount to. The importance of Tupper to Whitman is that *Proverbial Philosophy* demonstrated that rhymed metrical verse was not necessary for expression of impassioned ideas that were not suited for the prose essay. That *Proverbial Philosophy* was also obvious, trite, simpleminded, and sentimental did not really make any difference, for Whitman was not concerned with what Tupper was saying—what mattered was *how* he said it (or *printed* it).

If one could look at the early lectures and imagine Whitman listening to Tupper or reading him afterward and thinking of his own lecture notes while doing so, we can guess what must have gone on in his mind: "If my lecture were rearranged like that . . . !" Holloway presents these lecture notes in regular paragraph form (prose discourse going straight across the page to the right-hand margin and continuing on the next line as this line does), but it would give a clearer notion that these early lecture entries were a stage to *Leaves of Grass* if we see these lines arranged as Tupper does his. Here is a rearranged and early lecture of Whitman's:

True noble expanded American character is raised on a far more lasting and
    universal basis than that of any characters of "gentlemen" of aristocratic
    life...or of novels...or under the European or Asian forms of society or
    government
It is to be illimitably proud, independent, self-possessed, generous and gentle
It is to accept nothing except what is equally free and eligible to anybody else
It is to be poor rather than rich...but to prefer death sooner than any mean
    dependence.
Prudence is a part of it—because prudence is the right arm of independence.
    (*UPP:* 63)

This may still be some distance from "impassioned prose" or, as Herbert Read once said of D. H. Lawrence's poetry, "liturgical prose," but it is not an expository paragraph, either, despite the awkwardness of its opening line.

Let me go back to Tupper for a last and different sort of sample. At the beginning and end of *Proverbial Philosophy* he has poems, "Prefatory" and "The End," that are only remotely parallel to Whitman's "Proto-Leaf" (later entitled "Starting from Paumanok") and "So Long!," but there is one similarity that is not found anywhere else in poetry Whitman might have read. In these two poems (and occasionally elsewhere in the series) Tupper writes directly to the reader, as if the reader were listening to the poet's speech. Thus in the opening poem:

Wherefore, thou gentle student, bend thine ear to my speech,
For I also am as thou art; our hearts can commune together;

> To meanest matters will I stoop, for mean is the lot of mortal:
> I will rise to noblest themes, for the soul hath an heritage of glory:

And he concludes this invitation:

> I come a man of peace, to comfort, not to combat;
> With soft persuasive speech to charm thy patient ear,
> Giving the hand of fellowship, acknowledging the heart of sympathy;
> Let us walk together as friends in the shaded paths of meditation;

And "The End" has a summary that is remotely like the "To conclude, I announce" part of "So Long!" Tupper says:

> Nevertheless, I have spoken at my best, according to the mercies given me,
> Of high, and deep, and famous things, of Evil, or of Good. . . .
> I taught thee that nothing is a Trifle, even to the laugh of Recreation: led thee
>   with the Train of Religion, to be dazzled at the name of the Triune. . . .
> I scorned Ridicule; nor would humble me for Praise, for I had gained Self-
>   knowledge;
> And pleaded fervently for Brutes, who suffer for man's sin.

The question is not that Whitman and Bryant, and all the others who made Tupper's New York visit such a great success, approved of *Proverbial Philosophy* as poetry. As far as one can tell Bryant was not even embarrassed in sponsoring this triumphal week for the man whose books were pirated almost as much as Dickens' novels, and Whitman's own comments are mildly approving though mostly noncommittal. There is nothing much one can do about sudden popular success, except to wait it out and avoid hurting one's own reputation by knocking the venture at the height of its popularity and thus incurring the suspicion of envy. Indeed, who blasted *Jonathan Livingston Seagull*? But the chief value to Whitman of Tupper's appearance, it seems to me, would be to encourage him to reexamine his "barrels" of lectures.

Let me take a sample from Holloway to show what I mean. The reader might imagine himself in Whitman's position, having just heard Tupper or having just read his review copy of *Proverbial Philosophy*, and reflecting on what he might do with his own lectures if no lyceum wanted his oral presentation. How might this long complicated sentence be divided?

> I think the soul will never stop or attain to any growth beyond which it shall
> not go, when I walked at night by the seashore and looked up at the count-

less stars, I asked my soul whether it would be filled and satisfied when it should become a god enfolding all these, and open to life and delight and knowledge of everything in them—or of them; and the answer was plain to me at the breaking water on the sands at my feet: and the answer was No, when I reach there, I shall want to go further still. (*UPP:* 66)

A natural division is into six lines:

I think the soul will never stop or attain to any growth beyond which it shall
   not go,
When I walked at night by the seashore and looked up at the countless stars,
I asked my soul whether it would be filled and satisfied when it should
   become a god enfolding all these,
And open to life and delight and knowledge of everything in them—or of
   them;
And the answer was plain to me at the breaking water on the sands at my
   feet:
And the answer was No, when I reach there, I shall want to go further still.

An echo of these lines, in a different arrangement, is found in "Song of Myself" (ll. 1221–22). But—and here is the heresy to the metrists, the scansionists, and all critics so committed to the autotelic approach that to unsplit an infinitive is anathema—it really makes little difference how many lines are used as long as the prose discourse pattern is broken up. The rhythm in Whitman (with the exception of "O Captain! My Captain!," "Pioneers! O Pioneers!," the near-destructive opening six lines of "Song of the Broad-Axe," and a few other attempts at metrical regularity) is a prose rhythm based on syntax and grammar. The lines in *Leaves of Grass* are valuable for drawing attention to that rhythm, but other line arrangements are by no means impossible. Robert Peters, for instance, tries out some of the rhythmic principles of Charles Olson and Robert Duncan by rearranging lines from "Myself" in accordance with those theories (1979: 3–5). He takes the first five lines of that poem to make twenty-two lines with five sections, and the experiment is valid, albeit the length of this poem or *Leaves of Grass* itself when so presented is probably self-destructive.

But in the prose paragraph as Whitman wrote it for one of his projected lectures, the paralleling devices, the length of clauses, the repetition of guide words, all make a structure somewhere close to a six-line division fairly obvious. As such, the lines would be valuable in drawing attention to that rhythm (a prose rhythm, to be sure, but a rhythm nonetheless); they would also highlight the anaphora and other paralleling devices, would assist in the necessary eye and attention control as we finish one line and focus on the next, and, for admirers of the true first edition (or facsimile), would permit the extra pleasure of presenting all but the longest lines with a single line of type. The number and length of the lines, to repeat, are valuable for the above and possibly other reasons of emphasis, but they are not sacrosanct, as the 1860 Blue Book or any of the notebooks with trial lines will readily demonstrate.

What is necessary is that the appearance of prose discourse be broken up. In a major study for anyone trying to bring linguistic science to the aid of literary criticism, Jonathan Culler's *Structuralist Poetics*, this comment (with no snide allusion to Whitman the former journalist, I trust) makes the point: "If one takes a piece of banal journalistic prose and sets it down on a page as a lyric poem, surrounded by intimidating margins of silence, the words remain the same but their effects for readers are substantially altered" (p. 161). Those white margins framing the lines, those capital letters that begin a new line, plus the inherited social and cultural pressure about reading poetry, make us slow down and examine with appropriate seriousness what is written. They also separate the prose sentence or paragraph from the stanza, or strophe, that is the poetic unit in *Leaves of Grass*.

Here is another sentence to put into the *Leaves* form, but with inserted slash marks to indicate how it might be divided: "The soul or spirit transmits itself into all matter, / into rocks...and can live the life of a rock, / into the sea...and can feel itself the sea, / into the oak or other tree, / into an animal...and can feel itself a horse, a fish..or bird, / into the earth....into the motions of the sun and stars" (*UPP:* 64). Yes, the slash marks do help—but not enough. And page after page of prose discourse cut up by slash marks would lose this benefit by the irritation the insistent contradiction between the onflowing line and the slash-mark interrupter would engender. Note how the margins and initial capital letters do help:

> The soul or spirit transmits itself into all matter,
> Into rocks...and can live the life of a rock,
> Into the sea...and can feel itself the sea,

Into the oak or other tree,
Into an animal...and can feel itself a horse, a fish..or bird,
Into the earth....into the motions of the sun and stars.

Not a stunner, to be sure, but note the delight here in the synecdochic details, the shift from *can live* (l. 2) to *can feel* (l. 3), the shortened line 4 inviting us to make the application ourselves, followed by the longer line 5 with the neat substitution, at the end, of *or* for what might have been another *a*, which after two earlier determiners would have had a weakened semantic function. Indeed, the "Into" passage represents an order of thinking different from anything in Tupper, or in any other better poet in America before 1855.

In the late 1840s and early 1850s there was no way a man with a prophetic message like Whitman's could ever have been heard in or through any artistic medium open to him. No poetry of Edward Taylor's had been published, Barlow had been so much forgotten that Whitman probably never read him, no poetry of Freneau, Bryant, Halleck, Poe, Longfellow, Holmes, Lowell, or Whittier would have been even close to what he was doing. The last poems of McDonald Clarke, "the Mad Poet of Broadway," were clearly a possibility, but Whitman's own *Aurora* editorials about the career and bizarre death of that strange genius were something less than envious of his fate. Jones Very (if Whitman knew of him, which is doubtful) would have been too close to the kind of mystic Whitman did not want to be at all. Frederick Tuckerman was too late (*Poems*, 1860) and of a different bent anyway. Nothing in American dramatic productions, which Whitman knew well and attended often, would have suggested any theatrical avenue for prophet Whitman, for English imports dominated the stage, and the single American of talent, George Henry Boker, had only one major play that appeared in 1855 also. The novel of the Cooper and Simms kind that dealt with the American Revolution, and thus with American ideals in a way, was not open to a call for a new and continuing revolution of the sort Whitman advocated. Hawthorne's and Melville's "power of blackness" was so antithetical to anything Whitman stood for as to blind him to any literary form they worked in. Sylvester Judd's *Margaret* is a slight possibility, but Whitman's conception of the Real and the Ideal in an "I Sing the Body Electric" format cannot be imagined. Emerson's

LANGUAGE AND STYLE IN *Leaves of Grass*

Essays and Thoreau's *A Week on the Concord and Merrimack Rivers* were, indeed, the nearest thing in the standard, conventional literary forms that Whitman might have tried. But Thoreau's *Week* was known by only a few of his friends, and Emerson's *Essays* were copies of his lectures.

ORATORICAL CADENCE IN "SONG OF MYSELF"

For L.L.

What is it we miss when the oration is printed? Obviously, the human voice, but the old rhetoricians passed over that as being outside their jurisdiction. Indeed, the physiological aspects of "vocalism" are given far more attention in Whitman's notes (mostly to himself) than are rhythm, pace, emphasis, organization. But here too he studied and in fact copied (as Finkel discovered) the rhetoricians who were in a tradition that went back to classical times. Their influence is too complex to examine here, but let me take just one element—rhythm or cadence—to show one way he tried to get oratorical rhythm on the printed page. I was led to this investigation by D. W. Harding in his valuable *Words into Rhythm* (1976) and in particular by his brief treatment of the *cursus* (pp. 120–23). Harding makes no reference to Whitman, nor does Morris Croll, but there is a significant connection.

Early in this century there was considerable scholarly study of what we now call "prose rhythm." Much of the scholarship was English (George Saintsbury, Oliver Elton) and European, but the culmination was Croll's once famous article, "The Cadence of English Oratorical Prose." That article was written in 1919 in response to the quite intense discussion about the role and function of the *cursus* in shaping the beautiful rhythms of English religious prose, as best exemplified in the *Book of Common Prayer*. The state of Whitman scholarship in that centennial year of the poet's birth was such that no application would have been made to *Leaves*, but we are not obligated to continue to ignore the insights Croll provides just because Traubel and the other Whitmaniacs once aroused scholarly scorn.

The term *cursus* comes from the classical and medieval rhetorics and refers to a "conventional way of giving a beautiful flow at the end of a rhetorical unit" (p. 306). Croll's point of attack is the impact of this rhetorical feature in the early English prayers (the Collects), which were originally oral and which, even though written out, were written to be said. He goes into elaborate and fascinating detail to show that the *cursus* was not just copied by rote from the rhetorical theorists of the Continent, nor was it merely a literal translation of Latin prayers. Rather, the English divines "have allowed the English phrase to develop its own beauty, to perfect the oratorical form toward which we can see it slowly growing in the earlier translations. But in so doing they have also—perhaps unconsciously—tended to guide it toward one of the forms of final cadence to which their ears were habituated by their life long use of the Latin liturgy" (pp. 310–11).

All this may seem a far cry from Whitman's poetry, and it is. But the point is that the *cursus* is an *oral*, not a *metrical*, rhythmic device. The shapers of the *Book of Common Prayer* made revisions of the *cursus* theory to fit their quite different language needs (there were, for instance, a great many polysyllabic words in the Latin prayers from which most of the English prayers are drawn), so that adjustments were both inevitable and necessary. But the principles that evolved for the English *cursus* soon became a permanent factor in English style, not only in sermons and religious prose, which maintain the oral origins, but in such stylists as write for the eye only (Hooker, Browne, or later Gibbon and Macaulay, from whom Croll draws many of his examples) while still retaining the cadence of English oratorical prose. The American samples Croll uses are the Declaration of Independence and various writings and addresses of Woodrow Wilson. But how does a *cursus* work, and what are the variations Croll finds in English oratorical prose?

Croll explains through examples, and later I will take examples from Whitman to show his crucial adaptation of the *cursus*. Since we are now treating a form with oral origins, it is essential that we remind ourselves that the *cursus* is shaped even as it is limited by the physiological requirements of breathing and utterance. Within these limitations, the *cursus* marks the accents from the end of a phrase, clause, or short sentence (when in *Leaves*, in a line). There is no concern with the whole unit (unless it is very short) but only the termination. Accordingly, an investigation of stress, when it is marked, must go backward in the count; that is, one counts from the end of the unit (or Whitman line) marking the accented or stressed syllables. Thus the phrase

LANGUAGE AND STYLE IN *Leaves of Grass*

| | 9 | 8 | 7 | 6 | 5 | 4 | 3 | 2 | 1 |

(a) "eternal and glorious kingdom" is scored $8-5-2$;

| | 11 | 10 | 9 | 8 | 7 | 6 | 5 | 4 | 3 | 2 | 1 |

(b) "mercifully to look upon thy people" is $11-6-2$;

| | 10 | 9 | 8 | 7 | 6 | 5 | 4 | 3 | 2 | 1 |

(c) "the leaven of malice and wickedness" is $9-6-3$.

Note that one must think of the sounds of the words not only to mark or score the phrase but even to grasp the vocal relationship of the words to each other in the *cursus*.

Before making any application to *Leaves*, let me use the above examples to clarify the rules Croll supplies (pp. 348–49), which cover all of the various kinds of *cursus*. First: "English cadence ordinarily begins on one of the syllables, five to ten, counting from the end. It never begins later than the fifth, but sometimes the long cadence may begin as far back as the eleventh syllable" as in (b) above.

Second: "The first accent [*i.e.*, that furthest back: *ter* in (a) above] is the strongest in the cadence, as marking its beginning. It is the climax as to the height of pitch and strength of accent of the member in which the cadence occurs, and indicates the point at which the tendency to rhythmical form always observable in oratory, but restrained earlier by the necessities of logical statement, is finally allowed to appear without check. It marks the release of the rhythmic impulse which is half the secret of our delight in oratorical performance."

Third: Immediately following that strong first accent, "a trochaic movement begins which carries through to the end of the phrase and cadence." Croll is careful to point out that this "trochaic movement" is to be understood not as a metrical measurement, but as a movement in which the dominant accented syllable is followed by the unaccented syllable(s). In (c) above, the dactylic flow fits this rule. But "there is a striking exception to this rule in the case of the long cadence ending in $4-1$ (or $3-1$, or $5-1$)." This exception is an interesting one, for it is contrary to the medieval rhetorics (which were, to be sure, based on Latin oratory, where an accented final syllable would be an anomaly) but suited, indeed pleasurable, to the English ear long habituated to Anglo-Saxon strong endings. Examples here would be "pureness of living and truth" or "hope of thy heavenly grace," both $7-4-1$. There is a further ramification in this $4-1$ ending series, which Croll mentions but does not develop. He points out that for the standard 4̣–3–2–í there may be two variations, 4̣–3̣–2–1 or 4–3̣–2̣–1. An example of the 4̣–3̣–2–1 would be "those *things* which we *ask faith*fully" (7–4=3); of the 4–3̣–2̣–1, "thy *bene*fits and *great mer*cies" (7–3=2). The value of breaking the flow in this way would be to focus attention on key words. There is also the need to break the musical, sometimes lulling, rhythm, which may, on occasion, be too lulling. As we shall see, Whitman uses, very skillfully, the 7–4–1 pattern, as well as these variations.

Fourth: This is the key rule and concerns the necessary relative strength of the accented syllables. Every cadence must have at least "two accents, of which the first [*i.e.*, that furthest back from the end of the phrase or clause] is stronger than the second, and is followed by a greater number of unaccented syllables, or by an equal number which makes the *effect* of being greater, than the second." The principle here (contrary to traditional metrical prosody, it should be noted) is "an effect of decreasing length of period and strength of accent from the beginning of the cadence to the end." To Croll, rule four "is the most important of the five rules and gives the clue to the character of English cadence." Indeed, the "effect due to a three-, four-, or five-syllable period followed by a two-syllable one, or of four syllables followed by three, seems to be constantly heard in all prose that is euphoniously and flowingly written." Rule five is less important than the others but points out that when "the number of syllables following an accent exceeds three, a secondary subsidiary accent appears." This applies to long cadences (such as 7–2), when the voice may put a little extra stress on syllable 4 "to prop up or carry on the long run of syllables between the accent on 7 and the accent on 2."

Now Croll acknowledges that for the writers from whom he draws his examples (as I would acknowledge for Whitman) there is no presumption that the "cadence of English oratorical prose" could be obtained by some rote effectuation of the above rules. It is rather that the rules themselves are drawn from the practice of successful orators (from Cicero on) and are thus a formulation of thousands of trial-and-error efforts. If one of those rules, "the fourth, has an importance altogether out of proportion with the others," it is because "it states the general *character* of the English cadence." Indeed, "this principle taken alone

. . . reduces all the varieties of cadence form to a single psychological, or better, physiological law of movement" (pp. 350–51). And it is this fourth rule, or the principle it professes, that is found in *Leaves of Grass*, but notably in the early editions. Croll's final statement in the theoretical part of this article provides a useful caveat for me in the application to follow: "In English . . . cadence has always, in the first place, been more irregular than in Latin, and subject to whimsical, individual preference or even to deliberate intention to break rhythm noticeable in many authors. And in the second place, it is not apparent that either the theory of cadence or its forms have been known to any English author; and those who have practiced it have either been controlled by an undefined feeling for the oral beauty of style, or else . . . by a tradition which was transmitted from Latin to English during the formative period of English prose style" (p. 354).

I plan to make my case through an examination of Whitman's key poem "Song of Myself," but let us get our terms straight by examining a few lines from "Starting from Paumanok." The syllables are numbered backwards and the parenthesis at the end gives my way of reading the *cursus* part of the line. We may differ once in a while, depending on how we interpret the context that shapes the individual emphasis. If, after you check the context, there is still difference, it does not really matter too much. Go on to the next one, for there are so many of these manifestations of the *cursus* that our difference over a few lines can hardly alter the claim. Here are the opening lines:

Starting from fish-shape Paumanok where I was born,
12 11 10 9   8   7   6 5 4 3   2 1
Well-begotten, and rais'd by a perfect mother,   (7–4–2)
                         8 7 6   5 4 3   2   1
After roaming many lands, lover of populous pavements,   (8–5–2)

There is no explicit *cursus* element at all in the first line; it is, as in so many of the lines, devoted to "the necessities of logical statement," which, as Croll says, take place in any statement. Line 2 does show the cadence we are concerned with. Notice that it is necessary to start at the end of the line, that there is only one unaccented syllable, 3, between the accented 2 and 4, which is necessarily not more than the preceding pair, 5 and 6. Of special importance is the relative strength of the accented syllables. By the nature of things all accented syllables are stressed or emphasized to some extent, but in a *cursus* there must be a slight and gradual dropping down in intensity from *rais'd* to *per*fect to *mother*. I did not go back to include an earlier accent, the *got* of be*got*ten, for that comes too near to being a subjective judgment. Aside from the comma after syllable 9, which gives one pause, I see no reason against including an extra set. Indeed, the 10−7−4−2 would be preferable to the 7−4−2 if one really did put that much stress on *got*. To show the cadence of the line in another way, notice how it vanishes when we change a couple of words: "Well-begotten, and nurtured by an ideal mother."

The third line exhibits no interpretive problem but, coming just after the devoted reference to his mother, raises a possibly valuable side issue: Whitman seems to use (whether consciously or not) the *cursus* on matters of great personal concern and involvement. He was truly a city person of the "populous pavements." Here, in support of the foregoing but with a useful example of the *cursus* theory at work, is a later line in this prefatory poem:

I *stand* in my *place* with my *own day* here,   (9−6−3=2)

(From now on I will not mark the separate syllables but will underline the appropriate accents.) This line (l. 62) illustrates one of the variations in the 4−1 ending that Croll discusses. Many of the effective *cursus* lines appear at the end of the subdivisions of stanzas, which are usually long sentences. This line comes at the end of a subsection in which the persona is acknowledging, weighing, thanking, but finally turning his back on the traditional past. Any terminal line might, with a little fillip, conclude some point elaborated upon, so the *cursus* is appropriate. Croll points out the complication of the 4−1 ending and the added value of the two variations, the 4́−3́−2−1 or the 4−3́−2́−1. Line 62 uses the second of these to reinforce Whitman's (or the persona's) present-time commitment. Such a blunt interruption of the rhythmic flow could not appear earlier in the line without destroying the rhythm itself. But, coming at the end, after the established cadence, it makes the emphasis especially effective.

Here is the final line (l. 68) of stanza 5:

Yes *here* comes my *mis*tress the *soul*.   (7−4−1)

Stanza 6 continues the welcome to the soul, which he will celebrate in many different kinds of poems (or songs or leaves) he promises to provide. The stanza ends with a subsection, beginning "I will sing the song of companionship," and thus preparing for the Calamus cluster to appear later in the book. The nine lines exhibit his qualifications for writing the Calamus poems and end with this statement (l. 94):

> And who but I *should* be the *po*et of *com*rades?   (8–5–2)

The preceding eight lines provide the context that propels this *cursus* and enforces its meaning. Note that alone, or in a different context, the line might have a different emphasis, stressing the *I*, as "And *who* but *I* should *be* the *po*et of *com*rades?" or "*I* should *go* on a *di*et," or some other element, as "I *rea*lly should *get* at those *term* papers," etc. But Whitman's *should* is not to be read that way at all. What it is is a confident assertion, almost a boast, that with his experience (?), sensitivity, and poetic courage, he alone is best qualified to take on this assignment.

There are many other *cursus* in "Starting from Paumanok," the prefatory poem of the 1860 edition, and in "So Long!," the poem that concludes that volume, and all along the way. But there is a greater variety of uses in the first, major, and best-known poem, "Song of Myself." It is impossible here to demonstrate all the uses, but it can be shown that this oral feature appears at key places in the poem and thus provides a rhythmical and tonal quality that is in the text and on the printed page. It is a stylistic feature not found in any other poet because no other approached poetry as Whitman did.

Now in "Song of Myself" there are great blocks of the poem in which there are not only no *cursus* but no point in having any. These are the catalogs and the short narrative sequences, together making up about 500 lines, over a third of the poem. There are two, at the beginning of catalogs (ll. 148, 266), which if considered *cursus* are probably accidental:

> The *lit*tle one *sleeps* in its *cra*dle,   (8–5–2 ?)
> The *mar*ried and *un*married *chil*dren / ride *home* to their *Thanks*giving *din*ner,   (8–5–2 / 8–5–2 ?)

Both lines fit the spacing of accents by the unaccented syllables, but is *lit*tle stronger than *sleeps*, which in turn is stronger than *cra*dle? And is there a falling stress in the accented syllables of the two parts of line 266? I do not think so. Indeed, such stress would highlight the wrong features of these simple domestic situations. My own reading would keep the accents more or less the same. An important point to be made here is that these two lines *look* like *cursus* when seen on the page, but the test to be applied is not visual but vocal. Yet why should there not be *cursus* in the catalogs and narratives? Because they are the gathered materials (representing in the large sense the American experience) to which the *cursus* are a response. In a certain sense the material in the catalogs is just as valid in the printed text as in an oral presentation (and a movie version might be even better). With the *cursus* Whitman was able to suggest, imply, communicate, something of his response to these materials, to the American experience—a something that he might suggest in his voice but believed he could not do in conventional prose or in traditional metrical prosody.

Many of the *cursus* do, then, follow the catalogs, sometimes responding to individual items, as in lines 235 and 236:

?　　　?　　　?　　　? /　?　　　　?　　?　/
Oxen that rattle the yoke and chain or halt in the leafy shade,
　　what is *that* you ex*press* in your *eyes*?　　(9–6–3–1 / 6–3–1 / 7–4–1)
It seems to me *more* than all the *print* I have *read* in my *life*.　　(11–7–4–1)

Does *that* in the final set of line 235 deserve special stress that permits it to begin a *cursus*? In this context, yes, for he has just said about nature and American life, "not a person or object missing, / Absorbing all to myself and for this song." We are always caught by the enigma behind our dog's or cat's steady unblinking gaze, as Whitman was by the placid gaze of the oxen. If we could read behind it, we might grasp something of that great puzzle of animal consciousness and thus get closer to the greater puzzle of being. Notice that Whitman might have said "it"— "What is it you express in your eyes?"—which would make it a casual question undeserving of the *cursus* construction. For the first two sets of line 235, the question marks over the possible accents indicate that the *cursus* could embrace those extra sets, depending on one's reading of the line. My interrogations mean that I do not insist that these are *cursus* but acknowledge that others may read them that way.

And that brings up a key point: there is a danger that we, as readers, may overstress the *cursus* rhythm, read too rapidly, and achieve thereby a Procrustean, formulaic pattern destructive of poetic meaning. All Whitman lines, but especially the *cursus*, must be read with deliberation and with attention to the meaning of the words, not to the *cursus* pattern. The *cursus* effects will come by themselves as a higher or distant harmony enhancing, by echoing, the meaning of the lines. That correspondence may be shattered by the destructive force of the emphatic patterning. It is like reading Emily Dickinson while tapping out the hymn meters. The beauty of the cadence is in its extended form, the longer the better, but the danger is that the length itself may force direct consciousness of the pattern with the destructive results mentioned. There is no way to know how aware Whitman was of the *cursus* device. But even though he may not have had the term for it, he seems to have recognized this feature in the sermons, lectures, and orations he admired. From the little I know of the sermons of Elias Hicks and Father Taylor, there were some, and also in Emerson's essays (perhaps a carry-over from the original lectures). I have not examined Webster's or Ingersoll's speeches, but found a surprising amount, in a somewhat primitive but compelling form, in the selections in Bruce Rosenberg's *Art of the American Folk Preacher*.

Part of the reason for thinking that Whitman was aware of the value of the *cursus* is that he sometimes almost overdoes it. Some of that near-excess is found in the last eleven lines of stanza 14, which comes after almost one hundred lines of narrative sketches and catalog with no *cursus* at all. In these lines (ll. 253–63) there is no way but to see (or hear) that the *cursus* could be a curse if not used with Whitman's remarkable skill.

?

The *press* of my *foot* to the *earth springs* a *hun*dred
    *af*fections,   (14–11–8–5–2) or (7–4–1 / 5–2)
   ?   ?
They scorn the *best* I can *do* to re*late* them.   (11–8–5–2)

?

I am ena*mour*'d of *grow*ing out*doors*,   (10–7–4–1)
Of men that *live* among *cat*tle or *taste* of the *ocean or*
    woods,   (5–2 / 7–4–1)

STYLISTIC INNOVATIONS AND RENOVATIONS

Of the *buil*ders and *steer*ers of *ships*, and the *wiel*ders of *ax*es and *mauls*, and
the *drivers* of *hor*ses, $(7-4-1 \, / \, 7-4-1 \, / \, 5-2)$
　　？　　　　　　　　　　　　　？　　　　？
I can eat and *sleep* with them *week in* and *week out.* $(8-5-2)$ or
$(8-5=4-2=1)$

What is commonest, cheapest, nearest, easiest, is Me,
Me going *in* for my *chan*ces, *spen*ding for *vast*
*re*turns, $(8-5-2 \, / \, 6-3-1)$
A*dorn*ing my*self* to be*stow* my*self* on the *first* that will *take*
me, $(9-6-3-1 \, / \, 5-2)$
　　　　　　　　　　　　　　？
Not *ask*ing the *sky* to come *down* to my *good will,* $(11-8-5-2=1)$
*Scat*tering it *free*ly for*ev*er. $(8-5-2)$

Let me stop for this passage long enough to answer certain questions,
which may help to clarify the poetic value of the *cursus*.

Line 253: The only way to make such an extensive *cursus* of fourteen syllables would be to subordinate *springs* to an unaccented syllable. That is possible, but it would thereby force *hun*dred to a lower intensity than *earth*, which to me goes against the tenor of the line. We
must remember that the cadence of the *cursus* line comes from its falling rhythm, something like this for line 253, first in the long form and
then in the divided form:

```
        press
The              foot
      of my              earth
                to the              hun-
                       springs a           fec-
                                    dred af-    tions,
```

```
      press           .        .
The              foot     .        . hun-
      of my           earth . springs a .        fec-
                to the      .        .    dred af-    tions,
                         .        .
```

Although the long form would be preferable if the words corresponded,
when they do not correspond (with *springs* there must follow an up-
surge), adjustment to the thought is necessary.

Line 254: The grammatical referent of *They* is *affections*, and it would be a strain to make it the dominant word in the line and thus subordinate *scorn*. The 8–5–2 *cursus* is natural and appropriate to the thought.

Line 255: This is a well-known Whitman line, and the scoring is correct if one stresses the *I*, which would be appropriate enough in this poem. But there is a problem, not only for this line but for any *cursus* where the pattern fits. Almost all the lines (whether *cursus* or not) in this poem and in most of the early poems have the strongest emphasis early in the line. Often it is the first word that governs the rest of the line. This line does have a *cursus*, to be sure, but in my own reading the *cursus* begins with the *am* of ena*mour'd*, for that is the governing word of the rest of the line and of the next two lines also.

Lines 256–57: These lines make it clear that *cursus* are readily adaptable to a series. A danger to the oral presentation of any series of comparable items would be a singsong rendition that would detract from the serious intent of the lines. This danger might not be so apparent to the silent reader. In view of that, it is interesting that Whitman contrives the series to avoid the danger by changing the construction of each of the five items in the series (note that the semantic and syntactic structure is slightly different for each one). It seems, then, another small corroboration that the oral element was involved in the early stages of his poetry. Line 257, with its three *cursus*, is a rarity; however, there are others in a later remarkable group of *cursus*, lines 1063–1066.

Line 258: This line reveals another intriguing stylistic problem in the *cursus*: what happens when the *cursus* begins with the second of paired words. Certainly the *week in* and *week out* apply to *eat* as well as to *sleep*. There is no rule governing such a situation, but probably Whitman, in the imagined utterance of this line, would parallel *eat* and *sleep* with the same intonation and emphasis, and then drop down consecutively with each pronunciation of *week*. On the *in* and *out*, there is no way to show diagrammatically that there would be a slight deemphasis for each preposition.

Line 259: This famous line has not been scored as a *cursus*, for it does not fit the fairly rigid rules in Croll's article. But let me here quote again Croll's acknowledgment: English "cadence has always . . . been more irregular than in Latin, and subject to whimsical, individual preference or even to deliberate intention to break rhythm noticeable in many authors." This is what Whitman has done in line 259. He was not very bold or daring in himself and in his public relations, in fact he was anything but—except in his poetry. Here he practically stands the *cursus* on its head, with "deliberate intention to break rhythm" in order to obtain an emphasis by shock and surprise. There was no way the hearer (or reader) could respond to this line at its beginning except to accept it as another *cursus*, following the previous six. Prepared by the falling rhythm, we anticipate anything but that final startling *Me* assertion. I hate to be too obvious here but do want to make it clear what a brilliant poetic exploit has taken place. Let me use a scale again to demonstrate:

<pre>
              com-
                                                              Me,
  What is   cheap-
           monest,   near-
                     est,   eas-
                            est,
                                   iest, is
</pre>

Line 260: This is another of the famous lines in this poem, but note how (once we understand the *cursus*) this line will not be thought of as alone and separate. The *Me* (and even the capital letter is to do in print what his voice would do) that ends line 259 is followed not by an exclamation mark but by a comma. Whatever the voice level one gives to that final *Me* is the same level as the beginning *Me* of line 260. If this line were projected on a scale extended from that just above, the second *cursus* that starts with *spen*ding would probably not go as high as the opening *Me*. As I say the line, *spen*ding would be at the same level as the second element, *in*.

Line 261: This line is another in this series of participial phrases by which *Me* characterizes himself as "the American democratic" prophet, with a redefinition of *American* and of *democratic* and a show-and-tell demonstration of *prophet*.

Line 262: I always have trouble with this line, for I do not understand what he is asking the *sky*. Perhaps he means that he does not make ridiculous requests of life; he is a prophet, to be sure, but not one who expects to do the impossible. But clearly the *it* of the last line cannot refer to *sky*, so must refer to *good will*—but to what effect? My blind spot on the import of this line has nothing to do with the question mark over *my*. The question is whether *my* can be an unaccented syllable in this *cursus*; it perhaps should be accented and *good will* not stressed.

Line 263: The question mark here is to acknowledge that there are too many syllables in *Scattering* to fit the rule. But it can be made to fit by hurrying the pronunciation—to make it *Scatt'ring*. In the same way *easiest* in line 259 would be hurried, so that *iest* would be almost like *yest*.

But there is something of a problem in continuing to give examples of the *cursus* in "Myself." In a certain sense cumulative examples would be self-defeating, for such a listing would impose or inject a monotony that Whitman was always careful to avoid. Accordingly let me finish this explanation by picking out a few more lines to show his variations of the *cursus* pattern. For instance, there is nothing in Croll's explanation or examples to indicate that the *cursus* may be contrived to highlight parallel or contrasting ideas, yet Whitman does so with unusual success. He begins section 16 by explaining (l. 330) that he represents and speaks for all kinds of Americans:

> *I* am of *old* and *young*, of the *fool*ish as *much* as the *wise*,
>   (6–3–1 / 7–4–1)

and expands this notion in lines 332–33:

> Ma*ter*nal as *well* as pa*ter*nal, a *child* as *well* as a *man*,
>   (8–5–2 / 6–4–1)
> *Stuff'd* with the *stuff* that is *coarse* and *stuff'd* with the *stuff* that is *fine*,
>   (7–4–1 / 7–4–1)

This device of repeating the "as *well* as" in line 332 (the success of which overrides the slight *cursus* error in the second set: "*young*ster" or "*in*fant" would fit better than the one syllable "child" in the second *cursus*) or repeating the whole phrase except for the contrasting word at the end ("coarse" vs. "fine" in line 333) is one of stylistic markers of Whitman's early poetry. But what we should notice is that the line arrangement draws attention to this oral pattern, a form of "foregrounding" that will be discussed in a later chapter.

At the end of stanza 20, lines 413–21, he makes the bold assertion that he is independent of time. Among other claims, he says (l. 419):

> My *foothold* is *tenon'd* and *mortis'd* in *gran*ite,   (11=10–8=7–5=4–2)

as bold a use of the *cursus* as the thought itself. Croll points out the rare occasion when two adjoining syllables may have equal stress and so may be taken as one accepted member of the *cursus*. But it would be very unusual to find an arrangement to match this line with its daring gesture of tripling what singly would have been an anomaly to make a startling, and perhaps unique, *cursus*. Most of the time a double accent used for emphasis occurs at the beginning of a set, and when it is repeated it is especially effective, as in line 485:

> *Hurrah* for *positive science*! *long live* exact demonstration!
> (8=7−5−2 / 8=7−5−2)

Parallel or contrasting lines, such as those in lines 332−33 above, are spoken so as to balance the two phrases as well as the two lines. Once we adjust our speaking to fit the pattern, it will follow that we will even adjust our pace and emphasis to maintain the balance. Notice how we might respond to these lines (ll. 1269−71) if they were vocalized:

> I have *said* that the *soul* is not *more* than the *body*,   (11−8−5−2)
> And I have *said* that the *body* is not *more* than the *soul*,   (11−8−4−1)
> And nothing, not God, is greater to one than one's self is,

It is in the nature of the Whitman *cursus* that the vocalization of equal thoughts have equal words and equal emphasis and equal time-span of expression. Accordingly, the exchange of "body" and "soul" (l. 1270) will not change the established cadence, for we actually hurry up the pronunciation of "body" to keep the time allotment parallel. And notice how we hurt the cumulative effect of the passage if we should read line 1270 first, then line 1269, to be followed by line 1271. The passage needs the established pattern to start, and needs our contribution to maintain the pattern in the next line, and needs both to prepare us for the intended break in the cadence—the blunt, and therefore forceful, follow-up of line 1271, with its key statement on what the poem is all about. Was Whitman so expert in the subtleties of prosodic rhythm as to work all this out with the verse skill of a Longfellow or a Tennyson? I cannot believe it, and nothing in the "long foreground" provides any foundation for it. What he did was to transpose the imagined utterance of the imagined prophetic speaker to the printed page, and then to print the lines to draw attention to the oral patterns of his message.

Of course other features of the oral background are found in Whitman's lines: the two, three, and even four dots of the first edition to indicate not ellipses but breath pauses; the anaphora and even symploce to draw attention to the rhetorical schemata; the many antitheses and rhetorical questions; the use of punctuation for rhetorical as well as grammatical purposes. But the *cursus* has special importance in "Song of *Myself*" just because of its subject. Other speech-poems are *by* the prophet-poet but *about* the broad-axe, the open road, the rolling earth, the workmen, and so on: this one is both *by* and *about* the speaker himself. All of the *cursus* we have noted are personal, even those from "Starting from Paumanok," but in this poem the occasion for the *cursus* is not only more frequent but almost continual (except the catalogs already mentioned). The *cursus* seem, then, both intentionally and subconsciously, to reflect, to express, to manifest, the speaker. As such they warrant the extra attention given to them here, both in reading and interpreting this major poem.

The *cursus* feature is also important even as a structural device in many passages in which the *I* is the controlling but not dominant or assertive figure. Note in this famous passage (ll. 663–69) on the beauty and meaning of the humblest parts of nature, how all follows from and is embraced by the speaker's prophetic understanding of the world:

> I believe a *leaf* of *grass* is no *less* than the *journey-work* of the *stars*,
> $(14=12-9-6=4-1)$
> And the *pismire* is *equally perfect*, / and a *grain* of *sand*, / and the *egg* of a
> *wren*, $(8-5-2 / 3-1 / 4-1)$
> And the *tree-toad* is a *chef-d'oeuvre* for the *highest*, $(10=9-6=5-2)$
> And the running *blackberry* would *adorn* the *parlors* of *heaven*,
> $(12=11-8=7-5=4-2)$
> And the *narrowest hinge* in my *hand* / puts to *scorn* all ma*chin*ery,
> $(7-4-1 / 6-3)$
> And the *cow crun*ching with de*press'd head* / sur*pass*es any *stat*ue,
> $(7=6-2=1 / 6-2)$
> And a *mouse* is *mira*cle en*ough* / to *stag*ger sex*til*lions of *infi*dels.
> $(7-5-1 / 9-6-3=2)$

For these lines I have marked the accents and put in the slash marks for the end of a *cursus*, although if one has good breath control, it is possible to make each line a *cursus*. The breath pauses may not be precisely those indicated, but some pauses are necessary to capture and to savor the mutually contributing support of cadence and thought. For this sort of rhythmical passage Whitman had a remarkably sensitive ear, perhaps coming more from his listening to others than from practicing with his voice. But whatever the origin of their rhythm, these lines form a memorable *cursus*. The pattern is clearly not as regular and obvious here as in the earlier examples noted, but surely this is intentional, for it controls the presentation in a very delicate, unobtrusive, yet masterly fashion. I do not insist on my accenting of any of these *cursus* lines, and for this passage particularly one's subjective judgment of the importance of the individual items will shape the emphasis. But surely the stress goes more or less along the lines indicated. Whitman could, of course, have made each line regular in cadence, but the resulting insistent pattern would have detracted from the necessary focus on the lovely details of the experience he is describing. In a true sense the variety of the cadence is the appropriate expression of the variety in nature we experience.

There is no way to present all the variations in the *cursus* pattern, partly because many of them demand contextual understanding, but also because Whitman himself seems to be somewhat uncertain how to alert us as readers to the experiment he was engaged in. When he dropped the dots for breath pauses after the first edition, was it because the device was too obvious or not obvious enough (and therefore confusing) to an audience of the written not the spoken word? It is true, for the *cursus* pattern, that it is hard to miss the cadence in such a pat line as "I am the acme of things accomplish'd, and I an encloser of things to be" (l. 1148). Yet some of the most important lines are not obvious at all. Poetic closure, as Barbara Herrnstein Smith has convincingly demonstrated (1968), is a major part of a poem, and by extension the ending may be equally important to a speech-poem. But what of the ending of "Song of Myself"?

Having told us in a *cursus* line (l. 1339):

> I be*queath* my*self* to the *dirt* to *grow* from the *grass* I *love*,
> (6–4–1 / 6–3–1)

he concludes the poem (ll. 1344–46):

> *Fail*ing to *fetch* me at *first keep* enc*ou*raged,   (7–4–1 // 4–2)
> *Miss*ing me *one* place *search* an*other*,   (5–2// 4–2)
> I stop somewhere waiting for you.

The scoring of the two lines draws attention to the sharp division or separation of the terminal *cursus* from that which precedes it. These lines are the same in the first edition as in the sixth and final edition, but in 1856 and through 1871, Whitman put a comma after "first" in line 1344 and another comma after "place" in line 1345. Notice that the ending of the *cursus* foreseen, we push our voices up for the emphasis of the last two words, but are they a command or an invitation? In grammar we speak of command imperatives and hortatory imperatives. These seem to be hortatory, milder than a command. Perhaps Whitman really meant them as a strong wish, a hope, in which case the absence of the comma would be appropriate. The comma forces a break, makes the last two words stand out as an order, which Whitman may have felt like giving in 1856 when he seems to have been at his most prophetically aggressive. But by 1871 he finally realized that commands were not fitting for a poet who can only hope for and try to induce (but never demand) our attention. It is an interesting query and reminds us again how necessary it is that we say the lines of a poem to ourselves.

Near the beginning of this longest of his poems, he says (ll. 8–9):

> I, now thirty-seven years old in perfect health begin,
> *Hop*ing to *cease* not till *death*.   (7–4–1)

In a certain sense, we may say he began his poetic career with a *cursus*. But if so, it ceased to play a significant role a long while before his death. The poetry did continue, but the *cursus* pretty much ceases after 1860. It is not a sudden stop; indeed the 1860 edition, with its increasing number of lyrical poems, marks a transition. As he turned to writing lyrical poetry and, after the Civil War, to an altogether different kind of prophetic writing he turned away from the oral foundation of his art. The *cursus* is rarely used in the late poetry and, when spotted and examined, seems more accidental than intentional.

REVISIONS AND CHANGES

The two possible avenues for the new cultural revolution Whitman was pressing to proclaim were journalism and public speaking. As a practicing journalist he always worked for someone else, and no newspaper proprietor or magazine publisher depending on readership for survival would have increased his circulation with *Leaves* as a feature. As will be shown in Chapter VI, his journalism was important, but chiefly as training in language use. Even if he had the money to publish his own newspaper or magazine, he was sufficiently realistic to recognize the folly of publishing *Leaves* as a popular-press venture. What he did do was work out the original expression of his personal-prophetic message in those lectures sampled above, found he could not present them as oral performances, but then did find another way to do so (with or without Tupper's example). He called the result poetry, perhaps because he could find no other name, and his early critics themselves were at a loss to find a proper label.

In a key sense, the programmatic poetry that dominates the first three editions was possible only through the adoption of a persona, which it was the function of "Song of Myself" as well as the 1855 Preface to establish. But persona is not only a person, a voice, but a role, a person speaking in some imaginable situation. It has not been made sufficiently clear in comments on that key poem that the *speaking person* is essential to the presentation, so essential, in fact, that when Whitman later tried to emphasize the lyrical aspect of the poem he did so by de-emphasizing its oratorical base. He could not do so completely, of course, for that would destroy the poem, but notice the changes he did make. We cannot examine all of them, but to illustrate the direction of his revisionist trend consider these ten. Some of these, in a quite different context, have been pointed out by Malcolm Cowley in the last section of that well-known introduction to his edition (1959) of the first edition.

(1) The first manuscript version of the opening lines went this way:

> I am your voice—It was tied in you—In me it begins to talk.
> I celebrate myself to celebrate every man and woman alive;
> I loosen the tongue that was tied in them,
> It begins to talk out of my mouth.

It is not too difficult to imagine Whitman imagining himself walking up to the front of the platform and beginning his speech in such a fashion. It would fit with what he told Traubel years later: "When I was younger—way back: in the Brooklyn days—and even behind Brooklyn —I was to be an orator—to go about the country spouting my pieces, proclaiming my faith. I trained for all that—spouted in the woods, down by the shore, in the noise of Broadway where nobody could hear me: spouted eternally, and spouted again. I thought I had something to say—I was afraid I would get no chance to say it through books: so I was to lecture and get myself delivered that way" (pp. 5–6). It is true, to be sure, that as it became clear that he was not going to be invited to speak those opening four lines, he prepared them for the press and changed them somewhat, saying (or writing) in the 1855 edition:

> I celebrate myself,
> And what I assume you shall assume,
> For every atom belonging to me as good belongs to you.

These lines remained through the first three editions, but in 1867 he added "and sing myself" to the first line. That may seem inconsequential, but note the change in his own conception of his role that has taken place. Originally he was the speaker for the people, expressly so, as the manuscript version makes clear, and celebrating himself was his way of celebrating "every man and woman alive." That intention is not strengthened by 1855, but is still there with the addition of the 1855 second line. This meaning is by no means negated when he adds "and sing myself" or, in 1881, the title "*Song* of Myself," but there is a weakening (sort of by diffusion). Prophets, orators, public speakers, lyceum lecturers, are not really *singers*, and to inject this extra element is to diffuse the direct force, the audience contact, and the rapport of the original.

(2) Following the opening lines in 1855, in 1856, and 1860, Whitman had added, "I loafe and invite my soul / I lean and loafe at my ease....observing a spear of summer grass" (ll. 4–5), and then, after a blank space, "Houses and rooms are full of perfumes....the shelves are crowded with perfumes" (l. 6). But in the final version of 1881, the one we all read, the one made sacrosanct by Whitman's request that that form of *Leaves of Grass* alone be considered official, we find that he has taken two four-line stanzas from "Proto-Leaf" and inserted them between line 5 and line 6. The first four-line segment is autobiographical:

> My tongue, every atom of my blood, form'd from this soil, this air,
> Born here of parents born here from parents the same, and their parents the
>   same,

STYLISTIC INNOVATIONS AND RENOVATIONS

> I, now thirty-seven years old in perfect health begin,
> Hoping to cease not till death (ll. 6-9)

There is nothing wrong with the lines in themselves, but they are more appropriate to the poem they were taken from and they add nothing to "Song of Myself." "Proto-Leaf" was later retitled "Starting from Paumanok" and has always preceded "Song of Myself," so that line 8 is wrong on two levels; he was not thirty-seven, and this was not where he began. But the real problem with these lines is that they do not contribute to the assumptions which in line 2 he has told us we are to share with him. There are items which (in terms of line 7) he may assume, but we can hardly do so (where were your eight great-grandparents born?). Accordingly the rapport established between the persona and the reader by the first five lines of the poem is endangered, if not broken. The second set of added lines is:

> Creeds and school in abeyance,
> Retiring back a while sufficed at what they are, but never forgotten,
> I harbor for good or bad, I permit to speak at every hazard,
> Nature without check with original energy.

These are well-known lines, especially the last two, but again they serve a prefatory function here and might better do so in the prefatory poem where they originally were. But the problem is less with the quality of the lines than with their presence—interjected twelve years later—for by that time his view of his own poetry had changed. He was less concerned with imagined direct contact with the audience; there is no "you" in the added lines. He was then, as in so many other changes in this long poem, trying to bring out its lyrical side. And this is a central problem in many of these revisions, chiefly because he has committed himself (and us, as readers) to one form of expression (prophetic utterance in the American idiom) and now wishes to change it, to modify it. Let me say again that the stance he adopts (that of speaker, of native prophet) is admittedly a posture, a new poetic way of presenting himself. He is clearly under no obligation to take that stance. But once he does adopt it, does he have a responsibility to stay with it? It is a serious question for which no answer can be given in light of this one example, but we should hold the question in mind as we look at other changes and revisions.

(3) In the 1855 edition, following a series of encounters with various aspects of American life, the persona remarks:

> In me the caresser of life wherever moving....backward as well as forward
> slueing,
> To niches aside and junior bending. (ll. 226–27)

The passage remains the same through the first three editions, but for later ones there are additions:

> In me the caresser of life wherever moving, backward as well as forward
> sluing,
> To niches aside and junior bending, not a person or object missing,
> Absorbing all to myself and for this song. (ll. 232–34)

The phrase "not a person or object missing" hardly seems necessary in light of the wide variety of scenes and events that have been recorded, but as a reaffirmation it does not hurt the line, and may help. But the added line 234 does change the context. In the early versions he was not absorbing the multiple variations of American life for the purpose of the needs of his own ego and certainly not just to make a song of them. The original intention was to speak about the people for the sake of the people, not the poem.

(4) Similarly, the end of the first long catalog (which begins "the pure contralto sings in the organ loft") is: "And these one and all tend inward to me, and I tend outward to them, / And such as it is to be of these more or less I am" (ll. 324–25). These lines continued with only minor changes through 1860, but in the final version he added an extra line: "And of these one and all I weave the song of myself." The *these* and the *them* refer to the occupations and the people (some sixty-five in the whole catalog that forms section 15 in the final version), presented in vivid metonymic detail and with nonjudgmental acceptance. But the added line, as with the addition in (3) above, puts a different focus on the poet and the poem; there is, it seems, a pulling back from the prophetic stance in order to enhance the lyrical aspect of the poem. The added line, which became the source (in 1881) of the final title of this famous poem, is or is not a blessing, depending on whether the revisions to stress the lyrical intent of the poem are welcomed.

(5) At the end of section 22 in the final version the persona is concerned with his role as spokesman for a people of conflicting, indeed

contrary, impulses. It is a vigorous, challenging part of the poem that has remained central throughout all editions. But in the original, the persona is self-portrayed as almost aggressively on the side of those feared by the establishment. He first (in 1855) wrote:

I am he attesting sympathy;
Shall I make my list of things in the house and skip the house that supports
    them?

I am the poet of commonsense and of the demonstrable and of immortality;
And am not the poet of goodness only....I do not decline to be the poet of
    wickedness also.

Washer and razors for foofoos....for me freckles and a bristling beard.

What blurt is it about virtue and vice?
Evil propels me, and reform of evil propels me....I stand indifferent,
My gait is no faultfinder's or rejecter's gait,
I moisten the roots of all that has grown.

Did you fear some scrofula out of the unflagging pregnancy?
Did you guess the celestial laws are yet to be worked over and rectified?

I step up to say that what we do is right and what we affirm is right....and
    some is always the ore of right,
Witnesses of us....one side a balance and the antipodal side a balance,
    (ll. 464–76)

A complexity of changes occurs, most of them worked out in the Blue Book in the middle 1860s. First he kept line 464 as is, but put parentheses around line 465. There is only one parenthesis in the whole poem in the 1855 version, line 304, and it is truly an aside and so appropriately signaled. What his motives were when he added thirty-three more (not new words, just parentheses) needs to be investigated, and why he decided that line 465 was an aside, if that is what it is, is not clear. At any rate he dropped line 466, perhaps because it seemed to reply to its preceding question which had now become an aside. He then changed line 467 to begin with "I." The next line makes fun of polite folk who clean up and shave every day and proclaims his allegiance with the less refined—an appropriate stance for the spokesman of and to the American people. But he later decided that "foofoos" was not appropriate. It is hard to see why, for *foo-foo* was a slang word meaning an outsider, one not in on the secrets of a society, party, or band. Perhaps he felt it was New York City slang only, but in the context it seems sufficiently self-explanatory. At any rate in the Blue Book he changed it to "those that will." In softening the opposition between the two parts of the line, the line itself became somewhat innocuous, which presumably he recognized, for he dropped it altogether. In so doing he weakened not only this section but even the whole poem, for the subtly contrived and curiously dramatic situation of the poem is that of the persona as orator speaking to the people but wanting also to catch the sympathetic attention of the educated, somewhat disaffected members of that society. It was a very effective line in that context, but when he feared he might offend his educated reader, as the projected change and final dropping of the line indicate, he shows that he has lost some of the confidence that made the original version such a daring and successful poetic venture.

The rest of the passage continues without change up to line 475, a vigorous manifestation of the persona's role in the poem. The speaker, having assured the gathered people that (l. 470) he is not going to get caught in the endless palaver about the right and wrong of others' actions ("I stand indifferent"), next challenges his presumed hearers to speak for themselves ("Did you fear . . . Did you guess . . .") then speaks for them ("I step up to say . . .") and identifies with them ("what we do . . . what we affirm is right"). He does all this really to gain—or hoping to gain—the sympathy and possibly the support of his upper-middle-class reader (what would the actual common people, those he carefully does not call "the great unwashed," the farmers, the mechanics, have made of these dozen lines?). But a decade after writing the original line he backs away from this identification with the working people, drops line 475 and the first phrase of line 476, and collapses the two lines into one: "I find one side a balance and the antipodal side a balance." Now no present-day reader groans his dismay when he meets this line in some anthology of American poetry, for he does not know the positive affirmation the original carried, but to see the two is to see a clear manifestation of a shift in the persona's (thus, the poet's) role and function.

(6) These are the opening lines in 1855 for what later became section 35:

STYLISTIC INNOVATIONS AND RENOVATIONS

Did you read in the seabooks of the old-fashioned frigate-fight?
Did you learn who won by the light of the moon and stars?
Our foe was no skulk in his ship, I tell you,
His was the English pluck, (ll. 890–93)

The lines remained in the 1856 and 1860 editions but in the Blue Book
he did a great deal of revising and changing, finally reaching this opening for the 1867 and subsequent editions:

Would you hear of an old-time sea-fight?
Would you learn who won by the light of the moon and stars?
List to the yarn, as my grandmother's father the sailor told it me.

Our foe was no skulk in his ship I tell you, (said he,)
His was the surly English pluck, (ll. 897–901)

In the 1855 version, the lines still fit the speaker addressing a gathering. The "you" of the first two lines can be either singular or plural. In
line 892 the speaker is identifying with one of the participants, as he
has done for other episodes before and after this one. But note how the
import changes in the revised version. The incident is now not one of
the many metamorphoses manifesting the persona's prophetic, visionary powers, but is one of great-grandfather's recollection. The giveaway
that something has gone awry is the 1867 insertion of "list" in line 898,
an archaic "poetical" word totally unsuited to a persona presumably
speaking the idiom of the common people, for whom "foofoos" would
be no problem. There are other uses of "list" in the late poetry and they
show up in revisions like this one, but there is no poetical language of
this sort in the early editions—indeed, the 1855 Preface had blasted the
practice. As a clincher, note how the "I tell you" of line 892 was an
invitation to join the speaker in reliving the battle, and how it later becomes "I tell you, (said he,)," a tale of the battle addressed not to a listening audience but to the poet.

(7) The famous naval battle referred to above ends with one of the
great metonymic descriptions of the sort that led Jorge Luis Borges to
acknowledge: "So when I read Walt Whitman I got the feeling that all
the poets who had written before him, Homer and Shakespeare and
Hugo and Quevedo and so on, had been trying to do, and failing to do,
what Whitman *had* done. I thought of Whitman as having at last dis-

covered how poetry should be written, and so of course I could not but imitate him" (1962:44). Section 36 in its masterly accumulation of selected details is meant to compel imaginative involvement, and in the 1855 edition it is followed by the persona's parallel but even more intense involvement that fits (indeed, manifests) the prophetic role. Thus what later becomes section 37 begins this way in 1855:

O Christ! My fit is mastering me!
What the rebel said gaily adjusting his throat to the rope-noose,
What the savage at the stump, his eye-sockets empty, his mouth spirting whoops and defiance,
What stills the traveler come to the vault at Mount Vernon,
What sobers the Brooklyn boy as he looks down the shores of Wallabout and remembers the prison ships,
What burnt the gums of the redcoat at Saratoga when he surrendered his brigades,
These become mine and me everyone, and they are but little,
I become as much more as I like.

I become any presence or truth of humanity here, (ll. 933–41)

Whitman revised this quite intense presentation, partly in the Blue Book and sometime later, to make the still good but milder introduction to the rest of this famous section (which after the introduction remains the same). But the power of the identifications that the persona has undergone almost demands the opening outcry, which Whitman altered to "You laggards there on guard! look to your arms!" presumably because he worried that the profanity would offend. But had American gentility changed that much in five years? Had his projected ideal hearer or reader suddenly become squeamish? If not, who had really changed, the reader or the writer? The details in lines 934–38 are also dropped, which is unfortunate, for they provide a vivid spread of human reactions, but the loss is not as serious as that of the opening cry. The next two lines, 939–40, are surely more characteristic of the persona as portrayed elsewhere in the poem than is "Embody all presences outlaw'd or suffering" of the final version. The line that seems strongest, "I become any presence or truth of humanity here," is so because we can visualize the persona crying out those words to the surrounding crowd. As such, it is the line most committed to the prophetic stance enacted by the persona (note the so necessary "here") in 1855, which is why,

ten years later, when Whitman (and/or the persona) changed his out-
look, the line was dropped.

(8) In certain ways the very conception of "democratic prophet"
seems an internal contradiction, and perhaps Whitman realized this, for
in sections 38, 39, and 40 he elaborates on his (or the persona's) role,
insisting in 1855: "Behold I do not give lectures or a little charity, /
What I give I give *out of* myself" (ll. 991–92). The giving "out of myself" is a direct explanation of what has been going on in the poem thus
far, for he has been "absorbing" through his multiple identifications in
order to give back. When he later altered the line to "*When* I give I give
myself," the situation changes drastically. The *what* refers to what he is
saying, which is not a canned lecture or some token almsgiving, but the
utterance of the spirit of the nation which he has re-created in himself.
The *what* is, then, something tangible, to be distinguished from the
when, an indeterminate future occasion. The key changes, which are
italicized, may hardly be noticed in a quick glance at the lines, but what
was originally a significant statement of his prophetic function becomes
a sentimental overstatement of the "I give you my heart and soul," "I
give you all my love" sort.

(9) Section 41 ends with the well-known catalog in which the persona outbids "the cautious old hucksters" of earlier religions, and section 42, almost as an interrupter, begins: "....A call in the midst of the
crowd, / My own voice, orotund sweeping and final" (ll. 1050–1051).
It is the voice of the speaker, the persona, that is emphasized, and it is
important to recognize how, in the public speaker situation of "Song of
Myself," the pronouns are used. The "I" is obviously the persona, but it
is true that this is one of the few poems in the language in which the
persona insists he is the poet, "Walt Whitman, an American, one of the
roughs, a kosmos" (l. 499).

It is true that he was never known as Walt before, whether in his
journalistic career, as author of conventional poetry and fiction in the
1840s, or even in family correspondence. He even copyrights the first
edition as Walter Whitman. The Walt persona was, then, something of
a device, intended to draw attention to the first American poet to be
known by his nickname. When all the poets of his generation were being
referred to by the excessively formal three names, Whitman flouted
the custom by aggressively asserting his nickname. Indeed it borders

on the iconoclastic to refer to the author of "To a Waterfowl" as Billy Bryant, and to think of Hank Longfellow, Jimmy Lowell, Jack Whittier, Ollie Holmes. Formal names are part of the apotheosizing process going on in the mid-nineteenth century, with "Household Editions" and other testimonials to make these men the "living classics." The formality applies to titles of poems, too, which Whitman earlier did resist. What, by the way, would have been the consequence to its reputation if Bryant had given the waterfowl its ordinary name—"To a Goose"? "To a Duck"?

Be that as it may, in this poem, Walt Whitman, the "I," is speaker; the "you" would be his listening audience in the platform situation and the reader of the printed form; the "we" is the speaker and the audience together; and "they" would be those outside the range of the speaker's voice. Since the "I" identifies with the audience, the treatment of "they" is usually one of scorn, especially when "they" represent refined society. That seems to be the situation in the middle of section 42.

> They who piddle and patter here in collars and tailed coats....I am aware of
>   who they are....and that they are not worms or fleas,
> I acknowledge the duplicates of myself under all the scrape-lipped and pipe-
>   legged concealments. (ll. 1074–1075)

In 1856 he dropped the last half of that last line but kept the rest, for through the third edition he still maintained the scorn of effete society. In the Blue Book he worried about the "piddle and patter" as being too aggressively scornful, so he made the changes toward the presumably more tactful final version:

> The little plentiful mannikins skipping around in collars and tail'd coats,
> I am aware of who they are (they are positively not worms or fleas,)
> I acknowledge the duplicates of myself, the weakest and shallowest is
>   deathless with me, (ll. 1078–1080)

Both in 1855 and 1860, the admission of his scorn of the effete leads to his acknowledgment of his own egotism, as he says in 1855 (my italics):

> I know perfectly well my own egotism,
> And know my omnivorous *words*, and cannot *say* any less,
> And would fetch you whoever you are flush with myself. (ll. 1079–1081)

But note how by changing two words (in the Blue Book first) he changes the whole situation for the final version (my italics here too):

> I know perfectly well my own egotism,
> And know my omnivorous *lines* and must not *write* any less
> And would fetch you whoever you are flush with myself. (ll. 1082–1085)

Up to 1860, the persona is a speaker, from 1865 he is a poet.

(10) The stance or posture of this prophet-poet-priest of democracy speaking to "you," the audience, directly is the organizing principle of the poem. So section 44 is framed by acknowledgments of the speaker role: "It is time to explain myself....let us stand up" (l. 1133) to "Now I stand on this spot with my soul" (l. 1168), and these announcements remain without significant change through all editions. But, in adjoining sections, there may be seemingly small but significant changes of which those who know only the final version will be unaware. Let me finish this sampling of changes in "Myself" by directing attention to what I cannot but read as a major shift in his relation to his audience, both the assembled people listening to this wander-teacher on his journey through the states and/or the individual reader of the poem.

In section 45 there is the famous section on man's past and future evolution (1855 edition):

> There is no stoppage, and never can be stoppage;
> If I and you and the worlds and all beneath or upon their surfaces, and all
>   palpable life, were this moment reduced back to a pallid float, it would
>   not avail in the long run,
> We should surely bring up again where we now stand,
> And as surely go as much farther, and then farther and farther.
>   (ll. 1189–92)

These lines remained the same in all editions, and in 1855 they led to this conclusion:

> Our rendezvous is fitly appointed....God will be there and wait till we come.
>   (l. 1197)

This seems, both logically and psychologically, the natural (and supernatural, too, one may assume) result of the foregoing lines. But beginning in 1856 this stated consequence of our physical and spiritual evolution underwent various changes, ending up with this final version:

> My rendezvous is appointed and certain,
> The Lord will be there and wait till I come on perfect terms,
> The great Camerado, the lover true for whom I pine will be there.
>   (ll. 1198–1200)

Fine for Walt, we must say, but what about the rest of us? The original line is the proper one in the speaker-audience collaboration of the first edition; indeed it is carefully prepared for. But what a change when Whitman gave up this original platform stance and became the lyric poet who is only to be known as you read him! When the awareness of an audience in front of him no longer held his imagination, he no longer spoke with and for the people, his presumed audience, but for himself.

ᵃᵛ III ᵍᵃ

SPEECH ACTS AND
Leaves of Grass

ILLOCUTIONARY FORCE IN THE EARLY EDITIONS

So far no one has taken up J. L. Austin's implied challenge in *How to Do Things with Words* about the nontruth of poetic language in *Leaves*. One of the "parasitic uses of language" to which he objected was Donne's "Go and Catch a Falling Star," an imperative that was grammatically correct but semantically "not serious." His refusal to examine poetry was not because it did not employ the illocutionary acts he was defining but because in poetry "the normal conditions of reference may be suspended, or no attempt made at a standard perlocutionary act, no attempt to make you do anything, as Walt Whitman does not seriously incite the eagle of liberty to soar" (p. 104). I doubt that Austin had any particular passage in mind, whether from the late "To Soar in Freedom and in Fullness of Power" or "From Paumanok Starting I Fly Like a Bird" or any other poem. Indeed, Austin seems to have had a puckish sense of humor, and probably his reference had its origin in Max Beerbohm's delightful cartoon of Whitman standing on one foot, both arms aloft, a sprig of leaves in his teeth, but sufficient *embonpoint* to ground the bard if not his soaring rhetoric.

Austin's famous book has had far more influence in philosophy than in literary criticism, chiefly because he did not live long enough to work out the application of his "locution-illocution-perlocution" theory of speech acts to literature. But in 1969 John Searle published his *Speech Acts*, a development and classification of Austin's ideas. Since then this very important British contribution to the study of language has been fully studied and examined in this country, from my point of view most significantly by Richard Ohmann in five key articles.

Austin divides speech acts into three: locutionary acts, illocutionary acts, and perlocutionary acts. Locutionary acts are the basic physical and mental acts of saying or writing something. Illocutionary acts are those which carry out what they are saying as they are being said. Perlocutionary acts are those effects or results in the listener or reader of the illocutionary acts. Now the first and the third of these are the least recondite and need no elaborate explanation. A locutionary act is really just any statement that makes sense; it must comply with the grammatical and syntactical precepts of the language. The perlocutionary act is altogether outside the sentence or passage of the speaker or writer, since it refers only to the listener's or reader's response; it would thus be a concern of psychology, rhetoric, or questionnaires to sample audience response.

But if, in stylistic analysis, locutionary and perlocutionary acts are not very important, the whole notion of illocutionary acts is of serious import to a full understanding of Whitman's style. What was of concern to Austin, as a philosopher of language, was the inadequacy of then current language description to distinguish between different levels of speech or writing, or to capture the full force of the speaker's intention when he uttered or wrote what was in his mind. Here are some examples Austin used to start with: "I name this ship the *Queen Elizabeth*" and "I give and bequeath my watch to my brother" and "I bet you sixpence it will rain tomorrow" (p. 5). These are what Austin calls "performative sentences," and later he refers to the "illocutionary acts" they express. But what is the difference between those sentences and these: "The name of this ship is the *Queen Elizabeth*" or "I gave and bequeathed my watch to my brother, but now I take it back" or "I bet him sixpence it would rain tomorrow"? What has happened is that the action of dedication, with the breaking of the champagne bottle and all that, vanishes. Again, in the first sentence about my watch in my last will and testament, the illocutionary act is focused in the words *give* and *bequeath* and under the force of them the ownership of the watch is transferred. In the second *watch* sentence, the *gave* and *bequeathed* are now only declarative, and the illocutionary act has now moved down the sentence to its last four words. Of the two sentences about my rain wager, in the first one I am actually making the bet, but in the second I am only talking about it.

Let us go on about the rain bet a little further. The bet cannot take place just because I'm thinking about it, but I must *say* it and you must *hear* it and *agree* for the bet to be on. *Bet* and *name* and *give* and *bequeath* in the original statements are what Austin means when he claims that in illocutionary acts "the issuing of the utterance is the performing of an action" (p. 6). But remember that you have to understand my bet and agree with it for the bet to take place (it would not work with a speaker of another language, etc.). There is a convention in our society (custom, common practice, call it what you will) that we both understand about bets (and christening boats, bequeathing property, etc.), and my sentence ties me into it (and you too if you accept my bet).

Austin goes past these quite obvious manifestations of illocutionary force to more subtle examples covering the wide range of human interaction. It is fun to read *How to Do Things with Words*, for Austin takes his subject seriously but not himself. In fact, although much is said about illocutionary force, the book itself is more gentle (and sometimes whimsical) than forceful. Richard Ohmann says clearly what is so significant in this new understanding of language function: "The indicator or indicators of illocutionary force implant the meaning in the stream of social interaction; they are what make speech take hold, and what make language more than the medium of information exchange that philosophers and linguists long seem to have thought it" (1972:118).

Austin, to be sure, is chiefly concerned with direct and explicit performatives ("I hereby sentence you to five years") because in them the illocutionary act is obvious. But, as B. G. Campbell points out, "Overt performatives, however, are just one of several ways of expressing illocutionary acts in English. Stress and intonation in speech, punctuation in writing, the mood of verb, word order, are other modes of carrying the act's illocutionary force" (1975:4). Ohmann, too, recognizes the range open to the speaker or writer who wants his words to carry more than just information: "Some transformations make illocutionary force evident; negation often signals denial, the interrogative transformation signals inquiring, the imperative often signals command, and apposition contains the force of a 'verdictive' like defining or identifying. Sentence modifiers can show that the act is a conjecture ('perhaps'),

LANGUAGE AND STYLE IN *Leaves of Grass*

a concession ('admittedly'), an inference ('therefore'), or a denial ('on the contrary'). And there are many miscellaneous signals that every speaker recognizes: *You* & *future* is likely to be a prediction, an order, or a warning; *I* & *future* may be a promise; sentences with value words in them are in part verdictives; etc." (1972: 118). Many locutionary acts are statements only (*e.g.*, declarative sentences), which we read for their informational value. Statements as statements, per se, are true or false, but that is not enough for sentences of illocutionary force.

So what Austin does is to examine and propose "felicity conditions," that is, those conditions to which the illocutionary act must conform to be effective. One cannot ask of the judge ("I sentence you to five years") or the minister ("I now pronounce you man and wife") whether their utterances are true or not. But there are conditions that determine whether an illocutionary act is valid. One can easily imagine all sorts of illocutionary-destructive situations: the minister might have a gun at his head, both the bride and the groom might still be legally married elsewhere, etc. Austin spent four chapters working out these "felicity conditions," and although the examples he uses are not as blatant as those above, they are of the same sort. Ohmann, in a lively presentation of the speech-act theory as it applies to contemporary media, summarizes the "felicity rules" as he calls them under these four headings:

1. The circumstances must be appropriate.
2. The persons must be the right ones.
3. The speaker must have the feelings, thoughts, and intentions appropriate to his act.
4. Both parties must behave appropriately afterward. (1974: 50).

And Ohmann adds this explanatory comment: "The rules for illocutionary acts determine whether performance of a given act is well-executed in just the same way as grammatical rules determine whether the product of a locutionary act—a sentence—is well-formed. Doing an illocutionary act is acting by virtue of conventions, socially established and understood rules. But whereas the rules of grammar concern the relationships among sound, syntax, and meaning, the rules for illocutionary acts concern relationships among people."

The "felicity rules" themselves and their controlling action as to illocutionary validity or effectiveness are more significant features than the simplicity of their appearance might indicate. It is these rules that govern critical analysis in this new approach. Ohmann uses them brilliantly in an analysis of Thomas Carlyle (1972: 131–34), which was a revelation for me a few years ago as to the critical possibilities for *Leaves*.

Clearly not all illocutionary acts are as simple and obvious as "I bid three spades" or other examples used above. Indeed many of the differences among those who follow Austin arise in determining which organizational pattern is best for bringing together the various illocutionary forces available to the speaker or writer. The taxonomy used here is that proposed by Searle, originally in *Speech Acts* but since developed in more usable form in *Expression and Meaning* (1979).

> *Assertives.* The point or purpose of the members of the assertive class is to commit the speaker (in varying degrees) to something being the case, to the truth of the expressed proposition. (1979: 12)
> *Directives.* The illocutionary point of these consists in the fact that they are attempts . . . by the speaker to get the hearer to do something. (p. 13)
> *Commissives.* . . . Those illocutionary acts whose point is to commit the speaker (again in varying degrees) to some future course of action. (p. 14)
> *Expressives.* The illocutionary point of this class is to express the psychological state specified in the sincerity condition about a state of affairs specified in the propositional content. [The "sincerity condition" Searle refers to would be "felicity rules" 2, 3, and perhaps 4 in the Ohmann list above.] (p. 15)
> *Declarations* [*Declaratives*]. It is the defining characteristic of this class that the successful performance of one of its members brings about the correspondence between propositional content and reality (pp. 16–17)

The terms and their definitions are Searle's, and he gives fuller explanations of each. Let us now go down through the list of five again, adding some further explanations from Mary Louise Pratt (1977: 80–81) and giving a few examples for each from "Song of Myself."

Assertives. These are "illocutionary acts that undertake to represent a state of affairs, whether past, present, future, or hypothetical, e.g. stating, claiming, hypothesizing, describing, predicting, telling, insisting, suggesting, or swearing that something is the case." So Whitman says:

> This hour I tell things in confidence,
> I might not tell everybody, but I will tell you. (ll. 387–88)

selecting "you," his addressee, as special audience, as his confidant. (Following Ohmann and Campbell in this practice, I draw attention to illocutionary forces by broken underlining.) Again, near the end of the poem:

> I swear I will never again mention love or death inside a house,
> And I swear I will never translate myself at all, only to him or her who
>   privately stays with me in open air. (ll. 1250–51)

In both parts of this compound sentence the "I swear" is grammatically superfluous, but here as everywhere in *Leaves* illocutionary force is the key to the style. Sometimes to place effectively his stating his claim, his insistence on the truth of his utterance, he may prepare for it with a leading question:

> Has anyone supposed it lucky to be born?
> I hasten to inform him or her it is just as lucky to die, and I know it.
>   (ll. 131–32)

Perhaps the best-known sentence carrying the illocutionary force of this group is that of the affirmation following the so-called mystical experience of section 5. The whole eight-line sentence is an illocutionary act of the assertive class, in which these key lines are embedded:

> And I know that the hand of God is the promise of my own,
> And I know that the spirit of God is the brother of my own. (ll. 92–93)

Perhaps this is as good a place as any to point out that not only are illocutionary acts central to this poem (and to the work) but Whitman employs all the rhetorical patterns he can to draw the reader's attention to them—as here—with anaphora (the repetition of opening words) and epistrophe (repetition of closing words) as well as the rare symploce (anaphora and epistrophe in two or more adjoining lines). In fact here symploce has been given an artful extension so that the lines are identical but for the "hand / spirit" and "promise / brother" change.

Directives. Pratt gives this further explanation: "Illocutionary acts designed to get the addressee to do something, e.g. requesting, commanding, pleading, inviting, daring." These, too, are found in *Leaves* (especially before *Drum-Taps*) and are central to "Myself." Early in the poem, he asks: "Have you felt so proud to get at the meaning of poems?" (l. 33), so that he can follow with: "Stop this day and night with me and you shall possess the origin of all poems" (l. 34). This seems to be an imperative command (which would also be a directive, to be sure), but in the context it is really an <u>invitation</u>. Later he does make a request: "Eleves, I salute you! <u>Come forward!</u> / <u>Continue</u> your annotations, <u>continue</u> your questionings" (ll. 974–75). Near the end of the poem, the line, "<u>Shoulder your duds</u>, dear son, and I will mine, and <u>let us hasten forth</u>" (l. 1215), is as much an invitation as a <u>request</u>, but at the end of the stanza he does make a <u>command</u> (and note the usual but effective use of the verb *will*):

> Long have you timidly waded holding a plank by the shore,
> Now <u>I will you</u> to be a bold swimmer,
> To jump off in the midst of the sea, rise again, nod to me, shout and
>   laughingly dash with your hair. (ll. 1231–33)

And of course the famous last <u>request-plea-invitation</u> to conclude the poem:

> Failing to fetch me at first <u>keep encouraged</u>,
> Missing me one place <u>search another</u>,
> I stop somewhere waiting for you. (ll. 1344–46)

Commissives. These are "illocutionary acts that commit the speaker to doing something, e.g. promising, threatening, vowing." The last line of "Myself," quoted above, is a commissive. Since at the time the sentence is made the speaker is talking about some future action, the illocutionary obligation is usually expressed by the complement in the sentence:

> To cotton-field drudge or cleaner of privies I lean,
> On his right cheek I put the family kiss,
> And in my soul I swear <u>I never will deny him</u>. (ll. 1003–1005)

To reinforce this continual commitment to the lowly and despised, he also brings in an "I swear," an assertive previously discussed. Sometimes a supporting illocutionary element may come first, as in the famous lines:

> I speak the pass-word primeval, I give the sign of democracy,
> By God! <u>I will accept nothing</u> which all cannot have their counterpart of on
>   the same terms. (ll. 506–507)

Since the commissive is to emphasize the commitment of the speaker to some subsequent action, "Myself" by its internal structure would not be so likely to stress or emphasize that form of illocutionary act.

The purpose of most of the lines is self-revelation through immediate, present-time characteristic response to contemporaneous situations (thus there would be many more assertives). "Starting from Paumanok," by contrast, organizes whole sections around commissives, for it is a prefatory poem in which the speaker is committing himself to handle the many themes in the ensuing poems: thus in section 6 of twenty-six lines there are seventeen "I will" promises, and in section 12 with its twenty-one lines there are sixteen more.

Expressives. There are "illocutionary acts that express only the speaker's psychological state, e.g. congratulating, thanking, deploring, condoling, welcoming." The illocutionary force here is somewhat like that of assertives, but there is a difference. Searle points out that most illocutionary acts attempt either "to get the words to match the world," as do assertives, or "to get the world to match the words," as do directives and commissives. The feature of expressives, Searle believes, is that "the speaker is neither trying to get the world to match the words nor the words to match the world, rather the truth of the expressed proposition is presupposed" (1979: 15). Thus when the poet says: "I harbor for good or bad, I permit to speak at every hazard, / Nature without check with original energy" (ll. 12–13), he is not trying to find words to describe what he has discovered about the world—such assertives as "I guess it must be the flag of my disposition, out of the hopeful green stuff woven. / Or I guess it is the handkerchief of the Lord" (ll. 101, 102) would be doing that. Nor would he be trying to change the world, including "you" as addressee in directives, or himself in a commissive where he obligates himself to some activity that will alter some aspect of the world. There are a great many expressives in "Myself," for the poet takes the role of one trying to show the listener or reader what sort of person he is. Perhaps one might say that the whole poem had a directive intent to the extent that the poet is trying to get the reader to identify with him (in Kenneth Burke's sense of identification) as preparatory to making the subsequent poems more convincing, but even so these expressives clearly express, and intentionally so, the state of mind, the psychological state, of the poet:

> I am enamour'd of growing out-doors, (l. 255)
>
> I am of old and young, of the foolish as much as the wise, (l. 330)

I am he that walks with the tender and growing night, (l. 433)
Divine am I inside and out, and I make holy whatever I touch or am
　　touch'd from. (l. 524)

all the way to

　　　　Do I contradict myself?
　　　　Very well then I contradict myself,
　　　　(I am large, I contain multitudes.) (ll. 1324–26)

and "I too am not a bit tamed, I too am untranslatable" (l. 1332).

Declarations (Declaratives). These are "illocutionary acts that bring about the state of affairs they refer to, e.g. blessing, firing, baptizing, bidding, passing sentence." This class includes the obvious examples used earlier, in which the person speaking had the authority to make his illocutionary act perform his intention. He was, in a meaningful sense, doing what he was supposed to do: the judge sentencing the prisoner, the minister marrying the couple, even the bridge player who bids three spades has the authority to do so. But what authority does the speaker have in "Myself"? To begin with, he would have the authority of any person (speaker, orator, poet, or prophet) to say what was on his mind. So when he says "I celebrate myself," his words bring about or activate his declaration. But as the manifestation of the speaker continues, revealing him as the poet, prophet, cynosure, and conscience of democracy, he endows himself with the authority of that role. So: "I chant the chant of dilation or pride" (l. 428), or "I am he attesting sympathy" (l. 461). The following two lines were quoted above to show the second as a commissive, but the first of them is a clear example of a declaration for a spokesman of democracy:

I speak the pass-word primeval, I give the sign of democracy,
By God! I will accept nothing which all cannot have their counterpart of on
　　the same terms. (ll. 506–507)

By speaking (or writing) as he does, he is at the same time saying that he is accomplishing it. Sometimes declarations draw attention to themselves with an interjection, as in the effective "Behold, I do not give lectures or a little charity, / When I give I give myself" (ll. 994–95), in which he is intending to give (or is giving?—a key question) "the real Walt Whitman" in his utterance or in the lines of his poem, as he attempts again many pages later in "So Long!," in his most daring expressive:

> Camerado, this is no book,
> Who touches this touches a man. (ll. 53–54)

The final declaration in "Song of Myself" is one of many illocutions in that last stanza: "I bequeath myself to the dirt to grow from the grass I love" (l. 1339).

Such, then, are the illocutionary acts, of which there are more in Whitman than in any other American or English poet. It is indeed, *the* stylistic feature of *Leaves* up to and including the 1860 edition. One of the values of computer assistance would be to substantiate (or reject) such a claim. Edwin Eby's *Concordance* does, however, permit a rough estimate of major illocutionary verbs. I checked a list of some hundred performative verbs taken from a much longer list in Bruce Fraser, "Hedged Performatives" (1975), added some others from Charles Travis, *Saying and Understanding* (1975), and from Stephen Tyler, *The Said and the Unsaid* (1978), plus Ohmann's articles previously mentioned. The proportion seems to be over fifty to one (583 to 11); that is, for any illocutionary verb form used in the late poetry there would be fifty uses in the 1860 edition. Sometimes there would be only a few uses (for such performative verbs as accept, acknowledge, adopt, advance), other times (believe, know, say, swear, tell, think) a great many; "I believe" or "I swear," for instance, would each be used twenty-five times in the early poetry and then disappear altogether.

Of course, any sentence anywhere does carry some illocutionary force. Even the directions in a cookbook state something by someone who thinks it important, and the statement conforms without question to the "felicity rules." But such statements are nearly anonymous, and their illocutionary force so minimal as to be negligible. At the other end of the illocutionary spectrum, every sentence would be an illocutionary act, an oppressive and, indeed, offensive situation which Whitman would never desire. Illocutionary acts, whether in life or in literature, add such a burden of personal involvement and intensity (for both speaker and listener, poet and reader) that they can be destructive of perlocutionary effects. Whitman could not but know this. It is also true, however, that he strained this illocutionary tension so far that he can never be successfully imitated but can easily be parodied. There is nothing so much like a bump on a hollow (unless one is the hollow), and perhaps Whitman never realized the dangerous similarity of the serious and the comic, the sublime and the ridiculous, profundity and prolixity, prophesying and posturing. But before evaluating the effectiveness of Whitman's speech-act device, we need first to examine the central problem the critic must face in all this, and that is, What happens to the illocutionary act in literature?

This is the dilemma Austin faced twenty-five years ago, and he pointed it out and let it alone. There are, in fact, two problems here. What happens when the oral illocutionary act gets put in writing? What happens when the oral illocutionary act having been put in writing is then put in literature? Let us focus the problem on the first sentence quoted from Austin, the one about the christening of the ship, a standard illocutionary act of the declaration class.

Can the senator christen the ship by staying home and writing a letter to the captain with the declaration carefully written and even the name of the ship properly underlined? No, because there are *some* illocutionary acts that demand the physical presence of the person in authority, and the words must be spoken. If that declaration is written, as a reporter might or the senator herself in a letter to a friend, it is a report and has lost nothing but the most important element, the illocutionary force. So, here we are faced with a problem. Illocutionary acts are *speech acts* in Austin's sense and especially in Searle's sense, and many of the examples they use are best imagined as utterances spoken, presumably with gestures, voice intonations, eye contact, and such other aids to oral communication.

But if *some* illocutionary acts are thus circumscribed, not *all* are. I can *promise* to pay you next week, *will* my watch to my brother, *bet* a sixpence, even *bid* three spades by mail or some other written vehicle, and all these illocutionary acts are valid if the "felicity rules" have been met. Although illocutionary acts are usually oral, that is, spoken by the person expressing his illocutionary force, Ohmann does see that a bridge must be made, if we are to speak of illocution in literature. At first, Ohmann saw only a slight loss or diminution: "I should add, since I am addressing myself to a problem in literary theory, that all three kinds of acts [locutionary, illocutionary, and perlocutionary] may be performed in and through writing. The nature of the locutionary act is thereby altered in obvious ways. The illocutionary act is more or less attenuated, and the perlocutionary act is more or less delayed" ("Speech Acts," 10).

Nevertheless, the illocutionary act does involve direct personal interchange, whether by voice or by letter. To make *promises*, *bequests*, *bets*, and *bids* to everyone at the same time (even to those not yet born, as in much of Whitman's poetry) is to break all four "felicity rules." Now clearly Austin was probing his way through the then general ignorance of illocutionary forces and made mistakes that Searle and others have caught and corrected. But he did not hesitate this time: "A performative utterance [one conveying illocutionary force] will, for example, be *in a peculiar way* hollow or void if said by an actor on the stage, or if introduced in a poem, or spoken in a soliloquy." The "sea-change" that occurs in such circumstances is so strong that Austin, having trouble enough trying to work out the legitimate illocutionary function of his discovery, has no wish at all to consider literature: "Language in such circumstances is in special ways—intelligibly—used not seriously, but in ways *parasitic* upon its normal use—ways which fall under the doctrine of the *etiolations* of language. All this we are *excluding* from consideration" (1962: 22). Whatever initial excitement literary critics may have felt as word of Austin's formulations began to spread in linguistic circles was soon dashed, as the import of the above comment sank in. But Ohmann, the first to realize the potential of the speech-act theory for the critic, was also the first to find a way to use Austin's discoveries after all. The discussion, sometimes indeed rather heated argument, is still going on, and it is necessary to summarize it briefly before we turn to Whitman.

In a series of five articles from 1971 to 1974, Ohmann examined the ways in which the speech-act theory can be of aid to the literary critic. He answered Austin's relegation of literary language by acknowledging that "*A literary work is a discourse whose sentences lack the illocutionary forces that would normally attach to them.*" But literature does not have to be rejected as long as we remember that "*its illocutionary force* is mimetic." The reader will readily "imagine a speaker, a situation, a set of ancillary events, and so on" ("Speech Acts," 14).

In 1976, Samuel Levin corroborated this view but added a very useful new scheme for accepting illocutionary acts. His contribution, over-looked by later commentators, was that we as readers can and should always posit a "higher sentence, held to be implicit in the deep structure of all poems, and from which the facts follow as natural sequences" (1976: 148). Levin explains the value of the "higher sentence" concept in linguistic analysis and then offers the seemingly simple but shrewdly conceived all-inclusive higher sentence for poetry. This is the sentence that the poet (and the reader) recognizes as the unwritten preliminary to his poem: "*I imagine myself in and invite you to conceive a world in which . . .*" (p. 150). Levin continues: "The illocutionary force of this [implied but always understood] utterance is one of the poet's transporting himself or projecting himself into a world of his imagining, a world which he is free to make as different from [or as similar to] our world as he pleases. . . . It is a world which only the poet, or the transported image of himself [the persona], can know, and which we can discover only from his account of it. But the poet invites us to conceive that world with him" (p. 154). Levin demonstrates the usefulness of this higher sentence with an analysis of Blake's "Holy Thursday," to which he adds further useful comment in his *Semantics of Metaphor* (1977) and again in an important article in *Poetics* (1978).

Dennis Baron in "Role Structure and the Language of Literature" (1975) acknowledges Ohmann's rejection of true or real illocutionary force for literature, because the very structure and appearance of the literary work is an acknowledgment of its fiction. Baron writes, quite correctly: "The performative *I write* of literary language does not function like the parallel declarative *I say* of natural language. The statement made (text) is labeled by the matrix not as true or conditional, but as fake with respect to the participants in the communication, i.e., the author and audience." Yet, he too permits an avenue by which the illocutionary force is not altogether lost: "The literary speech act differs from other perlocutionary acts in that the reality brought into existence works a change on the audience (i.e., creates an effect) not by its literal truth value but by the principal means of foregrounding available to literature: the casting of the narration into a fictional mode within the communication event" (p. 51).

In 1975 also, B. G. Campbell made a test case of the speech-act theory by using Ohmann's classification of illocutionary acts as a critical approach to Masters' *Spoon River Anthology* and to Donne's "Go and Catch a Falling Star." The critical analysis in each case is very effective, but Campbell too believes it necessary to warn that the illocutionary force in the poem is not direct: "The fruitful area for study, therefore, is how the author effects his intended perlocutionary acts in the reader on the real world level through the reader's ability to individuate the characters' illocutionary acts within the instantial world at level two" (1975: 8).

Late in 1975, in Chicago, there was a lively conference on speech acts and literature, organized by Michael Hancher, editor of *Centrum*, a Minnesota journal, who later provided a transcript of the papers and of the discussion afterward. The participants in the conference were Stanley Fish, E. D. Hirsch, Barbara Herrnstein Smith, and Martin Steinman. *Centrum* continues to focus on speech-act theory, providing two bibliographies and the recent reprinting of the papers and discussion for another conference. That issue (Fall, 1978) also includes Charles Altieri's valuable article on the work of the legendary H. Paul Grice, who has extended Austin's theory to the whole cooperative role of conversational interchange.

The 1975 papers do not add significantly to the present explanation, but two participants (Fish and Smith) correctly warn of the danger to literary interpretation if one uses speech acts to characterize the author of the literary work when only the persona is responsible for the speech acts in the text. This is certainly valid (on such grounds Fish had, in 1973, objected to Ohmann's characterization of Carlyle) and posits an interesting problem as far as Whitman is concerned. We all acknowledge that Whitman is not the persona of *Leaves* but we do so against Whitman's continual insistence (except in that one letter to Mrs. Gilchrist) that he is the "I" of the poetry. But it is a moot point as far as this study goes, for the only concern is with the persona's speech acts as a stylistic feature of the poetry.

In this brief survey of speech-act commentary, the final view necessary to explain here is Pratt's. She is convinced (and has convinced me) that there is no such thing as "poetic language" as distinct in any essential sense from prose or everyday language. She does not give enough attention to the density of metaphor as a hallmark of poetry, but she shows clearly enough that metaphor is found in all language. But what is most important is her circumventing the long dominant contention that literature is not concerned with expression for the sake of communication but with expression for its own sake. Definitively stated most clearly by Jan Mukařovsky, but supported by the late Roman Jakobson, by Roland Barthes, Levin, and numerous others, this contention holds that "in poetic language foregrounding achieves maximum intensity to the extent of pushing communication into the background as the objective of expression and of being used for its own sake; it is not used in the services of communication, but in order to place in the foreground the act of expression, the act of speech itself" (1970: 43–44). This famous sentence from Mukařovsky's justly famous essay on foregrounding is actually not rejected or denied by Pratt or by Elizabeth Traugott and other generative semanticists. Rather, what they claim is that everyday language may also include what amounts to foregrounding. Through the skillful presentation of "natural narratives," drawn from the work of William Labov and others, and with the language discoveries of Austin and Grice, Pratt proposes "tellability" as a shaping motive for expression in jokes, anecdotes, tales, novels, plays, poetry, with no *essential* difference in the language used. There is, then, in her view, not a difference of kind but of degree between the language of poetry and anecdote. It is true that Pratt does not explore sufficiently the density of metaphor in poetry, and she occasionally quotes her adversaries out of context to make her points. There seems no great disservice to poetry or to literary criticism in agreeing with her conclusion. And the benefit in such an admission is that it embraces all the insights and clues to interpretation of earlier critics and adds to them the further critical tools of the speech-act discoveries of Austin and his commentators.

The question now is how all this relates to Whitman and to *Leaves of Grass*. When Whitman returned from New Orleans in 1848 to start a new career, there is no evidence that he intended to be a poet but a great deal of evidence that he intended to be an orator, speaker, lecturer, wander-teacher. The prophetic role he imagined for himself (of which the lecture notes in the early notebooks are the remnant) he never really had the nerve to enact, but the lectures (the notes for public speakers) are the first stage for the poetry. The key point here is that the change from prophet to poet was both a gain *and a loss*. The obvious gain is the evolution of *Leaves* through its successive editions. But the accompanying loss was a major one (Whitman even seems to think it a crucial loss), and the only way to estimate it is by the remarkable efforts Whitman made to prevent it, to overcome it, to compensate for it.

What he thought he had lost was the strength, the force, the charisma, the personal magnetism, the immediacy, the convincingness of the prophet. Unless we know someone who is truly a prophet, we have no way of comparing the prophet's utterance with the written version of it. The television replay of a Martin Luther King, Jr., speech is not even close, but note the enormous loss between that and the written version of the "I have a dream" speech. He was no prophet either, in the sense Whitman wanted to be, but even with an effective public speaker (as Winston Churchill) we can sense something of the loss. This is not to say that Whitman wanted to be a Bob Ingersoll or a Daniel Webster or a Wendell Phillips. His imagined role as the prophet of a democratic religion (or a religious democracy, as you will) was far more radical, profound, daring, disruptive, momentous than anything those fascinating speakers (that is, by their reputations, for they were very dull writers) ever attempted.

But what true prophets have is complete confidence and sincerity in their role, and there is nothing in the Whitman biography to put him into such company. If we accept near-total prophetic absorption and single-minded conviction as signs, we must also say that Whitman was not and never approached being a prophet. Nor would he have met the conditions Isaiah sets up in William Blake's *Marriage of Heaven and Hell*, plate 12:

> The prophets Isaiah and Ezekiel dined with me, and I asked them how they dared so roundly to assert that God spake to them; and whether they did not think at the time that they would be misunderstood, & so be the cause of imposition.
>
> Isaiah answer'd: "I saw no God, nor heard any, in a finite organized perception: but my senses discover'd the infinite in every thing, and as I was then perswaded, & remain confirm'd, that the voice of honest indignation is the voice of God, I cared not for consequences, but wrote."
>
> Then I asked: "Does a firm perswasion that a thing is so, make it so?"
>
> He replied: "All poets believe that it does, & in ages of imagination this firm perswasion removed mountains; but many are not capable of a firm perswasion of any thing."

There is nothing anywhere in the Whitman biography, his writings, or his character, which comes even close, but there is a great deal to show how much he tried to seem like one. Here is one of those self-revealing notes to himself: "The whole oration may be brief, yet illimitable by the manner, personality, style of me. No hurried gabble, as the usual American speeches, lectures, etc. are, but with much breadth, much precision, much indescribable meaning counterparting in the first person, present time, the divine ecstasy of the ancient Pythia, oracles, priests, possessed persons, demoniacs, etc." (*WWW*: 211). Notice that there is no yearning for true prophetic inspiration—he is thinking only of "counterparting in the first person, present time" the ecstasy of the prophet. Now prophets don't scout around learning how to proph, nor do many poets—or if they do, they are not so naïve as to leave notes telling us so. Indeed, and this is the key point, that Whitman successfully achieved a prophetic style (in the early, not the late, poetry) may have little to do with proving him a prophet, but it certainly reveals him to be an extraordinary poet.

A major difference Whitman faced in shifting from speaking to writing was credibility. As Reiss has shown, Whitman thought he possessed a great inner source of animal magnetism, never shushed his friends and followers when they made much of it (William Douglas O'Connor's "The Carpenter," for instance), and "wanted his poetic collection to assert a magnetic influence over his readers" (1963: 88). An impossibility, we must say, when we think of the literal implication of the claim. Again, he thought he had a great voice and was certainly fully aware of the contributing value of the spoken word: "The charm of the beautiful pronunciation of all words, of all tongues, is in perfect, flexible, vocal organs, and in a developed harmonious soul. All words spoken from these have deeper sweeter sounds, new meanings, impossible on any less terms" (*Daybooks and Notebooks*, III, 745). It was indeed through the spoken word that Elias Hicks and Father Taylor, the two speakers he most admired, demonstrated the "magnetic stream of natural eloquence, before which all minds and natures, all emotions, high or low, gentle or simple, yielded entirely without exception" (*PW*: 637–38).

There are many other values of the spoken address he thought would be in his lectures (the actual presence, the eye contact, the dynamic relationship with the audience, the prophetic authority, the power and force or tenderness and yearning of immediate self-communication), all of which he knew he would have to forgo or duplicate in some yet undiscovered fashion when he adopted the written form. For those who know Bucke's edition of *Notes and Fragments*, Furness' collection *Walt Whitman's Workshop*, Holloway's second volume of *The Uncollected Poetry and Prose*, Gohdes and Silver's *Faint Clews & Indirections*, Harold Blodgett's *An 1855–56 Notebook* with the struggle to achieve a form for "Crossing Brooklyn Ferry," William White's volume of *Daybooks and Notebooks* noted above, with its "Words," "The Primer of Words," and "Other Notebooks" (pp. 759–825)—as I say, for those who remember these works, the battle with language to achieve a new form will be remembered too, but perhaps overlooked or forgotten will be the enormous amount of self-education going on in those "foreground" years before *Leaves*. Stovall (1974) has probed and clarified much of the literal education of those years, the books he read, the journals he clipped, but these notebooks also show Whitman shaping the persona—and that crucial task has never been understood.

I am not denying or rejecting Edwin Miller's Freudian reading of *Leaves*, or Howard Waskow's *Walt Whitman: Explorations in Form*, or John Lynen's *Design of the Present*, or Albert Gelpi's brilliant *The Tenth Muse*. I even agree with much that they say, and fully agree with Quentin Anderson's *Imperial Self*, and his necessary additional essay "Whitman's New Man" (1974), and agree too with another dense essay by Harold Bloom in *Poetry and Repression* (1976). But for various reasons none of these books or essays explores the early notebooks. All of these studies tell us what Whitman was trying to say even though he did not know it, and none of them sufficiently explains what Whitman did think he was doing—and I do not mean psychologically or socially or culturally or religiously or patriotically or even prophetically; what I mean is, technically.

The skill, the art, the craft of any new poet is to make words do what words cannot do (or have not until then done), and it is a conscious, deliberate, disciplined, and intense effort: the sedulous rewriting of lines in different combinations, the different ways of writing about himself, the experiments in trying to reach his imaginary audience, the exercises in different tones, the search for words with emotive connotations, the tentative assertiveness (the tentativeness is Whitman's; the assertiveness, the persona's), the many reminders to himself about what was important. Years later, he tells us that "in the presence of outdoor influences" he "went over thoroughly the Old and New Testaments" and also read "the best translated versions I could get of Homer, Eschylus, Sophocles, the old German Nibelungen, the ancient Hindoo poems, and one or two masterpieces, Dante's among them" (*PW*: 722). One must always be wary with Whitman's PR recollections, unless there is independent support. In the early notebooks and workbooks, written only for himself, where the lecture notes, the "germs" and "spinal ideas" and "trial lines" for poems are found, there is no echo, no apparent influence of Scripture or Hindu literature or any other earlier prophetic writing. To me, the great value of these early notebooks is that they show us as much as anything ever can how *Leaves* came to be. And the great device he discovered was to fortify his lines with expressions of illocutionary force.

It is not that with an all-seeing yet discerning prophetic eye Whitman read Austin's book a century before it was written. Rather, this is to say that he recognized illocutionary force and responded to it in the speeches he admired, the actors he applauded, even the singers who overwhelmed him. He had read, and indeed imitated, enough conventional poetry to know that the prophetic force he wished to exemplify and exploit was not to be advanced in that channel, or in any other conventional literary form. The only free avenue was, literally, the "free speech" road. And when he could not speak, what could he do? Not publish his manuscript, but rework his speech so that his lines would exhibit and make manifest the illocutionary force that his voice and his presence could not. In the creation of what might be called his illocutionary style, the employment of the five types of illocutionary acts would be central, but they must be enhanced by contributing stylistic features.

One of these has already been examined, the *cursus*, an oratorical feature which he could draw to our attention by the arrangement of his lines so that many of them end with a cadence. But in relation to the speech act, there were two other characteristics of public speaking which he incorporated into his poetry: the immediacy of present-time involvement and the inclusion of the audience addressed. One essential of the speech act was that its words had to be uttered at the time of its action. So, one device he emphasized was the immediacy of the present tense. Here are the first lines or independent clauses of the twelve poems of the first edition:

I celebrate myself

Come closer to me,
Push closer my lovers and take the best I possess

To think of time....to think through the retrospection,
To think of today..and the ages continued henceforward.

I wander all night in my vision,

The bodies of men and women engirth me, and I engirth them,

Sauntering the pavement or riding the country byroads here there are faces,

A young man came to me with a message from his brother, [He later changed the tense for this line, making it "A young man comes to me bearing a message from his brother."]

Suddenly out of its stale and drowsy lair, the lair of slaves,
Like Lightning Europe le'pt forth....

Clear the way there Jonathan!

There was a child went forth every day,

Who learns my lesson complete?

Great are the myths....I too delight in them.

Of the twelve, nine are in the present. Of the other three, he changed the seventh to make it present (although it really would not have made any great difference, for it was only an introductory episode to get the poem started; after the first five lines the rest of the fifty-four line poem is in the present tense). The eighth had to stay in the past, for it is concerned with the revolutionary year of 1848, and when Whitman wrote the poem in 1850 it was in celebration of a past event. Indeed the only poem that seems to be in the past tense because the poet wanted it that way is the one that begins "There was a child," the beautiful account of the shaping of the poet's early sensitivity.

Now, of the 156 poems of the 1860 edition (which included all the poems up to that time), the 2 poems in the past tense noted above do continue that way. There is a two-line introductory beginning for

"Song of Prudence" in the past tense—"All day I have walked the city, and talked with my friends, and thought of prudence, / Of time, space, reality—of such as these, and abreast with them, prudence." But the rest of this fifty-four-line poem is completely present tense, so, like "Song of the Answerer," it is truly not a past-tense, reflective poem as "There Was a Child Went Forth." Two poems, and both of them major poems, "Out of the Cradle Endlessly Rocking" and my favorite "As I Ebb'd with the Ocean of Life," are mixed (a present-tense frame around a past-tense experience), but I count them both past to make my present point. Otherwise there are no past-tense poems in the program sections or anywhere else with the exception "Once I Pass'd through a Populous City" in the Enfans d'Adam section and 4 poems in the Calamus section, "When I Heard at the Close of the Day," "Of Him I Love Day and Night," "I Saw in Louisiana a Live-Oak Growing," and "I Dreamed in a Dream." So, what is the amazing result? Of the 156 poems in the 1860 edition, 9 are in the past tense, or of the total volume 94 percent of the poems are in the present tense. This figure becomes even more startling when we consider "Says" (8 small poems) and "Debris" (17 small poems) are counted as 2 poems. Furthermore, 5 of new past-tense poems given above are in the sections that show Whitman breaking away from the programmatic poems that dominate the first three editions.

There is no study that specifically examines the relation of verb tenses in a literary work to its illocutionary force or perlocutionary effects, although Lynen's *Design of the Present* has a valuable section on Whitman's use of the present tense. For my purposes, however, George Wright, "The Lyric Present" (1974) is more appropriate. This is an illuminating and sensitive study of the poetic values of the simple over the progressive present in English and American poetry, with some reference to Whitman.

The simple present is found in the five illocutionary forms (assertives, directives, commissives, expressives, declarations). Wright's concern is, in fact, the affective difference between the line "I *sound* my barbaric yawp over the roofs of the world" and a line using the progressive present which Whitman might have written "I *am sounding* my barbaric yawp over the roofs of the world" (Wright's italics). One can imagine either one as possible in a letter, in conversation, or in any other utterance, whether written or oral. It is also true that, grammatically, "Myself" might have started with "I am celebrating myself" and ended with "I am stopping somewhere waiting for you." Clearly the lyric present that Whitman preferred is also what we recognize as more affective—but why?

Let me paraphrase Wright, but with application to Whitman. The simple-present form ("I celebrate") describes an action that may be repeated but took place only that once, when Whitman began the poem. The word *celebrate* does relate, then, to some past occurrence, it is *past-like* but not really past. It is still happening, this celebrating, whenever someone reads the poem, even though Whitman's celebrating is long over, for the verb form used has established an action freed of time. "The actions described seem suspended, removed from the successiveness of our ordinary time levels, neither past, present, or future, neither single nor repeated, but of a different dimension entirely" (p. 565). This time-free tense escapes but includes the past and can also include a future sense, for we know the celebration is imminent; he will always sound his yawp and is somewhere ahead waiting for us. But if he had written "I am celebrating myself," etc., a portentousness, "a feeling of being on the verge of something to come" would be missing, and "we would not, as we do on hearing the line he did write, lean forward mentally in anticipation of the coming action" (p. 566).

Again, when Whitman uses this lyric present he makes himself his subject (Wright does not, but we all could point out manifold examples in "Song of Myself"), picturing himself and his actions "as he would observe the reticulations of a landscape at once dispassionate and involved." An even "more striking echo of this kind of generalization is to be heard sometimes when poets use lyric tense to describe persons other than the 'I.' On such occasions the persons described may acquire a strangely monumental character, as if, like landscape, they were there forever, conditions of life: 'The pure contralto *sings* in the organ loft . . .'" (p. 567; Wright's italics).

The simple present, this lyric tense, may also communicate "a sense of elevation and, often, of solemnity which seems appropriate to visionary experience. . . . When poets use the tense, therefore, to describe their own actions or those of others, these actions acquire a faintly or strongly ceremonial character." In "Song of Myself" *strongly* is most applicable; it is, indeed, conscious and intentional, although less so in other poems. "This is especially true in first-person examples, where the poet, in announcing his ceremonial actions, seems at times to be playing a priestlike role" (p. 568). Wright quotes as one of his examples, "I *give* you my sprig of lilac."

The suggestive powers of the lyric present "seem especially present when a first-person speaker describes his own physical actions," because that tense "far from describing a present action, more typically denotes an action envisioned, frozen, enchanted, recaptured, and in its use, in even the most ironic, the least sentimental poem, confers on the poem a touch of the sublime" (p. 570). To reach this timeless level, the expression must be freed of history even though it may use history (the Texas massacre, the John Paul Jones victory, etc.), must "withhold deliberately any definite information about the time level of the action." The poet would not ordinarily use *here* or *now*, and "even when he does ('Now on this spot I *stand* with my robust soul') we have no precise idea of when 'now' is. We know of 'now' only that it is the space of time (anything from a moment to an eternity) during which 'I stand'" (p. 565).

Now Wright in his very perceptive treatment had no occasion to treat of the speech-act theory, but his Whitman references (except for "the pure contralto") are examples of the illocutionary types I have been pointing out. Whitman had no notion that he was using the lyric present (indeed he never thought of his poems as lyrics), but he sensed what was needed to go from the fantasy eloquence of his public speeches, to the poems of the first edition. A comparison of the lecture notes with their final form in 1855 (Holloway gives the parallels in his notes, *UPP*) shows that he does remove the specific historical and precise time involvement that would limit his writing to "mere rhetoric" (with the exception of "Europe: The 72d and 73d Years of These States" and "A Boston Ballad," both earlier poems, written some years before the other ten poems of the first edition and without the lyric present and accompanying attributes Wright speaks of). It is true that the poems of the first three editions have a stronger programmatic tone and bent than do

LANGUAGE AND STYLE IN *Leaves of Grass*

most of the other poets Wright quotes, but such was the occasion for the creation of the poems, of which the present (including what Wright calls the "lyric present") was the prevailing tense.

AUDIENCE INVOLVEMENT, 1855–1860

Present tense (the tense of speech, of the oration, of the sermon, of Emerson's lectures) is necessary in any attempt to communicate illocutionary force, but there is also another necessary element, contact with the audience. The illocutionary act is directed to one or more persons to whom the promise, oath, direction, command, assertion, etc., is made. In *Leaves* the illocutionary acts are made by the persona, the "I" of the poems, and they are made to (*i.e.*, directed to) the audience, whether individually or collectively, signified as "you." We need to stop here to consider this second element of the speech-act style. Little has been done with the use of pronouns in theoretical discussions of the speech act. Indeed, the best place to start is an overlooked yet deceptively simple statement of Jakobson's in his famous "Closing Statement: Linguistics and Poetics"; "The particularities of diverse poetic genres imply a differently ranked participation of the other verbal functions along with the dominant poetic function. Epic poetry, focused on the third person, strongly involves the referential function of language; the lyric, oriented toward the first person, is intimately linked with the emotive function; *poetry of the second person is imbued with the conative function and is either supplicatory or exhortative, depending on whether the first person is subordinated to the second one or the second to the first*" (p. 357; my italics). The focus here, of course, is on the *first* and *second* persons. The presence of the first person in the first three editions is obvious enough, but it is extended use of the second person and the relation of the first to the second that have not received much attention. It is easy enough to see why, for (aside from Whitman) few poets permit an explicit *you* (referring to the reader or readers) to enter a poem at all. A check of the poetry in a text anthology of nineteenth-century British literature reveals one in Blake (in the Prologue to "The Gates of Paradise"), five in Wordsworth (in the fifteen-line opening section of "Michael"); one in Coleridge ("Epitaph"); at least ten in Byron's *Don Juan* (of the jocular sort); all through Shelley's "Song to the Men of England" (but only if the reader identifies the *ye* of the poem); one in Keats's "Ode on Melancholy" (in the sense that the opening imperative implies a *you*); one also in John Clare, Tennyson, Arnold, Clough; at least ten in Browning (mostly in "Rabbi Ben Ezra" and excluding the dramatic monologues); and even more in William Morris' Apology to *The Earthly Paradise*. None of these, however, is as direct as in Whitman.

While going through the *Norton Anthology* mentioned above, I looked specially for the standard device of oratory, the rhetorical question involving the audience. There were none. Nor were there any in American poetry, up to and including Dickinson. By contrast, this form of the rhetorical question is one of the style markers of much of Whitman's early poetry. It is not the use of questions, for they are found in the poetry of all of his contemporaries, but the direction of the question. In Whitman many of them are addressed directly to "you," the audience (the imagined crowd of the imaginary oration and/or the actual reader).

QUESTIONS IN *LEAVES*

Edition	Total	Direct to Audience
1855	195	149
1856	188	162
1860	173	76
1867–1881	202	7

Even those seven in the late poems are not directly to "you," the audience, as in the early poems: two are in "Hast Never Come to Thee an Hour," and they make up the whole poem:

Hast never come to thee an hour,
A sudden gleam divine, precipitating, bursting all these bubbles, fashions, wealth?
These eager business aims—books, politics, art, amours,
To utter nothingness?

Four are in "To a Certain Civilian," near the end of the Drum-Taps section. The questions are addressed to the Civilian, but since there is no indication that some specific person is meant, they may be counted as to the reader. The last one is in "As Consequent, *Etc.*," the introductory poem of the Autumn Rivulets section. In that poem, since lines 13–15

LANGUAGE AND STYLE IN *Leaves of Grass*

are addressed to the reader, the question that occurs in lines 19–20 may also be to the reader, though it is too generalized to make any claims either way.

To make clear what this discovery means, let me present these figures.

QUESTIONS IN *LEAVES*, 1855 EDITION

Poem	Total	Direct to Audience
Song of Myself	81	67
Song for Occupations	34	34
To Think of Time	19	16
The Sleepers	8	0
Body Electric	19	13
Faces	2	1
Answerer	8	5
Europe	2	0
Boston Ballad	7	0
A Child Went Forth	2	0
Who Learns My Lesson	5	5
Great Are the Myths	8	8

In "Song of Myself," section 11 treats the episode of the twenty-eight swimmers watched by the lady in the nearby house. At lines 200–201, midway in the episode, these lines occur: "Where are you off to, lady? for I see you, / You splash in the water there, yet stay stock still in your room." The question may be read as directed to the lady, or to the poet himself as an imaginary question, but in either case it is not directed to the reader. We may say it is *for* the reader, but not *to* the reader. But when he adds these two lines in 1855, "Do you guess I have some intricate purpose? / Well I have....for the April rain has, and the mica on the side of a rock has" (ll. 381–82), the question is directed to the audience, to the reader, even though the persona answers it himself. It is this sort of question that is unique in Whitman's poetry. It was a standard device in oratory and was recommended by all the rhetoricians (from Aristotle to Bishop Whately), but was never used in this direct sense by any established poet of the nineteenth century (unless one calls Tupper "established"). There may be occasional uses of the sort, in a prefatory poem, for instance, but not as a conscious rhetorical device (for poetic purposes) in poem after poem.

But it must be made clear that these direct questions to the audience occur only in the programmatic poems. Note that there are none in "The Sleepers" or in "A Child Went Forth," which are lyric rather than programmatic. The absence of these direct questions in two other poems of the first edition, "Europe" and "A Boston Ballad," supports the hypothesis made here, for they are pre-1855 poems and were written outside the impetus that characterized *Leaves*.

Now poetry that acknowledges its audience, that indeed involves that audience and attains many of its effects through the dynamics of that interchange, is not a discovery of Whitman's. It has been, in fact, a part of poetry from its beginnings up to the eighteenth century. But as M. H. Abrams reminded us years ago the audience has no modal existence in nineteenth-century poetry. In that well-known opening chapter of *The Mirror and the Lamp* (1953) he assures us that there is "something singularly fatal to the audience in the romantic point of view." Using John Stuart Mill's remarks on his poetic contemporaries, Abrams points out that "the poet's audience is reduced to a single member, consisting of the poet himself." To that contention, which has been generally accepted for the past twenty years, Whitman would be the major exception. He would also be (although some would differ— Murray Krieger, Allen Tate) to Abrams' further statement, "The purpose of producing effects upon other men, which for centuries had been the defining character of the art of poetry, now serves precisely the opposite function: it disqualifies a poem by proving it to be rhetoric" (p. 25).

If we use the direct question to the audience, to "you," as a sign of the programmatic poem, we will find that they are dominant in the first and second editions. But in the third edition there are major poems and groups that adumbrate the change to take place in Whitman's poetry after the Civil War. There are no questions at all in one of the best lyrics, "As I Ebb'd With the Ocean of Life." There are seven questions in "Out of the Cradle Endlessly Rocking," but none to the reader; of the twelve poems in the Enfans d'Adam section there are sixteen questions, but only four to the audience; of the forty-five poems in the Calamus section there are only ten I could count as to the reader, of the forty-one questions that are asked, and five of those were in "What Think You I Take My Pen in Hand?" On the other hand the 1860 edition begins with "Proto-Leaf" (now entitled "Starting from Paumanok") and ends with "So Long!," both programmatic poems (or platform poems). It is clear that Whitman meant to have even the growing number of lyrical poems enveloped in a programmatic frame, a structure for *Leaves* he maintained thereafter, even insisting to future editors that no other arrangement should be printed.

Perhaps with other English and American poets it was not considered "good form" to speak directly to a reader one did not know, but no such punctilious decorum hampered Whitman. The opening lines in 1855

> I celebrate myself,
> And what I assume you shall assume
> For every atom belonging to me as good belongs to you

are typical in that in addition to the present tense, there are four uses of the first person (including the *myself* and *me*) to two of the second person—a two-to-one proportion found in the poems in the first three editions. (It is not typical of this first long poem, however, for it is "Song of *Myself*," and the proportion is something like nine to one.) But the point is that these uses of the poet-persona speaking of and for and about himself directly and explicitly to "you," the reader, have never been found to this extent in any other poet.

He would have used *you* in an address or public lecture, and did indeed do so in the remnants of those "barrels" of lectures (found in *UPP*). For instance, here is a passage (p. 65) that uses the *you* for the audience even more in the lecture than in the poetry derived from it:

> The truths I tell to you or to any other may not be plain to you, because I do not translate them fully from my idiom into yours.—If I could do so, and do it well, they would be as apparent to you as they are to me; for they are truths.—No two have exactly the same language, and the great translator and joiner of the whole is the poet. He has the divine grammar of all tongues and says indifferently and alike, How are you friend? to the President in the midst of his cabinet, and Good day my brother, to Sambo, among the hoes of the sugar field, and both understand him and know that his speech is right.

In the first edition he uses this material for a key section of "Song of the Answerer":

SPEECH ACTS

Every existence has its idiom....every thing has an idiom and tongue;
He resolves all tongues into his own, and bestows it upon men..and any man
    translates..and any man translates himself also:
One part does not counteract another part....He is the joiner..he sees how they
    join.
He says indifferently and alike, How are you friend? to the President at his
    levee,
And he says Good day my brother, to Cudge that hoes in the sugarfield;
And both understand him and know that his speech is right (ll. 29–34)

In the poem of 1855, Whitman prefers to pronounce the man in the
above passage as the answerer, not the poet of the prose passage, for he
does not wish to confuse conventional poetry of his day with the new
assertive prophetic voice the poem is defining. Accordingly, the answerer, confident in his role, defies the conventional platitudes, and
Whitman asks his audience (l. 22): "Do you hear that mocking and
laughter? Do you hear the ironical echoes?" He makes this even clearer
at the end, when he does speak directly to the audience, the reader:

You think it would be good to be a writer of melodious verses,
Well it would be good to be the writer of melodious verses;
But what are verses beyond the flowing character you could have?
    ....or beyond beautiful manners and behavior?
Or beyond one manly or affectionate deed of the apprenticeboy?
    ....or old woman?..or man that has been in prison or is
    likely to be in prison? (ll. 51–54)

Not all the poems of the first edition employ this direct address to
the reader. Such use would break the mood of "The Sleepers" and
would be equally inappropriate in "Europe: The 72d and 73d Years of
These States" (the poem is addressed to Europe and the *yourselves* of
line 5 refers to the Europeans, as the scornful *you* of line 6 refers to the
kings and usurpers). In the ironical "A Boston Ballad," the *you* refers to
the spirits of the old revolutionaries who are dishonored by Boston's
support of the Fugitive Slave law, or to Brother Jonathan, the contemporary Bostonian who complies with that unjust law. Nor would a *you*
directed to the reader be fitting in "A Child Went Forth," which is in
the past tense throughout (it is possible that the reader might identify
with *him* or *her* of the last line, "And these become part of him or
her that peruses them here now," but that pronoun use is not one of
address).

LANGUAGE AND STYLE IN *Leaves of Grass*

Many of the other poems of the first edition make explicit use of the direct address to the audience. "Song of Myself" is so well known that it is not necessary to quote from it, but notice the others. In "A Song for Occupations" he is alarmed at the deferential and humble attitude he finds in workmen specifically, but also in all Americans (including his readers) who do not assert their dignity and independence:

> Why what have you thought of yourself?
> Is it you then that thought yourself less?
> Is it you that thought the President greater than you? or the rich better off
>   than you? or the educated wiser than you? (ll. 24–26)

So he challenges us, perhaps in the same words he might have shouted at his audience had he ever carried out his prophetic program:

> Souls of men and women! it is not you I call unseen, unheard,
>   untouchable and untouching;
> It is not you I go argue pro and con about, and to settle
>   whether you are alive or no;
> I own publicly who you are, if nobody else owns....and see
>   hear you, and what you give and take;
> What is there you canot give and take? (ll. 28–31)

And he reminds us: "The President is up there in the White House for you....it is not you who are here for him" (l. 83).

In "To Think of Time" Whitman is really asking us, his audience, to think of death, to actualize our suppressed thoughts and fears of death in order to free ourselves of those fears: "Have you guessed you yourself would not continue? Have you dreaded those earth-beetles? / Have you feared the future would be nothing to you?" (ll. 3–4). Let me stop here a moment to raise a question about this and the previous quotations from "Occupations." Is the *you* singular or plural? It is a central question, for if it is an address before a gathering of citizens the pronoun is plural, the collective *you* for all those within the sound of his voice. But if it is a line of poetry read by *you* as reader (as you are now reading this sentence), it is singular. The secret of Whitman's poetic maneuver here is that it is *both* or *either*. When the distinction between singular (thou, thy, thine, thyself) and plural (you, etc.) collapsed into the uniform combined form, this maneuver was possible for English and American poets (not for those who worked in French, German, Italian, Spanish, or any European language) and Whitman was the first—perhaps the only—poet to recognize and take advantage of this situation.

In a brilliant examination of the uses of the singular *tu* and the plural *vous* in French (and the corresponding pronouns from other European languages), Roger Brown and Albert Gilman trace the changes, clarify the differences in meaning, explain the temporary aberration of the Quakers in the steady decline of distinction between singular and plural forms in England, and show in their article "The Pronouns of Power and Solidarity" how significant the distinction was, and in a certain sense how great our loss (in English and American literature) has been. This makes sense up to a point, but even if the change was not already under way before the settlement of this country, it would not, indeed, could not, have been maintained in our frontier democratic society. Be that as it may, it was gone by the Age of Jackson, and Whitman could transfer a line from a lecture to a poem directly. Here are some lines from a collection of lecture notes on government, from which poetic lines for some early poems were transferred (I give the uncorrected words also to show what was involved):

<pre>
                            is
I have been informed that it∧expected that those who address
                will
the people are expected to flatter them—
                think I could taunt you
I flatter none—I come to rebuke, rather than flatter you.
What have you been about, that you have allowed those that scum to be
    floated into the Presidency?
</pre>

These lines and those that follow in the Notebook on Government (at the Library of Congress) have clearly a plural *you*, intended by Whitman as such, as "people" and "them" indicate. But nothing of that distinction is found in the poetry that was drawn from these lectures.

There is a plural pronoun in the poetry, to be sure, but it is either *they* (not important in the present connection) or, most significantly, *we* (a combination of the *I* of the persona-poet and the *you*—singular or plural, as you will—of the audience). Thus, to go back to "To Think of Time": "To think that *you* and *I* did not see, feel, think, nor bear *our* part, / To think that *we* are now here and bear *our* part" (ll. 8–9; my

LANGUAGE AND STYLE IN *Leaves of Grass*

italics). Similarly in the last poem of the first edition, "Great Are the Myths":

> Great are yourself and myself,
> We are just as good and bad as the oldest and youngest or any,
> What the best and worst did we could do,
> What they felt..do not we feel it ourselves?
> What they wished..do we not wish the same? (ll. 12–16)

In a certain sense, of course, all poetry is addressed to the reader, but the issue here is not really so simple as that. John Stuart Mill made the useful distinction: "Eloquence [*i.e.*, oratory] is heard, poetry is over-heard." That is, most poetry is either the poet talking to himself ("I wandered lonely as a cloud") or the poet talking to some animate or inanimate object, using an apostrophe ("Hail to thee, blithe Spirit!" or "O wild West Wind, thou breath of Autumn's being") or some other device by which or through which we play the eavesdropping role. Whitman is the first poet to write what Mill thought of as a disjunction, chiefly because he went from plans for oratory to poetry without giving up the immediacy of the speech act: present tense, first person (as speaker), second person (as audience), the illocutionary force of a message. Whether the result was eloquence, Mill did not say (he lived to 1873, but I have never heard that he read or responded to *Leaves*).

In this connection it is necessary to acknowledge that there is a fundamental question about the nature of poetry that cannot be answered in this study. Can "you" and "we" (meaning the audience or the speaker and audience together) appear in literature? The orator can use both pronouns, and they have been used in these pages, for oratory and critical essays are a form of discourse in which the audience participates, even if silently. But what of drama and fiction and poetry? We remember *Our Town* and the Prologue actor in some of Shakespeare's plays. In fiction, there is that great attention-capturing opening of William Saroyan's short story, "Did you ever fall in love with a midget?," as well as Ring Lardner's "Haircut" and the "Dear Reader" paragraphs in Victorian novels. And in poetry there are the occasional uses noted in the anthology of nineteenth-century literature. But all these are exceptions and are rare. Indeed much of the reason that these uses are memorable is that they challenge our expectation—an expectation shaped by our continual familiarity with literature from which the audience is officially excluded.

In a closely reasoned and illuminating essay on this problem in narration, Ann Banfield demonstrates "how arguments can be built using syntax as the evidence for one proposed division of linguistic performance identifying a category stylistically distinct from ordinary discourse" (1979: 186). She does this by isolating six characteristics of discourse, *i.e.*, direct speech, which are not found in any nondiscourse style. (She is not concerned with speech and dialogue that appear in quotation marks in novels and plays.) Of these six, the last, which is the second person, the *you*, is the most important and all-inclusive. "The second person can be taken as the essential mark of discourse or communication. The features given in (i) through (iv) in fact all follow from (vi). The absence of these features marks represented speech and thought as a non-discourse style" (p. 194).

The whole list and the other parts of this memorable article are important to stylistic criticism, but crucial to this study is the consequence for our literary classification of *Leaves*. In terms of Banfield's criteria (which one must use), many platform poems are suspect: not as to the "platform," which is, indeed, confirmed, but to these utterances as poetry. We may escape the dilemma (even as we admit we are "fudging") by accepting the truism that we do not use literary terms with much precision, that the label *poetry* is an evaluative as well as a formal term. We will continue to call "Song of Myself" and other speech-act writings (signaled by the use of *you*) "poetry," because we do not have any other name for them. But at least, with Banfield's clarification, we ought to acknowledge what an exceptional (in the literal sense) kind of poetry it is. She ends her essay with a full quotation from and acceptance of John Stuart Mill's famous article. In consequence of which, there are parts of *Leaves* that we should not, strictly speaking, call "poetry" even though we may applaud their eloquence.

Scholarship in stylistics is now advancing so rapidly that one needs to check the library new-book shelf as a last chore before sending out a book or article. A rewarding confirmation of that duty is the appearance of Banfield's essay as a chapter in her new book, *Unspeakable sentences* (1982). To this major study of the semantics of narrative, Whitman relates only as an exception, for his sentences are by no means "unspeakable." But to have that exceptional feature of *Leaves* confirmed in reverse, so to speak, is a happy by-product of her investigation. For obvious reasons, Whitman is not even mentioned in her book, but in terms of her last chapters it is now possible to place his unique role in a history of writing (in print) that is, intentionally, *not communicative* in any direct sense. It is necessary to examine the *you* in at least a few of these, for this direct inclusion of the reader is a unique feature of Whitman's style. Since it pretty much vanishes after 1860, and since the poems in the final edition are not in chronological order at all, many readers may have thought the first person, the *I*, was the dominant feature. Perhaps Allen Tate thought so, for he supported his dislike of *Leaves* by mentioning the many *I*'s, forgetting that on a percentage basis Dickinson uses even more.

Let us recall Jakobson's comment: "Poetry of the second person is imbued with the conative function and is either supplicatory or exhortative, depending on whether the first person is subordinated to the second one or the second to the first." And to make sure we understand the conative function, let me also quote: "Orientation toward the ADDRESSEE, the CONATIVE function, finds its purest grammatical expression in the vocative and the imperative, which syntactically, morphologically, and often even phonemically deviate from other nominal and verbal categories" (1960: 357, 355). Jakobson's statements are not exactly self-explanatory, but they will be clearer with some examples.

Let me demonstrate through a poem not widely discussed, "To You, Whoever You Are"—although it is good to acknowledge Waskow's valuable comments on this poem in his concern with didacticism in *Leaves*, a matter not relevant here. In "To You, Whoever You Are," a forty-eight-line poem, there are fifty-eight uses of the second-person pronoun (compared to twenty-five uses of "I") , and the *you* is not only significant, it is what the poem is all about. The poem appeared in the 1856 edition without any relation to other poems, but in 1860 it is the important introduction to and shaping force for a group called Messenger Leaves, not as important as other groups, perhaps, but the poems lost some of their impact when the grouping (and its title) was dropped and the poems diversified. In an as yet unpublished 1857 Autograph Notebook (Feinberg Collection), in which there are many preparatory lines for the 1860 edition, Whitman makes this note to himself, with a later cancellation line running through it, presumably because he had carried out the idea in Messenger Leaves:

> ?
> *Book of Letters*—Poem
> ?Poem
> Letter to a Prostitute
> Letter to felon
> Letter to one about to die
>   (end letter to prostitute—
>   "I salute you my love, with a kiss on your
>   lips, that you do not forget me—...

The idea was a fruitful one, but rather than "Letter to," the fifteen poems in Messenger Leaves are individually entitled "To....," as "To a Common Prostitute," "To One Shortly to Die." The first long poem, "To You, Whoever You Are" may be said to speak for fourteen specific identifications of the different sorts of persons Whitman imagined as the addressees of his lines. After an eleven-line introductory section, there is this key passage:

> I will leave all and come and make the hymns of you;
> None has understood you, but I understand you,
> None have done justice to you—you have not done justice to yourself,
> None but have found you imperfect—I only find no imperfection in you,
> None but would subordinate you—I only am he who will never consent to
>   subordinate you,
> I only am he who places over you no master, owner, better, God, beyond what
>   waits intrinsically in yourself. (ll. 12–17)

The poem goes on in this vein, but it is difficult to figure out exactly what Whitman's attitude to his addressee is. It is not supplicatory, in Jakobson's meaning, for clearly the *I* is not subordinate. And the last two lines above clearly indicate that "you" is not to be subordinated either. Does Whitman intend to convey an equality here, asserting that the addresser and the addressee are equal? If so, does that hold true for "Crossing Brooklyn Ferry"? In that poem, it does. But in this poem, there is something awry. The poem seems too programmatic; it is exhortatory and the reader (the addressee) is subordinated, even though the poet denies it in the last line quoted above. Indeed, the reader is always in the passive role, and any attempt to insist that the author and reader are on a par is almost impossible to carry out. After assuring the reader that the poet welcomes him, no matter what failings he may have, the poet says: "Silence, the desk, the flippant expression, the night, the accustomed routine, if these conceal you from others, or from yourself, they do not conceal you from me" (l. 30), and even adds what would have been line 33: "I track through your windings and turnings—I come upon you where you thought eye should never come upon you," in some sort of democratic "Hound of Heaven" pursuit that would be difficult not to think of as subordination, no matter how noble the intention (which is surely why Whitman dropped it). The exhortation comes in line 39: "Whoever you are! claim your own at any hazard!," which if "you" the addressee-reader will do, "The hopples fall from your ankles—you find an unfailing sufficiency" (l. 44).

The curious and very interesting point here is that Whitman wanted to motivate his audience to accept the democratic challenge, but could only do so by adopting a somewhat autocratic attitude. This is by no means an uncommon fault in politics, but it is rare in poetry, especially in poetry as otherwise ingenious, highly motivated, and successful as this poem. There is, indeed, a major problem in any poetry that directly addresses the audience, for example, Robert Frost nearly wrecked a fine poem, "The Pasture," with his arch remark "You come too." Whitman's problem did not involve trying to be speciously friendly to someone he did not know, but he comes near to overstressing the *you*, and by so doing reminds the reader that he is being talked to, perhaps even talked down to, thus threatening the reader's participation in the poem. If the *you* is presented in such a way that we cannot identify with him, then the poem becomes the poet's address to some other person—and accordingly we do become something like eavesdroppers rather than participants.

None of the other "you" poems is endangered by effusiveness or excess as is "To You, Whoever You Are," and one of them, "Ferry," is one of the exceptional poems of our language. But the great poetic skill here is in the delicate fusion of a number of poetic items, contributing elements which together make the whole greater than the sum of its parts, for even though in criticizing we must consider the parts seriatim, they are truly understood and appreciated only in the unity provided by the reading of the poem. But this famous poem has been so widely and vari-

ously discussed that there is no need for yet another full-scale interpretation, or even a summary of the various positions taken by Waskow,
James Miller, Jr., Edwin Miller, Anderson, Eugene Kanjo, Mark
Kinkead-Weekes, Susan Strom, and others. Rather let me point out
some features these critics had no occasion to consider.

As Whitman continually revised the poem through various editions
he clearly improved it, but at the sacrifice of some features that did have
a valid purpose. The part of the poem that is now (*i.e.*, in the final edition) section 3 began this way in 1860:

> It avails not, neither time or place—distance avails not,
> I am with you, you men and women of a generation or ever so many
>   generations hence,
> *I project myself—also I return—I am with you and know how it is,*

And what is now section 4 began, in 1860, with these lines:

> These, and all else, were to me the same as they are to you,
> *I project myself a moment to tell you—also I return.*

(I have italicized the lines that were dropped.) Obviously we do not
stop at the end of line 20 in our reading, nor at the end of line 49, waiting in expectancy for them—in the manner of the longtime resident in
a flat bordering the Forty-ninth Street El, who on the night after the
Elevated was shut down, suddenly rose up out of his sound sleep at
3:00 A.M. and cried, "What's that?" But the two near-duplicate lines
once framed that lovely catalog of the harbor scene through which (via
our common response) we recognized our affinity with the poet. We
still do so respond, but in 1860 he wants to remind us that we should
go outside or beyond or above his lines to initiate the affiliation. Presumably Whitman later thought these lines too obvious, but in 1860
these parallel statements tell us that he is projecting himself *in order to
remind us* that he too enjoyed the evening sights on the river, the slow-
wheeling gulls, the reflected sun in the water, the scallop-edged waves,
the furnace glare from the foundries on the opposite shore. Since the
catalog still does this, these framing lines serve to emphasize the reminder (much as in "To You, Whoever You Are") that we are being
told, being talked to, not in the sense of being talked down to but being
assured by one who is "in the know" or, perhaps, even being lectured
to. The lines are not necessary to the poet in any lyrical setting in which

he is recalling an experience in order to recapture its concomitant emotion for his own future enjoyment, but they were thought necessary to the audience.

A few lines later in the poem, the poet is probing for the remaining barriers between himself and the future audience (the audience is always future, even if only the day after the poem is finished), and he asks: "What is it then between us? / What is the count of scores or hundreds of years between us?" (ll. 54–55). And he answers that it cannot be "distance" or "place," for he can circumvent those barriers through our shared experience. But a much more profound barrier is our individuality and what we have done with it. As those fragments of the Over-Soul ("the float") are separated, to be incorporated (in the literal sense) in our bodies, we are made distinct, but we foolishly believe we have broken or lost our connection with the Over-Soul through our follies, our sins, our "dark patches." Whitman probably never read Hawthorne's *Marble Faun*, but it is curious to speculate on what he would have thought of Kenyon's reflections on evil and on what the "dark patches" had done for Donatello. The profundity of the idea that evil was educative, that evil—or our reaction to our own evil—was what made us human, would not have been as lost on Whitman as on Hilda, but clearly the whole notion is antithetical to *Leaves*. But Whitman does see that the separateness of the individual, the isolation of the sinner, because self-imposed, is a far more insurmountable barrier than the time and space he has already overcome.

Nor does he really overcome this final barrier, either, except by the famous "dark patches" section in which he acknowledges his own failures (comprehensive enough to encompass any sins of the reader) and dismisses them as unimportant and inconsequential in terms of the potential glory of confident participation in daily life. There is no attempt here, as in Baudelaire's "Hypocrite lecteur, mon semblable, mon frère!," to find our kinship as sinners. Rather, having "knitted the old knot of contrariety" himself, he rejects the privacy, the interior isolation, of the guilty. No sin, no wrong, no fault of the reader can bar him from spiritual fraternity with the poet, and nothing the past has done will prevent the reader from accepting the poet over the distances of time and place. That is, nothing but the one fault, sin, folly, weakness, or what have you, he admits to in 1856, but takes out of the poem thereafter.

In the final version of the "dark patches" section he acknowledges that he

Blabbed, blushed, resented, lied, stole, grudged,
Had guile, anger, lust, hot wishes I dared not speak,
Was wayward, vain, greedy, shallow, sly, cowardly, malignant,
The wolf, the snake, the hog, not wanting in me,
The cheating look, the frivolous word, the adulterous wish, not wanting,
Refusals, hates, postponements, meanness, laziness, none of these wanting.
    (ll. 72–77)

But in 1856 he also admitted, and included in the above list, that he was a "solitary committer," presumably, that is, a masturbator. Now clearly it was not necessary to put this in the list at all, but then, once he had included it, to take it out is comical—or seems so to us. Indeed, it seems that all of the other generalized faults were probably not really his at all, and that he dropped the one actual confession. But the point is that masturbation—or, better in his phrase, being a "solitary committer"—is the most private of all acts, the antithesis of the communion of spirits he is striving for with his reader. It is not that Whitman or his persona is too ashamed, for masturbation is more openly treated elsewhere in *Leaves* than in any poetry up to that time. Rather, the whole key section was undermined by the inclusion of an admission of weakness on his part that would accentuate the very privacy, loneliness, solitariness he was trying to overcome.

The only commentator who has noted this omission is Anderson (1971: 155) and he uses it in an altogether different context. He also quotes the five lines omitted between what is now section 7 and section 8. Here, too, we would differ, but only on his emphasis on the great gain to the poem by the omission. He believes that the lines "spoil the whole movement of the poem as we now have it by anticipating the generalization which catches up all sights and objects into the 'necessary film' in the concluding section" (pp. 152–53). They do anticipate, to be sure, for that is why Whitman put them there, and in the looser organization of the poem into 26 sections in 1860 they serve as a unifying link between what has been established, "It is not you alone, nor I alone, / Not a few races, not a few generations, not a few centuries," to the final truths to be revealed in the rest of the poem: "A necessary film envelops all, and envelops the soul for the proper time." To indicate this mild difference with Anderson is not to minimize the most profound and rewarding interpretation he has given this poem.

There is another omitted line which Anderson alone notices, a strange rhetorical question that would have been the final line in what is now section 8. Section 7 closes with three rhetorical questions, and section 8 adds nine more. But in the early editions there was a tenth concluding question. I quote the last four questions and put in italics the final one, which he later dropped:

We understand, then, do we not?
What I promised without mentioning it, have you not accepted?
What the study could not teach—what the preaching could not accomplish is accomplished, is it not?
What the push of reading could not start is started by me personally, is it not?

Anderson's explanation of this odd claim for an artist whose medium is the printed word is that this "assertion of an agency more inclusive and unmediated than print" (p. 120) is true, inasmuch as "the event of the poem is an apocalyptic event, and is brought about by an agent whose power to transform our consciousness goes beyond words because it is a power to transform the ways in which we apprehend words as well as the river or the sunset." For this reason, "The agent with whom we have to deal in 'Crossing Brooklyn Ferry' might provisionally be called a shaman; he has more in common with the practitioners of magic than with a publicly proclaimed poet" (p. 125).

If Whitman knew what the word *shaman* meant, he might well have smiled with satisfaction at such a remark. He never objected when Edward Dowden or Bucke or any of his contemporaries called him a prophet, a visionary, a seer, a bard. But, though Whitman was really no prophet, or shaman, he certainly did want to sound like one—or more explicitly write as he thought one would sound. In a very true sense, Anderson would agree with this way of seeing Whitman's prophetic role, for "the reason time, distance, and place do not avail is that the shaman, agent, magician, ghost, has satisfied the condition which fulfills 'soul,' makes 'identity' or 'role' 'complete'" (pp. 151−52). But my point is that the persona "has satisfied the condition" only by the artful use of language. When Anderson concludes that "we must take account of the shaman making his myth to act as a spell on us" (p. 165), he says more than is required of the most sensitive reader or the most sympathetic critic. The most we need grant is that through the skill of his language a poet achieves for us that "willing suspension of disbelief" for the duration of the poem and as long after that as we are uninterrupted by the pressures, interferences, concerns of our daily world.

An essay wholly independent of Anderson's interpretation, but like his in preferring "Ferry" to "Out of the Cradle" and "Out of the Cradle" to "When Lilacs Last," is that by Kinkead-Weekes, "Walt Whitman Passes the Full-Stop By . . .," an essay in a recent festschrift for the English philologist W. S. Mackie. In a brief but clear discussion of the uses of tenses in the poem, Kinkead-Weekes shows that Whitman "creates an experience which is pluperfect before the poem, perfect in the poem, present and manifestly happening as we read, and available in the future." There are other matters of language use, to be sure, that are to be examined in any full criticism of a poem (word choice, syntax, rhythm, figures of speech, rhetorical devices, etc.), but an important element in "Ferry" is the skillful shifting of tenses to achieve "the whole strange intersection of time that is the central experience of the poem" (1977: 177), and it is good to see it handled so well.

To return to the matter of the dropped line ("What the push of reading could not start is started by me personally, is it not?"), Whitman is always concerned that the illocutionary force that he thought he could communicate in an actual speech-act situation might not be carried by the written language. His belief that he had personal magnetism beyond the ordinary, that he had the vocal resonance, power, and capacity in projecting his voice to fortify his message, that a dynamic relationship ("the agonistic arena") would develop in his delivery, may have been only fantasy. Indeed, the only praise of his platform performance came from him (in his "anonymous" press notices) and from disciples who knew him first through the written word. But the point is that he believed it, and makes much of it in *Leaves*. It is not solely and strictly speaking a prophetic role he adopts as persona, for like priest, oracle, shaman, mystic, evangelist, that role implies a spiritually superior force or agency of which the prophet is the spokesman, agent, or messenger. Whitman takes no such subordinate role, through 1860 anyway. It is hard to find a single word to name the role he assumes—perhaps something like a democratic Christ (Thomas Edward Crawley has a very

LANGUAGE AND STYLE IN *Leaves of Grass*

revealing section on this [1970: 50–79])—and it is best seen in the role itself and the results he claims.

This role is certainly present in but not confined to a poem like "Ferry." In a lively article on the Bible and American literature, John Becker makes this good statement: "Whitman self-consciously asserted that he was writing more than the powerless 'pure' literature of the European past. He was writing the new American Bible, with all the power to shape a culture that the term *Bible* suggests. There is more than rhetoric and egoism in his claim. Whitman's poetry refuses to stay on the page. He is clearly striving to give words an almost supernatural, transtemporal force. He constitutes himself a new Providence as he looks over our shoulders today when we cross, or would if we could, Brooklyn Ferry" (1975: 257). But Anderson and Becker to the contrary notwithstanding, Whitman's poetry does stay on the page, and there is no true and real difference between "Ferry" and some fifty other occasions in the 1860 edition where the personal effect on the reader was intended, so that the persona might claim, "What the push of reading could not start is started by me personally." Some passages are more effective than others, but it is a difference of degree, not of kind, and in all instances the effect is a consequence of Whitman's language use, not of the amount of prophetic voltage he had on tap at the time the lines were composed. Let us examine a few of these, at different places in the 1860 edition, to get at their characteristic features.

The book has no preface, but has a poem "Proto-Leaf" (later entitled "Starting from Paumanok") to serve, quite as its title indicates, as the first, introductory, leaf (poem) in the series to follow. Whitman's readers are involved early in the poem and throughout by a series of illocutions: imperatives ("Take my leaves, America!," which means You, American readers, accept my poems), questions ("What do you seek, so pensive and silent? / What do you need, comrade?"), announcements ("Whoever you are! to you endless announcements"), personal assertions ("Hereby applying these leaves [poems] to the new ones [immigrants], from the hour they unite with the old ones, / Coming among the new ones myself, to be their companion—coming personally to you now, / Enjoining you to acts, characters, spectacles with me"). There is a warning ("For your life, adhere to me"), a challenge ("I have arrived, / To be wrestled with as I pass, for the solid prizes of the universe, / For such I afford whoever can persevere to win them"), a request ("Read the hints [the meaning of these poems] come at last"), a personal acceptance of *you*, the individual reader ("O my comrade! / O you and me at last—and us two only"), and a promise ("O now I triumph—and you shall also; / O hand in hand—O wholesome pleasure—O one more desirer and lover, / O haste, firm holding—haste, haste on, with me" [*i.e.*, with me as guide, move ahead through the poems to follow]").

All the above is obvious enough to need no further explanation, except for the last statement. Is it a promise? Yes, and this is an example of my earlier contention that Whitman is no shaman, that his poetry does stay on the page, for even on such a now minor and nearly forgotten language distinction, *shall* and *will*, he never blurs the two. He always uses the first person with *will* and the second and third persons with *shall* to imply promise (as well as the other standard implications: authority, command, consent, threat, determination, resolution, inevitability). The other features of this approach to the reader will become clearer as we look at a few more samples, but it is important to note that in 1860 this intimate approach to the reader was the first contact, before the reader read "Song of Myself" and before the later "Inscriptions." As Leslie Fiedler rightly if somewhat melodramatically says: "Only with the creatures of his fancy, with an imagined 'you' (sometimes conceived as a lost lover; sometimes as the perfect 'Camerado,' God; sometimes as an indiscriminate Everyman; often as the reader; most often as a second self, 'the real Me') could he enter into an orgasmic unity" (1960: 69).

However, we are concerned here with only one of the *you*s, the audience or reader. There are a number of references to "you" in "Song of Myself," especially near the end of the poem, but this poem is not so much *to* and *about* the reader as about the poet. There is, however, one fairly frequent interpretive mistake (l. 1321 in the final edition), which in 1860 goes like this: "Listener up there! Here you! What have you to confide to me?" The "listener" is not God, or the Over-Soul, but the reader. "Here you!" is a shout from the persona in the lines of the poem. Whitman often uses this spatial relationship, the reader is holding the book (where the persona is) and looking down on it—on him. Thus in the 1860 version of "By Blue Ontario's Shore":

LANGUAGE AND STYLE IN *Leaves of Grass*

> I am he who goes through the streets with a barbed tongue, questioning
>   every one I meet—questioning you up there now:
> Who are you that wanted only to be told what you knew before?
> Who are you, that wanted only a book to join you in your nonsense?
> Are you, or would you be, better than all that has ever been before?
> If you would be better than all that has ever been before, come listen to me,
>   and not otherwise.

But he dropped the "questioning you up there" thereafter, weakened the series of questions at the end by applying them to "O lands," and inserting this obstetrical parenthesis ahead of them: "(With pangs and cries as thine own O bearer of many children, / These clamors wild to a race of pride I give.)" (final ed., ll. 39–40). Labor pains in the birth of a poem can be understood, but only Whitman—in the late poems—has parturient pangs while in the very act of suffocating that poem. The direct thrust of the assertion to "you up there now," with the consequent defiant challenge to the reader, was an available device for a speech by changing the preposition only ("you *out* there now"). This successful stratagem he validly employed in a poem to gain and enhance audience participation, and then lost when he revised his poetry (in 1867 and thereafter) to meet some other and inexplicable need. He never tells us what he hoped to gain by the revision, but the price (the poetic effectiveness of a key section of a major poem) was no small outlay.

In "Occupations" there are a number of changes through the various editions, too many to be examined here. However, two uses of the audience-reader "you" are significant in the changing role of this poem. I group these changes into three instead of all six editions, and will show the difference between the 1855, the 1860, and 1881 versions. In 1855 the poem was untitled, and there is little indication that it was written for and about only those who worked with their hands. The poem follows directly after "Myself," and the persona of that poem is now speaking again. And it is *speaking*, for he makes it clear that *print* will not do.

> Come closer to me,
> Push close my lovers and take the best I possess,
> Yield closer and closer and give me the best you possess.
>
> This is unfinished business with me....how is it with you?
> I was chilled with the cold types and cylinder and wet paper between us.

I pass so poorly with paper and types....I must pass with the contact of bodies
and souls.

I do not thank you for liking me as I am, and liking the touch of me....I know
that it is good for you to do so.

Were all educations practical and ornamental well displayed out of me, what
would it amount to?

Were I as the head teacher or charitable proprietor or wise statesman, what
would it amount to?

Were I to you as the boss employing and paying you, would that satisfy you?

First, note that this is direct address. The scene seems to be the speaker
in the midst of a crowd through which he has just made his way, shaking hands, greeting, patting and being patted on the shoulder, and now
calling to those at the edge of the crowd to move closer. And what of the
lines themselves: why no commas in line 2 before and after "my lovers"?
What do the elliptical dots mean in lines 4, 6, and 7? Has something
been left out? To take the questions in inverse order, nothing has been
left out; the dots, which range generally from two to four, are not ellipses at all but for breath pauses, voice interruptions, of the presumed
speaker. There are few commas, for the speaker already knows that he
will pause briefly after "Push close," drop his voice slightly for "my
lovers," and then return to his former voice level and intonation for the
rest of the line. The point is that since these lines seem to be the repro-
duction of the manuscript of a speech, such punctuation is unnecessary.
The dots in lines 4, 6, and 7 are what specify the pauses, as of course do
the lines themselves. Some of the later changes in these lines were made
because the speaking role disappears. By 1860 there were commas
around "my lovers" in line 2, a comma after the second *closer* in line 3, a
dash instead of four dots and a capital *H* for "how" in line 4, the two
*and*s in line 5 are replaced with commas, and so on.

Punctuation adjustments to make the speech suit the printed page,
even when one is talking about the limitations of print for communicating personality, are by no means all that happens to this passage in
1860. Whitman also made a two-line subsection by putting "Male and
Female!" in front of line 6, "American masses!" in front of line 7, and a
four-line subsection by injecting "Workmen and Workwomen!" in front
of line 8. Now it is pretty farfetched to imagine Whitman ever actually
uttering the 1855 lines aloud, but still it could be done. But can anyone
be imagined gazing at the men and women surrounding him and cry-

ing out any one of these three exclamations? What has happened is that he has kept the speech-act format but added these inflated, pretentious, even condescending labels—why not "Men and women" or "Friends" for line 6, "American citizens" for line 7, "Fellow workers" for line 8?— that show only how much he had become out of touch with a real oratorical situation. Surely even a century ago one would never call the American masses by that name in their presence, unless one intended it as an insult.

It was not because Whitman realized how remote from reality these lines signified him to be that he dropped the first nine lines (the original seven plus the first two exclamations of 1860). What happened was that the untitled 1855 poem (in 1860 it was still untitled—he had dropped the awkward "Poem of the Daily Work of the Workmen and Workwomen of These States" of 1856—but was number 3 in the Chants Democratic group) became more specifically in content as well as in title a song for occupations. For instance, this line, line 32 in the first edition, remained with only punctuation changes through 1860, but was dropped thereafter: "I see not merely that you are polite or white-faced....married or single....citizens of old states or citizens of new states....eminent in some profession....a lady or gentleman in a parlor....or dressed in a jail uniform....or pulpit uniform." Because of that reorientation, plus the general weakening of the force of the speech-act situation when he revised the poem to minimize the oral aspect of his poetry, the opening lines vanished in 1881. They were replaced with what, comparatively speaking, are these rather flat and certainly less intimate three lines:

> A song for occupations!
> In the labor of engines and trades and the labor of fields I find the
> developments,
> And find the eternal meanings.

Here is another use of this audience-reader "you," this time at the heart of the poem, where he is trying to make the average person understand and act on his (the average person's) significance, power, place, meaning in the state, society, culture, and divine plan. Since its thought is central to the poem, the passage would not and could not be changed completely, as was the invocation, but even the apparently minor

SPEECH ACTS

changes are not minor at all. In 1855, the persona, still speaking as an orator, says after the first of the catalogs:

I bring what you much need, yet always have,
I bring not money or amours or dress or eating....but I bring as good;
And send no agent or medium....and offer no representative of value—but
    offer the value itself. (ll. 45–47)

There is something that comes home to one now and perpetually,
It is not what is printed or preached or discussed....it eludes discussion
    and print
It is not to be put into a book....it is not in this book,
It is for you whoever you are....it is no farther from you than your hearing and
    sight are from you,
It is hinted at by the nearest and commonest and readiest....it is not them,
    though it is endlessly provoked by them....what is there ready and near
    you now? (ll. 48–52)

He leads the audience on, with partial answers to that question, for another thirty lines or so, finally acknowledging:

All doctrines, all politics and civilization exurge from you,
All sculpture and monuments and anything inscribed anywhere are tallied in
    you. (ll. 87–88)

But, then, some ten lines later, just before he begins the notorious catalog of trades and occupations, he asks again:

Will the whole come back then?
Can each see the signs of the best by a look in the lookingglass? Is there
    nothing greater or more?
Does all sit there with you and here with me? (ll. 97–99)

As noted earlier, these lines are at the core of the poem. To Whitman, and indeed to anyone else, if the people (or enough of the people to shape the social attitudes of the day) think themselves inferior, humble, weak, second-class, then the rest of society, the government, the nation will treat them that way, so that democracy will lose ground, liberty will be lost, etc. The strength of democracy is in the people, but not unless the people are aware of it, are confident of their importance, and recognize that in institutions, religion, government, art, the same principle holds: "The President is up there in the White House for you....it is not you who are here for him" (l. 83), or "All architecture is what you do to it when you look upon it" (l. 92).

LANGUAGE AND STYLE IN *Leaves of Grass*

In Whitman's conception of his function there was no way to communicate confidence, to transmit it, by words alone, but by the contagion of his own confident manner he believed it was possible. Thus the speaker role and the use of all the rhetorical skills of the orator. Notice in lines 45–47 the traditional oratorical parallelism and repetition in the illocutionary utterances: "I bring . . . I bring not . . . but I bring . . . And send no . . . and offer no . . . but offer." Two-thirds of these are wasted (and thus a hindrance and frustration) if the intention is only to communicate ideas, information, facts. But their value here is to fix and hold the listener's ear (and eye, too, to be sure), to provide emphasis, to convey an emotional aura through the rhythmical shaping of the successive phrases. The series in line 46 with the separating *or* helps, of course, as does the idiomatic *as good* at the end, the parallel of the negative answered by the positive in both lines 46 and 47, the repetition (with a key difference) of "value" in line 47, and so on. If there is a weakness in line 45, as there is in reading, for students always miss it, I presume the persona in the imaginary speech would have enforced the true intent by intonation and vocal force. Students usually read the line as if the poet were saying, "I bring what you much need, yet I have always brought it," rather than Whitman's intent, which is: "I bring what you much need, yet you always have it anyway but do not realize it." Presumably Whitman recognized the possibility of misinterpretation and removed the comma after "need," which does help.

In 1860, as the oratorical shaping of this and other early poems faded, Whitman made some changes: line 45 remained as in 1855, but line 46 becomes: "Not money, amours, dress, eating, but as good," and by 1881 he had added "erudition" after "eating." In the next section, he replaced all the dots with short dashes, put in a comma for each *or* in line 49, a comma for each *and* in line 52, and also in line 52 put parentheses around the terminal question. By 1881, he had dropped the final question altogether.

Now these are not major changes. Indeed, in terms of the larger changes going on in Whitman and in *Leaves* after 1860 (in tone, subject matter, attitude, vocabulary, persona) they may seem inconsequential. My point is that, minor as is any one of these changes, considered alone, there are a great many of them, scattered all through *Leaves*, and they represent a conscious attempt to soften, weaken, lessen the blunt and forceful directness of the early poems based on the speech-act approach, the direct involvement of the audience-reader "you." To go through *Leaves* line by line noting the changes and evaluating each one would be a tedious process, for most of them would be like those in lines 45–52 above. Perhaps the best procedure is to evaluate this small group of minor changes, multiply it by 150 (the poems in 1860), and so estimate the cumulative effect.

But a change that was not minor is that for the question: "It is for you whoever you are....it is no farther from you than your hearing and sight are from you, / It is hinted at by the nearest and commonest and readiest....it is not them, though it is endlessly provoked by them ....what is there ready and near you now?" (ll. 51–52). The whole point of these lines, and of the five-line section which they terminate, is not to tell, that is, to *inform* only, the audience-reader how important they-he may be, but to have the truth discovered or rediscovered by the audience itself. For that purpose, the challenging question or riddle to push the audience to self-examination and find out what "it" is, is important, is indeed what this section of the poem is all about. To make it a parenthetical question, as he did in 1860, is to make it an aside, an afterthought, and so weaken the poetic impact of the line. But to drop the question altogether is to drop also, and intentionally, the direct relationship with the audience-reader that the poet has been at great pains to establish subtly and carefully in the poem up to this line, as line 51 immediately above it would demonstrate.

There is no way of knowing why Whitman should have dropped the question discussed above (even changing "endlessly" for "ever" in the preceding clause) to make line 52 finally look like this: "It is hinted at by nearest, commonest, readiest, it is ever provoked by them." We can, however, get some notion of what was going on in his attitude to this poem in Arthur Golden's facsimile edition (1968) of the famous Blue Book. As explained by its editor, and elsewhere in this study, the Blue Book was Whitman's working copy of the 1860 edition on which he made additions, omissions, emendations, and also private notations to himself. He never had a great deal of confidence about his lines, and the earliest notebooks show the continual rewriting, crossing out, rearranging, but once he finally got a poem in type he seems to have been able to leave it alone and turn to a new poem or new problem. Indeed, much of the reason for his getting printer friends to set in type a poem of his long before the book it was to go in was finished must have been this need to resolve the creative crisis of the not-finally-complete draft. For later changes, the Blue Book is witness to the great indecision, worry, and uncertainty, not only about this poem, but about many others. At least five different titles were tried out (there are that many varieties of ink, pencil, and handwriting); he makes this note at the top of the first page:"? take this out [*i.e.*, the whole poem] to alter it + vivify [or verify?] for future volume"; but a later (?) note on the other side of the page reads, "This is satisfactory as it now is—Dec. 7, 1864." The "as it now is" is in reference to the many revisions, including those noted above, so it really was not satisfactory after all. But what the changes do show (whether they remained permanently or not) is that he never makes a change to augment, reinforce, or render more realistically explicit the speech-act situation with which the poem began—rather he seems to have forgotten that aspect (or perhaps taken it for granted) and directs his attention to making other changes, without realizing they go against the speech-act foundation of the poem.

To demonstrate, let us return to the lines quoted above. The original lines 87 and 88, and farther on lines 97, 98, and 99, were guidelines to the audience-reader leading them or him to the long catalog of various occupations, from which the lesson was to be drawn by the reader himself. But in the Blue Book, Whitman injects a new line to precede the summation in lines 87–88 and all the subsequent lines of the poem. This new line is "List well now my scholars dear," which he finally changed again to the "List close my scholars dear." If we were looking for a date and place for the turning point in Whitman's poetic career, the date he made this revision, or really this addition, December 7, 1864, would fit.

What is *list*? It is an archaic (chiefly poetical) form of *listen* (according to dictionaries then and now), has not and never did have much currency in American English, and the only way Whitman could have got the word was from some poet of the sort he abjured in the 1855 Preface and in all his work up to 1860. The only thing we can believe is that he had decided to be "poetical," not for any ironical purposes but

with the awful sincerity of the self-deceived. It might be thought a typographical error, except that there are other "poetical" uses. In the
Blue Book for "As I Ebb'd with the Ocean of Life" he substitutes *list*
for *listen* in "As I listen to the dirge," for "Song of the Answerer" he
inserts the new opening line "Now list to my morning's romanza," and
as we have noted in "Song of Myself" he inserts a new introductory line
to the account of John Paul Jones' naval victory, "List to the yarn."
Others have noted this change, notably Asselineau (1960: 226–27),
but few of us have been sufficiently severe in holding Whitman to account for that worst of literary sins, the sin against language.

The use of *list* for *listen* may seem a literary peccadillo of an inconsequential sort. But the trouble is that this change reflects an attitude to
the reader, to himself, and to his earlier poetry that can never be reversed. Let me clarify by returning to lines 97–99. These lines remain
the same in 1855 and 1860, and they serve the same purpose, to lead
into the well-known catalog, which permits realistic support for the
poet's claims that he speaks for all workmen. In the Blue Book he
changed line 99 from "Does all sit there with you and here with me?" to
"Does all sit there with you, with the mystic unseen soul?" Then he
adds these new lines:

> Strange and hard that paradox true I give
> Objects gross and the unseen soul are one.

What has happened is that by adding these lines he has removed himself, or he has moved the persona, to a different position or different role
in relation to the subject (the workers) and to the audience. The original organization of the poem was to guide the worker (and the audience) to a discovery of each individual's need to throw off the shaping
pressures of society and to assert his true independence. For Whitman
now to *tell* the worker (in the sense of informing him, preaching to him,
or even explaining things to him in any obvious manner) is to debase
the whole approach. It is a very delicate and fragile relationship that is
carefully developed in 1855 and 1856, endangered (by such gaffes as
speaking to the American masses as "American masses!") although still
maintained in 1860, but given up late in 1864 when he revises the
poem to do with it something he had not desired to do earlier.

Who are the "scholars dear" who are requested to "List close"? How did they get to be the persona's property; "my scholar"? Even if they are rarefied workers, which is (remotely) possible, there is still the patronizing tone that makes one wince. Again, further in the poem, when he changes the rhetorical question "Does all sit there with you and here with me?" to "Does all sit there with you, with the mystic unseen soul?," what does the "mystic unseen soul" mean? Is it sitting out *there* with the workers? More plausibly, is it Emerson's Over-Soul? The pretentious language that was Whitman's way of disguising his floundering poetic powers is seen here for the first time. And why, after earlier carefully avoiding generalizing too soon and setting up one of his more spectacular catalogs out of which at the end the generalization was to be drawn, does he now give the answer ("Objects gross and unseen soul are one") to all the questions he has been asking before the catalog?

It is still one of the better poems, because it was such a good poem that it survives the revisions. Some—to my mind, only a few—of the changes Whitman made in the early *Leaves* were advantageous, but this was not one. In the present connection, the discussion of the personal effect on the audience-reader, the *you*, the original poem reached an intimate relationship that later changes as the language diminished.

A poem he did not change for the worse, perhaps because he hardly changed it at all, is "Song of the Open Road." It has the direct relationship with the audience-reader "you"—indeed much of the poem is based on expanding that relationship. But parts of that poem can also be used to explain through example a point mentioned earlier, Whitman's adept use of the *shall-will* distinction. As will be noted, the selections also show a developing bond (on the persona's part, at any rate) to which the use of these auxiliaries contributes. Since the changes are so slight, the text of the final edition is used.

The many uses of "you" in the early sections of this poem refer not to the audience, but to the road and the assorted items on the road that capture his attention (section 3). But in section 5 he is ready:

> All seems beautiful to me,
> I can repeat over to men and women You have done such good to me
>   I would do the same to you,
> I will recruit for myself and you as I go,
> I will scatter myself among men and women as I go,
> I will toss a new gladness and roughness among them,

Whoever denies me it shall not trouble me,
Whoever accepts me he or she shall be blessed and shall bless me.
   (ll. 62–68)

The first "You" in line 63 is intentionally capitalized, probably because it follows the "men and women" but now becomes the first pronoun for the audience. There was a comma after "women" in earlier editions, and no gain in dropping it—it may be one of the few typographical errors that escaped Whitman's sharp proofreader's eye. But to the *shall-will* matter in the last five lines, can any difference even be noticed? When I was in high school we were still taught the distinction. A few days after we had a session on it, there was a theme due. As a stunt, I carefully switched all the *shall*s for *will*s and vice versa, planning to tell Miss Reed (my favorite teacher) after she had corrected them, that I had done it on purpose—that she was very observant to have noted it, and that I now realized the distinction between *shall* and *will* made a difference after all. The distinction, she had contended, was a sign of the distinguished writer. When I got the theme back, there was not a single red mark on my *shall*s and *will*s. I was much too embarrassed to say anything about it, but it made the *shall-will* distinction stay in mind for some years.

A century ago the use of *shall* and *will* was a valuable aid in shaping audience reaction. What lines 64–66 are truly saying can be seen by writing out what the *will* implied to the reader of a century ago:

I intend to recruit for myself and you as I go,
I promise to scatter myself among men and women as I go,
I am determined to toss a new gladness and roughness among them.

The *shall* lines (ll. 67–68) would go this way:

Whoever denies me, by my authority I announce it cannot trouble me,
Whoever accepts me, he or she is going to be blessed for so doing by my authority and is going to bless me in turn.

The revised lines are a bit awkward, but the purposiveness of the statements Whitman intended is clear. A few lines from this poem will illustrate Whitman's practice. The rule he was following is still current, although as Julian Boyd and Zelda Boyd indicate (1980) it is rarely followed in this country.

Shall	I; we: simple futurity
	you (sing. & plur.): authority, command, promise, inevitably
	she, he, it; they: authority, command, promise, inevitably
Will	I; we: consent, promise, determination, resolution
	you (sing. & plur.): simple futurity
	she, he it; they: simple futurity
Questions	*shall* is used when *shall* is expected in answer
	will is used when *will* is expected in answer

This question-answer matter is important in *Leaves*, with its many sometimes-more-than rhetorical questions, for answering "we will" or "you shall" implies commitment on the audience's part. Whitman is also careful and correct in his use of the past participle: *should* (for all persons) to denote duty, propriety, expediency; to make a statement less direct or blunt; or to emphasize the uncertainty in conditional and hypothetical clauses; *would* either to express a wish or, in place of *will*, to make a statement or question less blunt or direct.

In "Open Road," up to line 62, the persona has been expressing his delight in and need of the open road, speaking for himself. Thereafter he brings in the audience-reader to the extent that the poem becomes by the end a joint venture. He explains to the audience the challenge of the road, the need to travel with like persons; he defines *adhesiveness* (one of his favorite phrenological borrowings, as Arthur Wrobel has shown) as the "efflux of soul," exemplified in "the fluid and attaching character" (presumably the persona) toward whom "heaves the shuddering longing ache of contact." Thus established, the persona becomes international and cries out, "Allons!" (l. 114), not once but ten times in the remainder of the poem (and the only uses of this famous "Marseillaise" cry in *Leaves*).

But even as he promises, both for himself and the audience, "We will sail pathless and wild seas," he warns, "None may come to the trial till he or she bring courage and health." He acknowledges in a statement which only in the final edition did he put in parentheses: "(I and mine do not convince by arguments, similes, rhymes, / We convince by our presence.)" (ll. 138–39), and then proceeds to convince, not by argument, simile, or rhyme, but by precept, in the well-known section 11:

> Listen! I will be honest with you,
> I do not offer the old smooth prizes, but offer rough new prizes,

SPEECH ACTS

These are the days that must happen to you:
You shall not heap up what is call'd riches,
You shall scatter with lavish hand all that you earn or achieve,
You but arrive at the city to which you were destin'd, you hardly settle
  yourself to satisfaction before you are call'd by an irresistible call to depart,
You shall be treated to the ironical smiles and mockings of those who remain
  behind you,
What beckonings of love you receive you shall only answer with passionate
  kisses of parting
You shall not allow the hold of those who spread their reach'd hands toward
  you. (ll. 140–48)

Notice the *will* of determination in line 140, and the *shall* of command
in lines 143, 144, 147 (with the *only* for extra emphasis), and 148.
Line 146 fits the *inevitably* of the definition best. For anyone old enough
to have once used this *shall-will* differentiation, it does not take long to
get resensitized. But even if not, it is (or was) a real and valid distinction that we ought to keep in mind in reading literature written before
World War I. It has special import in the early Whitman, for whether it
is used consciously (as in the *shall* lines in the passage above) or habitu-
ally (as in "I will be . . .") the poet's attitude of mind is revealed without explicit verbalization.

Notice how the closing section uses these auxiliaries in a fashion to
bring to culmination the whole intent of the poem:

> Camerado, I give you my hand!
> I give you my love more precious than money,
> I give you myself before preaching or law;
> Will you give me yourself? will you come travel with me?
> Shall we stick by each other as long as we live? (ll. 220–24)

Ending a poem with a question is a tricky maneuver that does not always work (there are a couple of dozen of these in *Leaves*, many of them
short poems), and "Open Road" is the only major poem that uses the
device. It is successful here chiefly because of the *shall-will* usage. Remember that the form used in a question (whether *shall* or *will*) antici-
pates the same form in the answer. Here, when the answer is not vocalized at all, it nevertheless flashes through the reader's mind. The
poet expects (and presumably will get) from the each "Will you?"
in line 223 the "I will" reply, implying consent, promise, or resolve.
For the last line of the poem—and note that he shifts to the first-person

plural—the answer is consequent upon one's having just vowed to take to the open road with the poet. Accordingly he expects a "We shall" in simple agreement, which is automatically given him under the impact of the poem. The point here is that the persona speaks directly to the reader, in the present tense and time, with sufficient seriousness and sincerity that we give him that necessary "willing suspension of disbelief" and respond, however fleetingly, to his query.

Many other poems in the 1860 edition have this direct relationship with the reader, with the implication that the poet goes beyond the poem to affect the reader with his own personality. Whitman, I sometimes think, was so convinced that he had to get beyond the printed line to communicate the force of his belief with the direct immediate effect he found in listening to Elias Hicks and Father Taylor that he wrote as if he were doing so in order to make it come about.

This device is rarely used after 1860, and it is not always successful in that edition. Many poems of the Calamus section are involved in intimate relationship, although I agree with Russell Hunt that a major critical error of the past few decades of Whitman scholarship has been to read that section as if its intention were primarily and solely to give expression to the poet's homoerotic and homosexual bent. Hunt shows clearly and convincingly that many of the Calamus poems are concerned with the poetic process, with Whitman's attempts to clarify for himself and his reader the special nature of his poetry. One cannot agree for every poem that "Calamus is an *ars poetica* in which Whitman explains what act is being performed in the writing and the reading of *Leaves of Grass*" (1975: 485). But certainly all the poems he cites and many others are best interpreted in this way. For instance, "To a Stranger," which Hunt does not have space to refer to, is a direct statement to the reader, and to prefer a homosexual reading of the poem would be more perverse on the critic's part than on Whitman's.

But the point here is that these poems are all addressed to the individual "you" and as such escape the net being used here, which includes all the audience as well as the individual reader. The poems called elsewhere "platform poems" are those in which the persona can be imagined speaking to an audience, to a group of people; the *you* can be taken as a plural or a singular, sometimes indeed it starts out as a plural but becomes a singular as the poem advances. The Calamus poems, and a few others scattered throughout the 1860 edition but chiefly near the back, are not and cannot be read as having a group audience, as the persona uttering the lines from a platform.

It has been necessary to go into this matter of the single or multiple audience at some length, for one of Whitman's great contributions to poetry was this audience relationship, particularly for such poems as "Open Road," in which the audience is multiple but permits (with Whitman's encouragement, of course) the individual reader to feel that he or she is the one to whom it is directed. Whitman begins the 1860 edition with a use of "you" which permits that sort of reading with "Proto-Leaf," and he ends it with one of the triumphs of this poetic device, "So Long!" This cannot but have been intentional, for he even hints as much in an overlooked short poem in the middle of the volume. One of the intended features of the book is that the longer title, *Leaves of Grass*, refers to the whole book, which includes a major section of twenty-four poems under the subtitle Leaves of Grass (pp. 195–242). The last of these untitled poems is short and goes this way:

> Lift me close to your face till I whisper,
> What you are holding is in reality no book, nor part of a book,
> It is a man, flushed and full-blooded—it is I—*So long*!
> We must separate—Here! take from my lips this kiss,
> Whoever you are, I give it especially for you;
> *So long*—and I hope we shall meet again.

The poem is unsuccessful for a number of reasons, but chiefly because it is too short for the intense intimacy of the central episode. The identification of the persona with the book (a form of metonymy) and the attempt to make the reader holding the book a participant in a relationship with the persona come as something of a surprise. There are many problems Whitman faces in identifying himself with his book, but here I am concerned only with the handling of the *you* of the second line to whom the poem is addressed.

As those acquainted with "So Long!," the final poem in *Leaves*, will recall, the thought of this poem and many of its words are used again there, but not until there has been considerable preparation, lines 2–3 above not coming up in "So long" until lines 73–74, and lines 4–5 not until lines 84–85 in what was then a poem of eighty-nine lines. The short poem does, however, make its point clearly enough, which is that the book, the poetry, this poem has a life of its own, that since the persona speaks through or out of the poem, the persona is in the poem. In the Blue Book Whitman tried out some changes for his six-line poem which he didn't carry through, but they show how carefully and painstakingly he went over the lines trying to help the poem accomplish an ultimately impossible task.

The crossings-out and revisions can best be comprehended in Golden's facsimile, but here the line is repeated with each revision. After the third line of the poem Whitman thought of putting in this line, but it took four attempts:

> At every leaf I feel the pressure of your hand and return it;
> At every leaf I have felt the pressure of your hand and return it;
> At every leaf I have felt the pressure of your hand more than you know;
> At every leaf I felt the pressure of your hand more than you know;

With this new fourth line the present fourth line of the poem now seemed too abrupt, so he put in a new beginning word: he wrote in the margin *For*, crossed it out for *But*, crossed that out for *Now*, liked that, drew an arrow over to the beginning of the line and wrote *Now* again. Accordingly the line would become "Now we must separate—Here! take from my lips this kiss." Still not satisfied, he inserted *a while* after "separate." My conjecture may have the time sequence of his changes somewhat awry, but note that he is thinking not about changing the startling notion of secular transubstantiation (this is my body, this is my blood: *i.e.*, this book is me) as too incredible to be accepted, but is experimenting with words, phrases, times, and tenses—to make the unbelievable a continuing, ongoing, everyday happening.

Jarrell's original essay on Whitman's language manipulation was first entitled "Walt Whitman: He Had His Nerve," and that fine critic wrote out his responses to many of the great lines in "Song of Myself." It was from Jarrell's essay that I first learned that Gerard Manley Hopkins knew Whitman's work, and I have often wondered with what sort of delight-dismay, holy-heresy, shock-surprise Hopkins would have read "Lift me close to your face till I whisper" or the longer poem "So long." Jarrell's essay did not go into that, but I like to think he would have considered this effort or the later

> This is no book,
> Who touches this, touches a man.

of "So Long" a nervy venture of an even more spectacular variety.

No poet tries so hard to make contact with his reader, and the final poem of the 1860 edition is the culmination of the volume in this regard. Fiedler quotes the passage just below the famous utterance and says, "No poet engages the reader with so fervid and intimate a clasp; no writer describes the act of reading so erotically" (1960: 69). To the extent that this compliment is true, it is because Whitman went over and over his lines asserting, then clarifying and emphasizing, their illocutionary force.

≈ IV ≈
NEGATION IN POETRY AND IN
Leaves of Grass

There is one important treatment of negation for the novel (Maire Kurrick, 1979) but no comparable study for English and American poetry, and certainly no one has done so for Whitman. Nor can it be done here, both because of limitations of space and because I do not have the necessary computer assistance for a complete study of this unusual feature of language which shapes poetry in unexpected ways. My curiosity was originally aroused by the comments in Chaim Perelman and Olbrechts-Tyteca's *New Rhetoric* (1969) that "negation is a reaction to an actual or virtual affirmation by someone else" and that "negative thought only comes into play if one's concern is with persons, that is, if one is arguing" (p. 155). Kenneth Burke in *Language as Symbolic Action* (1966) makes a similar point, developing his contention "that there are no negatives in nature where everything is simply what it is and as it is." Indeed, "the negative is a peculiarly linguistic resource. And because it is so peculiarly linguistic, the study of man as the specifically word-using animal requires special attention to this distinctive marvel, the negative" (p. 419). In both studies, the major reference for the theory of negation was Henri Bergson's *Creative Evolution*, which is concerned with the negative chiefly in the sense that it is and has become a problem in philosophy.

Most discussions of negation are by philosophers to other philosophers, or by linguists to their colleagues. Burke's discussion ties into his explanation in "Dramatistic View of the Origins of Language," and as such has more reference to rhetoric than to poetry. As he says: "Bergson approaches the problem of the negative in terms of the negative *proposition*; but we would approach it in terms of the negative *command*." Burke believes, in fact, "that the negative must have begun as a rhetorical or hortatory function, *as with the negatives of the Ten Commandments*" (1966: 421). There is, to be sure, a significant hortatory element in Whitman, although Burke, in this book and in his specific studies of Whitman elsewhere, does not pursue that avenue of investigation.

Bergson's point is that any description of nature (nonhuman nature) can only be positive. He states: "That which exists may come to be recorded, but the nonexistence of the nonexisting cannot" (p. 318). If we are speaking literally of what we see, "we shall affirm that such or such a thing is, we shall never affirm that a thing is not" (p. 316). It is a difficult concept to accept, for immediately we begin to search for exceptions, but it is true, and after a while we do see that negatives reflect our reaction and only that. Burke has great fun in extending the implications of this idea—he includes brief treatments of William Ernest Henley's "Invictus," Clough's "Say Not the Struggle Nought Availeth," and Milton's "When I Consider How My Light Is Spent" (in the five-page section 13)—particularly as it supports his own theory of language. But what the negative does for poetry, and what it reveals of the poet's response to nature, life, society, is also worthy of investigation.

The first, and for many years the definitive, treatment of the negative was Otto Jespersen's *Negation in English* (1917), which I found still valuable, particularly in its liberal use of examples from literature. The standard linguistic treatment in this generation, which is referred to by other linguists so frequently that I presume it is definitive, is Edward Klima's "Negation in English" (1964), a seventy-eight-page classification and grammatical description of the large variety of negative constructions in the language. Klima's article is most useful in identifying the different forms and degrees of negation, especially in terms of how to handle such prefixes as *un-*, *in-*, and *dis-*, which are sometimes negative but by no means always, the suffix *-less*, and such words as *seldom*, *doubt*, and *without*, plus assorted indefinites which may or may not be negative, depending on the contextual frame.

Another valuable linguistic study in this respect is Talmy Givón's "Negation in Language" (1978), because of its pragmatic orientation.

Many negatives in everyday conversation are forms of denial, and denial is one of the speech acts first formulated by Austin, classified by Searle, elaborated by Ohmann, and systematized as a critical apparatus by Campbell, Hancher, Pratt, and others. There has been serious objection to the literal interpretation of speech acts in criticism (for example, by Fish and Hirsch), especially as clues to the poet's psyche, since the speech act in a literary work must inevitably reflect the persona, and not necessarily the author at all. It is clear that the negatives or any other speech acts in Browning's dramatic monologues are not of much use in characterizing Browning, but the situation is not so clear with Blake or Byron or Wordsworth, and still less clear with Whitman, who went to such elaborate lengths to identify himself with the "I" of *Leaves*. Be that as it may, two of Givón's six conclusions were shaping influences on my own reading of negatives in nineteenth-century English and American poetry. These are his two well-substantiated claims: "Negatives constitute a different speech act than affirmatives. While the latter are used to convey new information on the presumption of ignorance of the hearer, negatives are used to correct misguided belief on the assumption of the hearer's error. Negatives are consistently more marked in terms of discourse-pragmatic presuppositions, as compared to affirmatives. More specifically, negatives are uttered in a context where corresponding affirmatives have already been discussed, or else where the speaker assumes the hearer's belief in—and thus familiarity with—the corresponding affirmative" (p. 109). The use of these two claims in what follows is basic, even though continual documentation and acknowledgment have not seemed necessary.

Whitman uses many negatives, but is that use distinctive? Can we say that the negative is a style marker? To answer these questions we must know whether he uses more negatives than do his contemporaries, and whether there is anything special or unusual in his use. To make a simple check to see if there were more negatives in *Leaves*, a standard text anthology (*Norton*, Vol. II, for English; Vol. I, for American, plus *Final Harvest* for Dickinson) was used and the negatives in a group of Romantic and nineteenth-century poems were counted. For this rough count, anything for which there might be interpretive difficulty was not tabulated. Since the number of lines of poetry for each poet varied widely, the number of negatives was related to the number of lines to get a percentage, which is the important figure in this sort of comparison. This is what resulted.

NEGATIVES IN SOME ENGLISH POETS

Poet	Negatives	Lines	Percentage
Blake	73	762	9.6%
Wordsworth	408	4,323	9.4%
Coleridge	131	1,869	7.0%
Byron	750	4,300	17.4%
Shelley	294	2,983	9.9%
Keats	299	2,355	12.7%
Tennyson	324	3,703	8.8%
Browning	378	2,919	12.9%
Arnold	160	1,541	10.4%

Two observations should be made about this list before we turn to the American poets: the Blake figure may be suspect, in relation to the others, because of the limited number of lines available (I would have guessed a higher percentage); the Byron percentage was higher than anticipated chiefly because of the large sampling in the anthology from *Don Juan*, which in its mocking style uses negatives liberally.

NEGATIVES IN SOME AMERICAN POETS

Poet	Negatives	Lines	Percentage
Bryant	83	717	11.6%
Poe	125	927	13.5%
Emerson	97	907	10.7%
Thoreau	41	349	11.7%
Longfellow	140	1,598	8.8%
Whittier	123	1,517	8.1%
Holmes	51	567	9.0%
Lowell	219	1,865	11.7%
Melville	51	384	13.3%
Dickinson	722	7,187	10.0%
Whitman	2,070	10,659	19.4%

Again, the number of lines to be examined was low, especially for Thoreau and Melville, but they were included to give a sense of the use of negatives in what anthologists considered representative poems. We are

LANGUAGE AND STYLE IN *Leaves of Grass*

all more acquainted with Thoreau's prose style, which is strongly negative; the opposite (more positive) for Melville; it is curious to see the extent to which the poetry is or is not corroboratory. For Lowell, the selections from *The Biglow Papers* were not included (nor was Tennyson's "Northern Farmer"), for dialect poetry is too difficult to analyze.

The reason for beginning this negative-use investigation was a conviction of a radical change in Whitman's poetry after the Civil War—not in subject matter or theme, but in style. Still, to have a general feeling about a change in style is much too vague and impressionistic to be very convincing, so it was necessary to find style markers that would demonstrate the change, if there really were one. A number of other stylistic changes could have been documented to support the claim, but the use of the negative caught my attention, chiefly because it had not been examined before (as diction has) and because negation is significant not only for *Leaves* but for poetry in general. Accordingly the negatives in the first three editions were checked against the poems written after 1860.

NEGATIVES IN *LEAVES OF GRASS*

Edition	Negatives	Lines	Percentage
1855	583	2,316	25.1%
1856	439	1,849	23.7%
1860	537	2,439	22.0%
	1,559	6,604	23.6%
1865–1881	413	3,243	12.7%
Annexes	98	812	12.1%
Leaves total	2,070	10,659	19.4%

If we make a broad division of Whitman's poetry into *early* (up to and including the 1860 edition) the *late* (after the Civil War), the late poetry is in no numerical fashion notable for the use of negatives. It can also be demonstrated that there is not only a numerical but a qualitative difference in the negations in the early poetry. The startling disproportion between the use of negatives in Whitman's early and late poetry is important for a number of reasons, to be sure, but two seem especially significant. If the strong use of negatives is a feature of the first edition, and even of the first three editions, what does that signify as to the nature and impact of the poetry itself? And if the employment of negatives then drops to a level more or less in the range of other poets in his century, why did this happen? Some attempt will be made to answer these questions, but after we explore how the negative has been used in poetry.

It is unlikely that the use of negatives is a fully conscious and intentional practice in everyday conversation. Even in writing on an occasion when our attention is on some specific subject, we are rarely aware of when or how we use negatives. To check myself on this notion, I re-examined a book review written yesterday in which I could not remember using any negatives at all. Of the eleven negatives I found, seven were in one paragraph, and I now realize that paragraph was, after all, mildly contentious. The point is that negatives seem to come automatically to the voice or pen without conscious shaping. But in poetry every word is supposedly consciously drawn and placed.

Certainly, the opening of Keats's "Ode on Melancholy" ("No, no, go not to Lethe, neither twist") was beautifully contrived to take full dramatic advantage of the negative warning. We are not likely to remember, however, that of the ten negatives used in that poem, nine of them are in the first seven lines. We will, of course, remember the four in the first line because the line itself is so memorable in its surprise negative command that it springs to mind when someone mentions the title. Anthology selections are not appropriate for any full-scale treatment of the negative in English poetry, but let me draw attention to a few notable usages which others may wish to follow up. In Keats, for instance, the tendency sometimes is to group negatives (much as in the seven-line opening noted above) with a remarkably successful double focusing of attention on a turning point in the poem. They are not used as an opening device anywhere else, but the placement in other poems is just as adroit and skillful. For instance, eleven of fifteen negatives in "Ode to Psyche" are in the third stanza; ten of thirteen in stanza 2 of "Ode on a Grecian Urn," with two more in the opening two lines of stanza 3; and for both odes the use of negatives changes and shapes the direction of the poem.

Sometimes negation is used for some special occasion. In Blake, for instance, in "The Book of Thel," it is peculiarly appropriate that Thel, the virgin, defines herself by negatives in sections 2 and 3, which fits her characterization as timid desire afraid to venture into life. In a quite different situation, that section in *The Marriage of Heaven and Hell* called "Proverbs of Hell" ("A diabolic version of the Book of Proverbs in the Old Testament," the footnote assures us) uses many negatives and does so very appropriately, indeed almost necessarily, in view of the contravening going on. What is surprising in Blake is the near-absence of negatives in the lyrics, eighteen of them in twenty-eight poems (altogether some five hundred lines).

In Wordsworth's poetry there are many variations of negation usage, some in passages that have been much admired although it is not generally recognized that it was the negation that supplied or helped supply the added character that made the line or passage memorable. Arnold recognized, for "Michael," that "And never lifted up a single stone" was an "expression of the highest and most truly expressive kind," but he almost insisted this was a self-evident truth that needed no textual support. Yet any poetic statement is evaluated aesthetically as well as semantically, through its language, its context, its prosodic impact. The *never* is not only placed in the line in the governing position for both sound and meaning, but it is prepared for by almost one hundred preceding lines with no negatives at all. A textual critic would find other support for Arnold's high praise, to be sure, but the negation, especially in its use at this place in the line and in the poem, should not be overlooked.

There are other features in Wordsworth's negation that cannot be explored fully here. But notice such items as these: the argument between William and Matthew in the famous paired poems is light and friendly, but also shrewd and skillful, especially in use of negatives— William uses many more negatives in his "Reply" than he does in the reverse situation, "The Tables Turned." Again, there are many of what might be called "positive" poems, those which mirror nature or are so in tune with nature that negation is not involved. Some "positive" poems, then, are notable by the absence of negatives, as "The Green Linnet," "I Wandered Lonely As a Cloud," and even "We are Seven." In a key sense, the graceful tribute to Dorothy, "To My Sister," only uses its three negatives ("no book," "no joyless forms," "no book") to reject whatever of human products may interfere with their positive engagement with nature. On the other hand, how many negatives are in the brief "A Slumber Did My Spirit Seal"? There are eight and superbly placed.

But more interesting to me are the mixed poems, poems which do use negatives but in complex fashion to suggest, explore, resolve, or not resolve human problems. "Tintern Abbey," indeed, seems almost a theory and demonstration of this negative principle, a sort of show-and-tell use with no negatives, then the key uses (ll. 23, 31–32, 40, 50–54), but also the affirmations in the blocks of lines between these negatives. Then there is the recognition, at about line 70, of the grades of involvement with nature, from childish joy to mature but passionate intensity. He says (with my italics for negative use here and through the rest of this chapter, unless otherwise indicated), at line 75, that "I cannot paint what then I was" and yet goes on to describe with ten negatives the critical period in his reevaluation of nature, ending with "Nor harsh, nor grating, though of ample power / To chasten and subdue." We all remember the famous lines that follow, "And I have felt / A presence . . . Of all my moral being," but are not conscious that these nineteen lines are positive in the literal sense of being without negatives. Yet they are, and are indeed framed by negatives, for two negatives follow, to be confirmed by five negatives in three lines (ll. 127–30): "that neither evil tongues, / Rash judgments, nor the sneers of selfish men, / Nor greetings where no kindness is, nor all / the dreary intercourse." There are significant uses of the negative in the closing exhortation to Dorothy as well.

The very sensitive, sometimes shaping use of negatives, often so deftly placed that we are not consciously aware of their influence when reading, is duplicated in other poems, particularly in The Prelude, but a study of that must be someone else's pursuit. But one passage may be used as a transition to Byron and thence to Whitman. We do not think of Wordsworth as needing to defend his character, publicly at any rate; but once in The Prelude, book 14, he does so:

> Never did I, in quest of right and wrong,
> Tamper with conscience from a private aim;
> Nor was in any public hope the dupe
> Of selfish passions; nor did ever yield
> Willfully to mean cases or low pursuits. (ll. 150–54)

We rarely know the explicit occasion or accusation that leads to impassioned defense of this sort, or even if we do know what the outward calumny was, we cannot know how it affected its victim except by the temper and quality of his reply. But I must say that these defenses almost never work, as even in these lines of Wordsworth's, for we who are reading the lines are not the original slanderers. Consequently, the lines seem a bit overstated almost as if the poet were telling us what a fine person he is. This is a minor, almost inconsequential faux pas in Wordsworth (if it is even that, for there is only this one occasion). But the point here is that there is no way to defend oneself against such attacks except by the use of negation.

Byron uses more negatives than any other English poet, and, aside from the wide variety in *Don Juan*, many of the uses arise from the need to rebut what he considered unjust accusations. That this reaction was made through the guise of Childe Harold or Lara or Manfred or any other Byronic hero might presumably make the defiant gesture more palatable, but it is still based on negation. And it seems, the greater the need for justification the greater the number of negatives. This is an example from *Childe Harold's Pilgrimage*, canto 3, stanza 113:

> I have *not* loved the world, *nor* the world me;
> I have *not* flattered its rank breath, *nor* bowed
> To its idolatries a patient knee—
> *Nor* coined my cheek to smiles—*nor* cried aloud
> In worship of an echo; in the crowd
> They could *not* deem me one of such; I stood
> Among them, but *not* of them; in a shroud
> Of thoughts which were *not* their thoughts, and still could,
> Had I *not* filed my mind, which thus itself subdued. (ll. 1049–1057)

The negative thrust has never been any deterrent to literary popularity. It is easy (perhaps even so facile that it can be abused) to identify with, to respond to, to experience vicariously, etc., and that is why the classical rhetoricians made much of this device. Of course all of Byron is not like stanza 113 above, or like the excerpt from *Lara* with its 25 percent of negation-carrying lines, for spacing is important, as Byron surely knew.

There are important uses of negation in the other English poets, particularly in Browning, whose use of negatives in the dramatic monologues as a means of his speaker's self-characterization is quite skillful. As for American poets of the period, the importance of negation to Poe's poetry is momentarily surprising, as is the low percentage for

Dickinson. Comparisons of the use of negation seem appropriately done in tables and percentages, but to determine whether negation is a stylistic trait in a poet's work, a more detailed examination would be necessary (as has been done here in small part for Wordsworth). And that is what I wish to do for *Leaves*.

But there are some areas of negation not treated here. First, there is the vexing problem of hidden negatives, words that are inherently negative but do not manifest as much on the surface. Such words as *cease*, *murder*, *refuse* may be understood as *not continue*, *make not alive*, *not agree*, but there is no surface indication that they are negatives. As Gunther Kress and Robert Hodge say: "It seems that the negative has been completely absorbed into the new unit" (1979: 24). It would be interesting to investigate these, for what they really do (whether consciously on the poet's part or not) is to present as a positive action something that is inherently negative. Also, I have not included some words with negative signs. The prefixes *dis-*, *im-*, or *in-*, and *un-* are commonly used to make a word negative, although some words, such as *dismay*, *immediate* or *inform*, *unless*, are difficult to determine. Accordingly, any word that could not be read by substituting *not* for the prefix (is *disappoint* really *not appoint*?) is not counted as a negative. It is possible that the above tables may be, therefore, incomplete, but that determiner was applied to all poets alike, so the comparisons should not be too much awry.

A final caveat is a bit more complicated—one that relates to Whitman more than to any other poet checked. Every poem has its own autonomous world, which may or may not have a parallel in the real world. When it does not, the difference, if intentional, may be so strongly unlike contemporary society as to be antilanguage with an antisociety intent. There is, then, a much more basic negativity, sometimes of a subversive sort, which again may have no obvious, immediately apparent signals. In its present-day application, this form of aggressive negativity has been most usefully analyzed by Herbert Marcuse in "The New Sensibility" (1969) and, in its broader cultural context, in his well-known *Negations* (1968), but it is not a contemporary language and cultural phenomenon only. Antilanguage can appear in any age, and in the poetry of that age, as shown in the interpretive argument over Donne's "Nocturnal upon St. Lucy's Day" by J. P. Thorne

(1965) and G. R. Kress (1978) summarized in Kress and Hodge (1979: 70–77).

Now in the first three editions, when Whitman, on social, religious, and sexual matters, professes a world and conduct within that world so pointedly contrary to the world as presented by other poets and writers of the 1850s, he may be said to be using antilanguage in the sense defined by Kress and Hodge (1979) and by Marcuse (1969). Whitman partially acknowledges as much himself in a draft paragraph, to be used in one of those self-reviews of either the first or the second edition, in which he puts himself against "the cultivated classes." The paragraph is one that Bucke collected, this one number 59:

> We suppose it will excite the mirth of many of our readers to be told that a man has arisen, who has deliberately and insultingly ignored all the other, the cultivated classes as they are called, and set himself to write "America's first distinctive Poem," on the platform of these same New York Roughs, firemen, the ouvrier class, masons and carpenters, stagedrivers, the Dry Dock boys, and so forth; and that furthermore, he either is not aware of the existence of the polite social models, and the imported literary laws, or else he don't value them two cents for his purposes. (*NF*: 70)

This is a very shrewd statement, not for the workmen (note the "ouvrier") but for the democratic but educated reader who is also opposed to the "imported literary laws" yet will not be bothered by the idiomatic "don't value them" of the last line. But analysis of this sort of "negation by implication" is not my present concern, and indeed it has been brilliantly treated elsewhere by Anderson (1974: 37–49). I mention it here to explain that there is a strong negative connotation in the early poetry that goes beyond the negative signs here investigated.

In similar fashion, negativity is involved or implied in some humor and much irony, but there is not enough of either in *Leaves* to warrant an analysis. The humor Richard Chase (1955) finds in certain lines of "Song of Myself" may be there, depending on one's mood, but there is no evidence that it was intentional. Mark Twain is a humor*ist*, but Huck Finn is not. Huck is indeed completely, and naïvely, serious throughout, which is why he is and is made to be humor*ous*. To think that Walter Whitman Junior contrives situations to make us laugh at Walt Whitman, the persona, is surely to misunderstand the prophetic role intended. There is only one poem of effective and intentional ironic import, "Poem of the Propositions of Nakedness" (1856), later known as "Respondez!" But that bold poem was dropped from the 1881 final edition. It was yet one more of the many changes and deletions Whitman made to fit a revised notion of the kind of poet he wanted his book to reveal.

We can start with a negative feature garnered from that model essay on comparative stylistics, Gilman and Brown's analysis of the stylistic differences in Emerson and Thoreau. In their section on aggressiveness, they say: "The strong use of the first person singular pronoun is a formal feature of what may be called aggressiveness, especially if it occurs with another set of features, the negative forms *not*, *none*, *no*, and the like" (1966: 107–108). This is so obvious, once it is mentioned, that examples almost provide a synopsis of "Myself," but here are a few: "I am *not* an earth *nor* an adjunct of an earth" (l. 135), "I do *not* snivel that snivel the world over" (l. 394), "I do *not* trouble my spirit to vindicate itself or be understood" (l. 410), "I am *not* the poet of goodness only, I do *not* decline to be the poet of wickedness also" (l. 463), all the way to "I too am *not* a bit tamed, I too am *un*translatable" (l. 1332). What makes this form of negative aggressive is that we recognize an affirmative view that the poet must emphatically negate. Gilman and Brown go on to point out that "a series of *first person* plus *negatives* represents a pre-occupation with mistaken ideas that the writer or speaker must set aside so that he can establish his own truth,—thus . . . aggressively warring against the conventional ideas of his society" (p. 109). And of course, this is how much of "Myself" is organized.

In their article, Gilman and Brown have captured a key difference between two Concord friends—a difference in character that reflects itself in a difference in style. Whitman had no philosophic and literary companion with whom we might draw a like contrast, but one might usefully compare and contrast the early and late Whitman. Not Walter Whitman Junior, the person (he was so secretive about himself and had such a profound psychological need to manipulate the facts that he can never be trusted on what he says for the record), but Walt Whitman, the persona. Even that persona changes, some roles are dropped and others added. One of the roles that was dominant in the early poetry was that of the prophet-poet-priest of democracy, that imaginary public speaker whose presumed utterances make up about two-thirds of the poetry in the 1860 edition. We have already seen that the speech act was dominant in those platform poems, and to that feature we should now add another rhetorical feature, the antithetical stance with its many negatives.

That feature of Whitman's early style is mentioned but not developed by Harold Bloom in *The Anxiety of Influence* (1973) and its follow-up *Poetry and Repression* (1976), for his is a thematic not stylistic approach. Otherwise there is no comprehensive treatment of antithesis, with its inherent negative side, for Whitman or for any nineteenth-century English or American poet—for antithesis is a rhetorical device found chiefly in prose (and in ornate and mannered prose, at that). Indeed the best study for those who wish to go beyond the brief treatment here is that model for stylistic analysis, W. K. Wimsatt's *Prose Style of Samuel Johnson* (1941). His introductory paragraph states clearly the rationale for so many negatives in a poet so fundamentally affirmative as the persona of the platform poems:

> The negative defines the positive. The more peculiar and complex the affirmation the more it may need the emphasis of negation, the more negation itself, elaborated in its own aspects, may become a relevant and parallel meaning, until which is and which is subordinate is hardly to be told, rather the two as a pair of reflecting, reciprocal movements are the true theme of the discourse. This is characteristic of all thoughtful writing, that the author is interested not only in what is now but in what was or will be, what is in any other respect, what might be or ought to be—what he does mean and what he does not mean—in a word, in distinctions. When these distinctions crystallize into enough formality, they may be called antitheses. (p. 38)

Whitman is rarely as formal as Johnson in his antithetical practice (the balance, the exact paralleling), perhaps because refinement and polish would not fit his notion of what his prophetic role should be, but the thrust of affirmation by negation is central to his self-definition in "Myself."

Whitman also goes beyond this emphatic negation by which he describes himself to bring his views to others in many of the programmatic poems of the early editions. The negative techniques are equally applicable when applied to others, and they are the feature of those poems in which he challenges his fellow Americans to be independent, self-assertive, and unafraid of death. To maintain the admiration of institutions and libraries, the regard for the country and its Constitution, the reverence for church and Scripture, and at the same time to convey the danger of excessive admiration, regard, and reverence, is not easy, but it is the intention of many of these early poems, and it was through negation that he did so. "Occupations" follows "Myself" in the first edition and redirects many of its contentions. In "Myself" he could say for himself, "I do *not* despise you priests, all time, the world over" (l. 1096), and in "Occupations":

We consider bibles and religions divine—I do *not* say they are *not* divine,
I say they have all grown out of you, and many grow out of you still,
It is *not* they who give the life, it is you who give the life,
Leaves are *not* more shed from the trees, or trees from the earth, than they are
    shed out of you. (ll. 78–81)

This challenge, with its four directive negations, is handled with considerable shrewdness: the beginning *We*, including the persona and the listening workers, is followed by the persona, the *I*, who takes on himself the reduction of religion by reaffirming the divinity of man, but who then directs the life of religion to the people, "you," the audience. This device is repeated in different words and phrases but with the same use of negation and the same involvement of the audience for public institutions, business, "our Union grand," the President who "is there in the White House for you, it is not you who are here for him," art, sculpture, architecture, music. He then proceeds with a long metonymic catalog of trades and occupations, almost one hundred lines with no negatives, to conclude:

I do *not* affirm what you see beyond is futile, I do *not* advise you to stop,
I do *not* say leadings you thought great are *not* great,
But I say *none* lead to greater than these lead to. (ll. 133–35)

These lines conclude the negatives (75 of them in 178 lines of the first edition), but note the difference if the same thing were said without the negatives:

I affirm that what you see beyond is hopeful, I advise you to proceed,
I say leadings you thought great are great,
But I say that all lead to less than these lead to.

Sometimes for rhetorical reasons Whitman uses more negatives than are needed, as we shall see shortly, but he could never be accused of not using enough.

But before leaving the clues provided by Gilman and Brown, let me draw one final suggestion of a further degree of negative aggressiveness. They find that "Thoreau's combativeness can also be measured by his use of contrasting conjunctions—*but, though, yet*, etc. These encode a negative implication, for in the beginning of the sentence an expectancy is generated only to be violated by the *but, yet, etc.*" (pp. 109–110). Whitman uses most of the contrasting conjunctions, especially *but*. The negative implication seems even more pronounced than that in *Walden*, probably because the line arrangement often draws attention to the word. Here are a few obvious examples that do not require a summary of the context to be understood:

> I have heard what the talkers were talking, the talk of the beginning and the
> end,
> *But I do not* talk of the beginning or the end. (ll. 38–39)

> These come to me days and nights and go from me again,
> *But they are not* the Me myself. (ll. 73–74)

> *No* shutter'd room or school can commune with me,
> *But* roughs and little children better than they. (ll. 255–56)

> You will *hardly* know who I am or what I mean,
> *But* I shall be good health to you *nevertheless*, (ll. 1341–42)

The use of *but* in the above lines and throughout "Myself" alerts us again to that special characteristic of Whitman's practice, the use of antithesis. There is, indeed something of a paradox here, for Whitman— surely the most optimistic of American poets—leads them all in use of negatives. There is clearly no place for Whitman in Gaston Bachelard's *Philosophy of No*, and *Leaves* would not be quoted in Charles Glicksberg's *Literature of Nihilism*. What happens is that the negative is used as an emphasis for the positive; it is a stylistic, a rhetorical, device, especially in "Myself," and in no way suggests or relates to personal doubts, despair, solipsistic rejection. Notice the preponderance of negatives in a typically positive affirmation:

> These are really the thoughts of all men in all ages and lands, they are *not*
> original with me,

If they are *not* yours as much as mine they are *nothing*, or next to *nothing*,
If they are *not* the riddle and the untying of the riddle they are *nothing*
If they are *not* just as close as they are distant they are *nothing*. (ll. 355–58)

This confidence, a near-assertiveness, of the early platform poems is regularly expressed via the rhetorical device of antithesis, as can be noted in many of the quotations in this chapter.

Whitman tended to use more rather than fewer negatives than were semantically or syntactically needed. Without rhyme or meter to signal the poetic intent, other forms of parallelism were essential. Guided more by oratorical parallelism, especially of the anaphora variety, than by the Bible, he shaped lines and series of lines to emphasize the negative feature as well as other values. In "Occupations" when he wrote

Souls of men and women! it is not you I call *un*seen, *un*heard, *un*touchable and *un*touching, (l. 29)

the four adjectives were surely chosen partly because of the prefix. In "Myself" he ends section 43 with a series:

It *cannot* fail the young man who died and was buried,
Nor the young woman who died and was put by his side,
Nor the little child...
Nor the old man...

and so on for six more lines beginning with "Nor" (ll. 1124–33). Sometimes a whole poem can be built with this sort of anaphora, as "Not Heaving from My Ribb'd Breast Only," a Calamus poem of 1860 on the adhesiveness theme, with sixteen of the seventeen lines beginning with a negative. Similarly, the 1856 poem now known as "Assurances" has nine of its twelve lines beginning with "I do *not* doubt."

It is not easy to determine how much anaphora of this sort is enough, for the decision must be made on the quality of the lines that are so united. But most of the poems of the first three editions reveal a common fault, excess. Whitman employed many of the oratorical devices, with negatives, and occasionally he intentionally misused some of the parallel devices to gain the value of the repetition without making it appear that he had forced words out of their natural place for the sake of the pattern. One of the most difficult rhetorical patterns is called "symploce," each line in a series beginning and ending with the same word or phrase. In "To Think of Time," an 1855 poem in which he experimented with a number of oratorical devices, there is such a skillfully organized negative symploce:

> *The law of* the past *cannot be eluded,*
> *The law of* the present and the future *cannot be eluded,*
> *The law of* the living *cannot be eluded*....it is eternal,
> *The law of* promotion and transformation *cannot be eluded,*
> *The law of* heroes and good-doers *cannot be eluded,*
> *The law of* drunkards and informers and mean persons *cannot be eluded.*
>   (ll. 84–89)

For the final version, he joined "it is eternal" to "eluded" (l. 86) by putting a comma for the four dots, and not so strangely changed the last line (l. 89) to read

> *The law of* drunkards and informers and mean persons, *not* one iota thereof
>   *can be eluded.*

A last novelty in this very artful poem is the rare use of the double negative. Emerson had believed that it would have the value of strong emphasis, similar to what he had noticed in the speech of uneducated persons, but he himself never tried it. But Whitman did, a few lines beyond the symploce above. He has presented the scene of the burial of the stage driver on a bleak December afternoon and is now commenting on death. He has said every death is important, is significant, not only the heroes and good-doers but the drunkards, informers, and mean persons. He admits that we notice the death of the distinguished,

> But there is more account than that....there is strict account of all.
> The interminable hordes of the ignorant and wicked are *not nothing,*
> The barbarians of Africa and Asia are *not nothing,*
> The common people of Europe are *not nothing*....the American aborigines are
>   *not nothing,*
> A zambo or a foreheadless Crowfoot or a Camanche is *not nothing,*
> The infected in the immigrant hospital are *not nothing*....the murderer or
>   mean person is *not nothing,*
> The perpetual succession of shallow people are *not nothing* as they go,
> The prostitute is *not nothing*....the mocker of religion is *not nothing* as he goes
>   (ll. 94–101)

Poetic exploits of this sort are rare anytime, anywhere, and indeed there are not many as bold as this elsewhere in *Leaves.* Even Whitman pulled back a little in 1856 and dropped line 98 about the zambo, but kept the rest until 1860. After that, as he became more circumspect, he dropped the last line, and by 1881, lines 99 and 100 went also. So the poem as we now have it prints the first three lines (ll. 95–97) only. It is difficult to know whether he was correcting excess or giving way to squeamishness—probably the latter, for he continued the excess of squeamish lines after 1860.

At the beginning of this chapter it was asserted, with Bergson and Burke, that there are no negatives in nature, only in man. It would follow that man in complete accord with nature, man in his original natural state, would be without negatives, since he would be without the need for negatives. That primitivism of this sort might still be possible, probably no Romantic poet fully believed, but Whitman was sufficiently in accord with the principle to use it frequently as a means for criticizing contemporary society. He does so brilliantly in section 32 of "Myself" with his opening statement, "I think I could turn and live with animals, they are so placid and self-contained" (l. 684), and the famous tribute to animals for their nonhuman virtues:

> They *do not* sweat and whine about their condition,
> They *do not* lie awake in the dark and weep for their sins,
> They *do not* make me sick discussing their duty to God.
> *Not one* is *dis*satisfied, *not one* is demented with the mania of owning things,
> *Not one* kneels to another, *nor* to his kind that lived thousands of years ago,
> *Not one* is respectable or *un*happy over the whole earth. (ll. 686–91)

In that beautifully perceptive essay on "Song of Myself," John Berryman responds to that passage: "But what I am interested in is how little is said about animals that is not negative—only 'placid and self-contain'd' . . . and 'Not . . . unhappy' which comes to an affirmation" (1976: 230).

The paradox these lines exemplify is that the only way to describe a negative-free society (with all that that implies) is with negatives. Earlier three negative lines from "Occupations" (ll. 133–35) were rewritten using positives. The result lost much but it was still possible. But how can one restate the above six lines? Is there such a thing as a negativeless language (*i.e.*, a completely and totally positive language)? Perhaps there is no answer, although one cannot but agree with Ernst Cassirer that "in language taken as a whole . . . every meaning is linked with its opposite, and that only the two together become an adequate expression" (1953: 120). Whitman seems to agree also, for that paradox is basic to his great poem on language, "A Song of the Rolling Earth," of 1856.

The poem had different titles, originally "Poem of the Sayers of the Words of the Earth," with this introductory, all-inclusive (except for negatives) definition of natural language: "Earth, round, rolling, compact—suns, moons, animals—all these are words to be said, / Watery, vegetable, sauroid advances—beings, premonitions, lispings of the future, / Behold! these are vast words to be said." For some reason, Whitman dropped this opening, substituting "A song of the rolling earth, and of words according," which is now the opening line of the final version to which line references will be made henceforth. Now what is involved here is the ideal of language, which is that the "substantial" word is the thing itself not the sign of that thing. In their opening note to this poem, Harold Blodgett and Sculley Bradley in their indispensable edition (1965) remind us of the Emersonian parallels to this definition in "Nature." Emerson is probably the source of the idea itself, but Whitman's brilliant expansion is noteworthy for its central paradox, which is that he can only define natural language by the unnatural negative.

He follows the opening lines or line with a question: "Were you thinking that those were the words, those upright lines? those curves, angles, dots?" The answer: "*No*, those are *not* the words, the substantial words are in the ground and sea, / They are in the air, they are in you." There are two things to note here. First is the direct involvement of the audience, the *you* of the question, but also the audience as participant, as an example, as a sort of corporate QED, the *you* of the answer. In Whitman's most effective programmatic poems, this *you* is always expressly present, and, as indicated in the previous chapter, he is the only major poet to so involve the reader. Second, "No" and "not" in the reply, of which there are eighty-one more to follow, are words for which there is no representation in nature; in terms of his answer, *no* is not a substantial word, and yet its employment in the poem is integral, essential.

He establishes through the next twenty lines that the "truths of the earth," even though "untransmissible by print," are "imbued through all things" and therefore are "conveying a sentiment and an invitation," which (and here the *I* is the earth)

NEGATION

> . . . I utter and utter,
> I speak *not*, yet if you hear me *not* of what avail am I to you?
> To bear, to better, lacking these of what avail am I? (ll. 25–27)

By poetic license, we can admit this personification of the earth, although the central problem remains, namely, that the earth cannot speak through negatives, for negation is not in nature but only in man. But then we come to an interpretive problem, the well-known parenthesis:

> (Accouche! accouchez!
> Will you rot your own fruit in yourself there?
> Will you squat and stifle there?) (ll. 28–30)

Is this the earth's aside to the audience? Is the *you* of line 26 the *you* of lines 29 and 30? There is no parenthesis in the 1860 version and no correction in the Blue Book, and since it comes soon after, that seems to be the case. But the tone of the statement, the outburst really, does not fit lines 31 and following, so Whitman must have put in the parentheses to indicate his, the poet's, own aside. As such, the outcry reflects the poet's momentary indignation that we enfold ourselves in our own ignorance, enwomb ourselves in some sort of Joanna Southcott stupefaction. After this aside, the poet returns to his original role as interpreter, but note the inevitability of the negatives:

> The earth does *not* argue,
> Is *not* pathetic, has *no* arrangements,
> Does *not* scream, haste, persuade, threaten, promise,
> Makes *no* discriminations, has *no* conceivable failures,
> Closes *nothing*, refuses *nothing*, shuts *none* out,
> Of all the powers, objects, states, it notifies, shuts *none* out. (ll. 31–36)

The negative description continues through the rest of this first section, the earth seen first as one of the sister stars and finally as "the divine ship" that "sails the divine sea," the universe.

Section 2 serves as a transition but, as directed to the audience, specifically reaffirms that the "divine ship sails for you." Yet now the *you* seems to be less the crowd, the collective *you*, but rather the singular *you*, the reader.

> You are he or she for whom the sun and the moon hang in the sky,
> For *none* [no one?] more than you are the present and the past. (ll. 76–77)

and

> *No one* can acquire for another—*not one*,
> *No one* can grow for another—*not one*. (ll. 80–81)

Then, after another artful brief catalog, of the symploce sort, the stanza ends "The oration is to the orator, the acting is to the actor and actress, *not* to the audience, / And *no man* understands any greatness or goodness but his own, or the indication of his own" (ll. 88–89). In section 3, the poet, who has thus far (except for the parentheses noted) been an observer, a reporter, now assumes an active role. In a series of speech acts of the assertive class, those which Searle says "commit the speaker . . . to the truth of the expressed proposition" (1979: 34), the persona swears to truth of assorted discoveries about the language of nature he has made. The fourth commitment is: "I swear I begin to see *little* or *nothing* in audible words" (l. 98), and the fifth: "I swear I see what is better than to tell the best, / It is always to leave the best *un*told" (ll. 102–103). He elaborates through ten more negatives to show that we must understand, not through language but through experience, that "The earth is just as positive and direct as it was before" (l. 111) and that the soul, too, "is positive and direct," for even though "*No* reasoning, *no* proof has establish'd it, / *Un*deniable growth has establish'd it" (ll. 114–15).

Section 4 concludes the poem with a salute to the reigning artists of the future. Surprisingly, these major artists will be neither word artists, the poets, nor spokesmen of the Word, the prophets, for committed to language they must ever be, once removed from the truth of the earth. But the persona begins with a reflection on all he has said: "These to echo the tones of souls and the phrases of souls" (l. 116), and in an aside to the reader he adds:

> (If they *did not* echo the phrases of souls what were they then?
> If they *had not* reference to you in especial what were they then?)
>   (ll. 116–17)

He encourages the lesser artists, himself included I presume, to "Say on, sayers! sing on, singers!" (l. 121), to "pile the words of the earth," to "work on, age after age," since "*nothing* is to be lost," for finally

> When the materials are all prepared and ready, the architects shall appear.
>   (l. 125)

When Louis Sullivan in Chicago made all his apprentices read Whitman, one may be sure that "Rolling Earth" was not overlooked, and certainly not by Frank Lloyd Wright, who later in unabashed humility had the poem's conclusion on his studio wall:

I swear to you the architects shall appear *without* fail,
I swear to you they will understand you and justify you,
The greatest among them shall be he who best knows you, and encloses all
    and is faithful to all,
He and the rest shall *not forget* you, they shall perceive that you are *not an iota*
    less than they,
You shall be fully glorified in them. (ll. 126–30)

But the point is, of course, that the architect, whatever the other limitations of his medium may be, is freed of the passion and the curse of the poet, to make words do what they cannot do. I once read a long, very intense, almost agonized letter of Dylan Thomas about his (but any poet's) battle with language. Since the letter will perhaps never be published, let me explain what I remember about it. The famous Whitman collector, Charles Feinberg, had other literary interests and treasures also, one of which is this letter. The circumstances were that a German refugee in World War II was in London during the blitz at the time that Dylan Thomas was giving regular BBC broadcasts. The young refugee knew some English and had written some poems, which he sent to Thomas, asking for advice on whether they might be publishable. Thomas, perhaps moved by the odd circumstances of the request (a refugee in an enemy country trying to crack the poetry market), started to write a gentle but honest answer, explaining the difficulties for anyone new to the idiom and urging the young man to try some other line, for it would take him too long to master the language.

Then, perhaps realizing his response could not seem anything but a rebuff, or a put-down, he went on to explain, patiently and quietly at first, his own continuous battle with words. As he went on, one could almost feel the growing intensity as, caught up in his explanation, probably half forgetting the person he was writing to, he went on, page after page (some dozen pages, I recall, of clear but very small writing), pouring out the frustrations, the momentary successes, the destructive rage in slashing out and starting over, the endless groping for another word

or another order, and so on, in one of the most poignant personal out-
pourings, mixed with strange triumphal almost celebratory overtones
for the emerging poem, that has ever been written. A fine, well-known,
and somewhat worldly American poet was visting Mr. Feinberg one
evening when I was there, and was given the letter to read. He started a
casual reading, got caught, sat down to concentrate, then cried out,
"Listen, everybody," and began to read aloud, weeping openly in the
process. All that was some twenty years ago, but when I think of the
great folly of Whitman's poem, trying to use language to suggest what
is beyond language, Thomas' strange wonderful letter comes to mind. I
do not mean that Whitman had the savage intensity about his writing
that we associate with Thomas, for he did not, but the exploit itself of
using more negatives than any other poet in any other poem to create a
positive response to nature is the sort of achievement Thomas might
have gloried in.

As the table listing negatives in *Leaves* demonstrates, the change in
Whitman's poetry after the Civil War is drastic; there are other altera-
tions as well: the speech act with use of "you" almost vanishes, the vocabulary becomes more abstract and strongly latinized, rhetorical questions continue but not addressed to "you," the Whitman catalog is no
more. But the strong use of the negative is one of the style markers of
the first three editions, and when it stops there must be a reason.

There is; in fact there are two reasons. First, and most obvious, is
the near-absence of negatives in the catalogs. There are 311 negatives
in the 1,336 lines of "Myself" for 23 percent, but if the catalogs were
not there (*i.e.*, omit only three, sections 8, 15, 33) the figure would go
up to 26 percent. "Occupations" without the catalog of trades would
have 63 percent instead of 42 percent of negative lines. From another
perspective, the new poems of the 1856 edition had close to 24 percent
negative lines, but if we drop "Salut au Monde" (the poem nearest to
being one long catalog) the negative figure would be 30 percent. One
can play around with percentage tables for negatives in a number of
ways to show the difference the catalogs make, but the more interesting
question, is, Why there are so few negatives in the catalogs? Essentially,
because they are the nonjudgmental presentation of synecdochic details
reported seriatim just as they come to the poet's inner or outer eye.

They are part of the prophetic role Whitman imagined for himself in the oratorical beginnings of *Leaves*. In a fantasy picture of himself as orator-prophet (some of it plagiarized from Nairne), he describes his gestures and voice through a challenging confrontation with his audience, but then goes on to explain: "But all converging sooner or later into the clear monotonous voice, equable as water—sometimes direct address to you, the hearer, without a pause afterward, as if an answer was expected. *Then perhaps for many minutes total abstraction and travelling to other fields, the vocalism limpid, inspired, no account made of the material place, the audience, but only of that other more spiritual world in which the speaker is now roaming*." The final sentence, which I have italicized, seems to be the rationale for the catalogs, Whitman in his mind's both panoramic and telescopic eye roaming over America, focusing on the significant detail to represent the life of the nation, "absorbing all to myself and for this song." And in his doing so, there are no conscious rejections, no arguments, no exhortations, no protests—no negatives. In many of the early poems, then, Whitman joins negative and positive passages but does not blend or fuse them.

The second reason for the decline of negation after the third edition is that Whitman gave up the role of prophet-poet-priest of democracy that had manifested itself in a direct address to his audience. Whether the audience is the individual reader or the crowd gathered around the persona of the platform, the language of direct address is present with all its rhetorical devices, of which negation is a principal feature. There are other features of direct address (the speech act, the rhetorical question, the present tense), but they are only other style markers along with negation which together helped *Leaves* make such an impact on the world's poetry.

Not all the poems written before 1860 are strongly negative, but when negation is absent it is usually because the poem is not one of direct address but of some other more traditional poetic form, such as apostrophe, elegy, lyric, etc. In the first edition, the negation is 16 percent for "The Sleepers" and 12 percent for "There Was a Child Went Forth" and in 1860 "As I Ebb'd" is 19 percent and "Out of the Cradle," 15 percent. And that is the sort of poetry that continues in the later editions: "Song of the Banner at Daybreak" (1861–1862), 29 percent;

"When Lilacs Last" (1865), 3 percent; "Pioneers!" (1865), 9 percent; "Centenarian's Story" (1865), 10 percent; "Return of the Heroes" (1867), 14 percent; "Proud Music" (1869), 11 percent; "Song of the Exposition" (1871), 13 percent; "Passage to India" (1871), 8 percent; "Thou Mother with Thy Equal Brood" (1872), 15 percent; "Song of the Redwood Tree" (1874), 15 percent. These ten poems are the only ones after 1860 that are over 200 lines each. The apparent exception, "Banner at Daybreak," is one of those that proves, for it was written in 1861 long before the change in his mind-set of 1865. But the forty-one negatives did not help; it is one of Whitman's disasters.

There are only two other shorter but significant poems that use negatives sufficiently to merit comment: "Prayer of Columbus" (1876) and "Chanting the Square Deific" (1865). Both are something like dramatic monologues, but not exactly. "Columbus" is nearer a soliloquy, although Columbus is speaking to and praying to God as he walks along the beach. Blodgett and Bradley, in their informative note, feel more kindly about this poem than I can; to me it is Whitman's poem about Whitman, and thus vitiated by its sentimental self-pity. But, even if we do assume it is Columbus speaking, there are problems, many of them related to the nineteen negatives in its sixty-six lines (29 percent). The first three of them are in lines 8–10:

> Haply I may *not* live another day;
> I *cannot* rest O God, I *cannot* eat or drink or sleep,
> Till I put forth myself, my prayer, once more to Thee.

There is nothing in the six-line opening stanza to prepare us for the "poetical" *Haply*. Many students (admittedly not very familiar with archaic language and certainly not expecting it in Whitman) think it is either a typographical error or a telescoped version of *Happily*, with resulting confusion. But it is the psychology predicated in lines 9–10 that is false. If he "cannot rest" because he will be troubled about not saying his prayers, he ought to say them instead of saying (or thinking) that he cannot rest until he does. And then the paralleling of the two *cannot*s seems unfortunate. Certainly he *can* eat and drink, whether he prays beforehand or not. The line implies either that he will gag if he has not said his prayers, or that he is so passionately intent on making that prayer that there is some sort of near-hysterical compulsion involved. "I will not" or even "I shall not" would be better.

NEGATION

A bit later there are four more negatives, presumably as part of that prayer:

> Thou knowest I have *not* once lost *nor* faith *nor* ecstasy in Thee,
> In shackles, prison'd, in disgrace, repining *not*,
> Accepting all from Thee, as duly come from Thee. (ll. 19–21)

"Thou knowest" is the last of six such openers, each telling God that he (Columbus) has done his part. It hardly seems appropriate to tell God again what He already knows, and it really seems less a prayer than a tabulation of his virtues. The first *nor* in line 19 is perhaps another archaism, but it is not clear how it was supposed to help the poem. That he has not lost ecstasy is hardly true, for ecstasy is a sudden, intense rapture which, if he has not lost it, he still has—and no one in ecstasy could be thinking or saying these lines. The negative in line 20 is mistaken also, for the opening six lines of the poem are just that, he is repining for all he is worth. The other negatives do not seem quite as misplaced as these first seven, but they add little to restore the credibility of the poem.

But "Square Deific" is a different poem altogether. It too is not a dramatic monologue, although it might be better thought of as four such. It also has more negatives than other poems after the 1860 edition, eighteen in forty-five lines (40 percent), which might indicate its earlier origin. Yet the notebook jottings, going back before 1855 and continuing to about 1860, are not worked out sufficiently to demonstrate that the negatives were intended at the beginning. It so happens that most of the negatives are in the first section, that devoted to Jehovah; indeed, rather surprisingly, he defines himself:

> *Not* Time affects me—I am Time . . .
> *Un*persuadable, relent*less* . . . (ll. 5–6)

> Relent*less* I *forgive no* man . . . whoever sins dies . . .
> Therefore let *none* expect mercy—have . . . the appointed days mercy? *no* more have I,
> But . . . as all the appointed days that *forgive not*,
> I dispense . . . judgments *in*exorable *without* the least remorse. (ll. 9–12)

Here Jehovah is a little more on the defensive than is generally recognized. Perhaps, as we saw for "Rolling Earth," there is something of a problem in explaining time, law, and justice, except through their opposites. Since the opposite of time is too difficult to comprehend, that characteristic is announced, not explained. But the requirements of law, justice, and authority are characterized as overriding pleas to moderate their severity.

The Consolator, the Christ-Hermes-Hercules, is more readily explained by example, with no negatives needed, which is what happens in the first eleven lines of the stanza. Only at the end, in the last two lines, does the negative help strengthen the effect of the lines:

> But my charity has *no death*—my wisdom *dies not, neither* early *nor* late,
> And my sweet love bequeath'd here and elsewhere *never dies*. (ll. 24–25)

To say "my charity continues," "my wisdom goes on," "my sweet love lives" might literally mean the same, but would not work in the poem. "Neither . . . nor" in line 24 does not help in the same way, but it supports and emphasizes the other negatives so that the lines are better with than without them.

But even though the poem is meant to reach its high point in the unifying role of Santa Spirita in the fourth stanza, it is the third stanza —the incorporation (in the true literal sense) of Satan into the Godhead —that gives this poem its challenge and commands continual attention.

> Defiant, I, Satan, still live, still utter words, in new lands duly appearing,
>   (and old ones also)
> Permanent here from my side, warlike, equal with any, real as any,
> Nor time nor change shall ever change me or my words. (ll. 33–35)

Although adding an extra side to the Trinity to make room for Satan in the Square Deific may seem something of a feat, it is hard not to take Whitman seriously when we realize that he does not have Satan use negatives to define himself. There are three negatives in the stanza but they are slight, almost casual: in line 32, in a parenthetical aside he acknowledges that it was thought he had been "baffled and dispel'd," but, he says that "that will *never* be." And in the last line, acknowledging that he represents defiance, he asserts, "*Nor* time *nor* change shall ever change me or my words." The importance of this stanza, then, rests not on these somewhat perfunctory negatives, but on the characteristic of Satan as a positive figure, force, or idea.

A scholar who has explored this notion about language is the French philosopher and critic Michel Foucault, in two essays. One is in *The*

Archaeology of Knowledge (1972), where in Part 4 under the larger title "Archaeological Description" is the section "Contradictions" (pp. 149–56); the other, "A Preface to Transgression," a brilliant examination of transgression as a form of the negative, but negative used as a challenge to test limits, is in his recent *Language, Counter-Memory, Practice* (1977). Both are valuable in understanding the fascination of this poem (and this stanza) and of *Leaves* itself. Foucault's thesis that transgression, contradiction, defiance, have more important positive than negative meanings is what Whitman's poem also asserts. Perhaps Foucault does not know Whitman's poem, for it is hard to think there would not be a reference. But in the terms of his analysis, there are really no contradictions in Whitman. This claim seems controverted by the well-known lines in "Myself": "Do I contradict myself? / Very well then I contradict myself" (ll. 1324–25). But Whitman himself makes an immediate qualification, "(I am large, I contain multitudes.)" The rhetorical (and in this case, poetical) value of seeming contradictions would be, in Foucault's words, to prod the challenged reader to find the fundamental coherence of the poet's utterance: "In all these forms, a coherence discovered in this way always plays the same role: it shows that immediately visible contradictions are merely surface reflections; and that this play of dispersed light must be concentrated into a single focus" (1972: 150). The seeming contradiction of Satan as a true member of the Godhead, of divinity (how can evil be part of the All-Good?) is to challenge us to find that necessary truth that Satan can represent.

That truth can be grasped in Foucault's explanation of *transgression*, which is the antithetical but necessary opponent of *limit*. "The limit and transgression depend on each other for whatever density of being they possess: a limit could not exist if it were absolutely uncrossable, and, reciprocally, transgression would be pointless if it merely crossed a limit composed of illusions and shadows" (1977: 34). Satan, the principle of transgression, is essential to the Godhead in a different way than Christ, for Jehovah as authority, as justice, can only rule over something which does not want to be ruled. "Transgression carries the limit right to the limit of its being; transgression forces the limit to face the fact of its imminent disappearance, to find itself in what it excludes" (pp. 34–35). Perhaps this is a more profound conception that Whitman may have realized; it certainly seems a deeper truth that Nietzsche could explain. In Foucault's explanation he frees this concept from morality, from ethics, from conventional notions of right and wrong, good and bad. In the same fashion Whitman does not portray Satan as the arch-sinner (as the epitome of transgression understood as evil or wrong or bad), but as the epitome of defiance: "Defiant, I, Satan, still live, still utter words . . . / Permanent here from my side [of the square] . . . / Nor time nor change shall ever change me . . ." (ll. 33–35).

Foucault frees transgression from its negative association. "Transgression is neither violence in a divided world (in an ethical world) nor a victory over limits (in a dialectical or revolutionary world) . . . Transgression contains nothing negative, but affirms limited being—affirms the limitlessness into which it leaps" (1977: 35). If not negative, then positive? No, for "correspondingly, this affirmation contains nothing positive, since, by definition, no limit can possibly restrict it. Perhaps it is simply an affirmation of division." Indeed, "this philosophy of non-positive affirmation is, I believe, what [Maurice] Blanchot was defining through his principle of 'contestation.' Contestation does not imply a generalized negation but an affirmation that affirms nothing, a radical break in transitivity" (p. 36).

It is amazing to me that Whitman should have grasped this subtle, complex, and profound truth, but there seems no other way to read "Square Deific" and Satan's role in it. What happens is that Satan, in this stanza and in the poem, is not the corrupter, the personification of the Great Denial; what he stands for is the necessary challenge, "Defiant, I, Satan." Foucault classifies this point also in this further characterization of transgression: "Nothing is more alien to this experience than the demonic character who, true to his nature, 'denies everything.' Transgression opens out onto a scintillating and constantly affirmed world, a world without shadow or twilight, without that serpentine 'no' that bites into fruit and lodges these contradictions at their core. It is the solar inversion of satanic denial. It was originally linked to the divine, or rather, from this marked by the sacred it opens the space where the divine functions" (p. 37).

This is not an easy truth to grasp, but it is what Whitman dramatizes by restoring Satan to the Godhead. Foucault himself seems to have recognized the difficulty in explaining this set of abstractions, so he himself tries a figurative explanation, which Whitman might have applauded: "Transgression, then, is not related to the limit as black to white, the prohibited to the lawful, the outside to the inside. . . . Perhaps it is like a flash of lightning in the night which, from the beginning of time, gives a dense and black intensity to the night it denies, which lights up the night from the inside, from top to bottom, and yet owes to the dark the stark clarity of its manifestation, its harrowing and poised singularity" (p. 35).

In this reading of the poem, the third stanza, the Satan stanza, becomes the center of the poem, its high point, which is what Whitman intends. That also makes the fourth and final stanza, the Santa Spirita, the uniter, the reconciler, something of a "foregone conclusion." The standard way of reading the poem is to have it build up to the last stanza in an ascending order of importance. But that implies that God and Satan would destroy each other if the bringer-together were not present; it even admits that fond hope of sentimental Christians that some fine day Satan will give up and submit, and peace and goodness will reign thereafter. But as we have seen, Satan as defiance, as challenger, as transgressor in Foucault's definition, needs God as God needs him. Whatever reconciliation there is, is already present, if undefined. The Santa Spirita does the defining. Accordingly, negatives are not essential to the last stanza—they are there, to be sure, but in parentheses, something as an aside or afterthought.

ᔤ V ᖇ
METONYMY IN WHITMAN AND IN
Leaves of Grass

Jakobson's Theory

The grid below is a device for illustrating Jacques Lacan's rediscovery and explanation of Sigmund Freud's original discovery of the two principles of association found in all language, whether poetry or prose. The letters, A to D, indicate on the horizontal dimension the relations of contiguity (association via metonymy and/or synecdoche). The numerals, 1 to 4, indicate on the vertical dimension the relations of similarity (association via metaphor and/or simile).

$$\text{organization} \longrightarrow \text{contiguity}$$

		(metonymy)		
A1	B1	C1	D1	
A2	B2	C2	D2	selection
A3	B3	C3	D3	↓ (metaphor)
A4	B4	C4	D4	similarity

When Lacan talks about the "horizontal dimension: relations of contiguity" he means the associative patterns by which one item we perceive, A, reminds us of some other item B close to it in our actual or imagined experience. On the "vertical dimension: relations of similarity," Lacan refers to our perception of likeness in items not contextually related; if in thinking of *2*, one then associates it with *4*, it will be because of some similarity between the items outside of their proximity. Lacan says, rightly, that "these two axes divide language in its totality," but it is necessary to explain the background of that statement before applying it to *Leaves*.

Opposition to established practice often provides the spur for new hypotheses, especially as with Freud, when he felt excluded by the medical profession. Up to 1890, the medical establishment considered as nothing more than random babbling the speech of patients who had suffered strokes (in medical terms, aphasic disturbance). Freud set out to show the profession wrong. He demonstrated in 1891 that aphasic speech was a form of dislocated communication, to be sure, but that it did have its rationale. Normal speech, he maintained, was the result of two separate operations of the mind, selection and combination (later on, in dream interpretation, he saw these as identification and symbolism, and as condensation and displacement, respectively). Just now, for instance, from the lexical storehouse at my command, I *select* (I could say *pick*, *choose*, *isolate*, etc.) one or more words and *combine* it or them with another selection of words to express what I have in mind.

The processes of the mind may or may not be physical but they are seated in a physical part of the brain, and it may be assumed that one part of the brain is involved in the selection process, and that some other part is where the combination process takes place. A disturbance in one area (usually from a small hemorrhage occasioned by the rupture of a nearby blood vessel) may impair its contribution to speech without infringing on the activity of the other area of the brain where the other part of the speech process is carrying on. Freud's interest was not really in linguistics, or at that time in literary criticism, and his hypothesis (finally accepted by the medical profession) had little impact outside of medicine. He himself went on to develop a system for the interpretation of dreams, using this same hypothesis in the process, and his interest in puns, jokes, Freudian slips, etc., is a later consequence of this early investigation.

But between Freud and the contemporary French structuralist-psychologist Lacan there are two other figures, neither a professional psychologist, but both concerned with literature. In 1941, Burke's *Philosophy of Literary Form* was published, a collection of studies developed in the 1930s. The title of the book comes from the first long article (pp. 1–137), in which Burke recommends a textual analysis of the association patterns of poetic language as opposed to those of standard speech. Particularly in the section titled "Open Words for 'Symbolic'" (pp. 25–33), he adumbrates the position established by Jakobson in the 1950s, although to my knowledge there was no awareness of each other's work.

Burke is such an amazing pioneer in so many areas of literary criticism that it is a shame he has not been properly recognized for his insight into this polar structure of speech (the metonymy-metaphor axes of Lacan's grid), now so much talked of. Indeed, Floyd Merrell (1978) seems the only person to know of this connection. World War II took attention elsewhere in 1941, and Burke's resistance to standardized literary terms, his use of these terms in a different context in *A Grammar of Motives* (1945), plus his unintentional subordination of this first essay to other eye-catching essays in the book ("Hitler's Rhetoric," for instance), seem to have prevented the pioneer quality of this major essay from being recognized.

Jakobson may have explored the implications of Freud's discoveries about aphasia before his famous essay, "Two Aspects of Language and Two Types of Linguistic Disturbances" (in his and Morris Halle's *Fundamentals of Language*, 1956), but clearly this is the key statement. Jakobson alerts us to the "two basic types of aphasia," that in which the major deficiency lies in selection or substitution of words and phrases "with a relative stability of combination and contexture"; and the reverse, the impairment of "combination and contexture, with relative retention of normal selection and substitution" (p. 63). Let me explain in terms of the grid at the beginning of this chapter.

If the contiguity faculty is injured, a person will find it difficult, perhaps impossible, to combine sentence elements or to impose any kind of order in his speech. He will adopt the typical telegraphic style and depend more and more on that part of the speech function which has not been injured, *i.e.*, selection. Consequently, since selection depends on seeing similarities, the dependence will be on primitive metaphors and similes to convey meaning. Thus, someone who wants to but cannot say "microscope" will say "spyglass." If unable to say "fire," the aphasia victim may say "light" to communicate what is in his mind. On the other hand, if one has trouble with the similarity axis, he will have difficulty in finding the word for the idea in his mind and will not be able to make the association. He may wish to tell someone that his brother is a "bachelor" and cannot find the word, but to say his brother is "single" or "unmarried" will not be an available substitute. Again, in his desperation at not knowing the word for "knife," he will probably rely on what is available at the opposite facility, *i.e.*, contiguity, and say "fork," or "table" for "lamp." As Jakobson puts it: "Such metonymies may be characterized as projections from the line of a habitual context into the line of substitution and selection: a sign (e.g., *fork*) which usually occurs together with another sign (e.g., *knife*) may be used instead of this sign" (p. 69).

Aphasics are entitled to our sympathy, but the understanding of the language principle that their speech reveals is the key here. What is apparent is that these are clearly two different and separate functions at work in all speech, writing, prose, and poetry. As Jakobson acknowledges: "In normal verbal behavior, both processes are continually operative, but careful observation will reveal that *under the influence of a cultural pattern, personality, and verbal style, preference is given to one of the two processes over the other*" (p. 76; my italics). The two different, indeed almost polar, semantic lines along which discourse may develop are the metaphoric (through similarity) and the metonymic (through contiguity). What is involved here is, in fact, more than just the use of words, for the hypothesis, Jakobson declares, concerns the workings of the mind, the results of which should serve as one (and a major one) of the distinguishing features of any mental activity, in art as well as in any other human activity—such as style.

Jakobson is generally thought of as a linguist, but he is something of a cultural analyst in his critical application of this principle. A list, comparing and contrasting the two emphases, metaphoric and metonymic, will provide a quick insight into the dichotomy Jakobson finds. The list below is a composite of six different lists (listing pairs to highlight contrasts is a favorite classroom device, and in itself would indicate these six as teachers, which they are) taken from Gérard Genette (1972: 30), Lacan (Lemaire, 1977, pp. 34, 200), Claude Lévi-Strauss (Leach, 1976, p. 12), David Lodge (1977: 81), Hans Osterwalder (1978: 22–23), Brian Wicker (1975: 14, 5). Some of the points made in the list are not explicitly Jakobson's but have been developed by others as a consequence of his initial distinctions.

It is also imperative to remember that these terms are not mutually exclusive; both are necessarily involved in varying ways in all human expression (which is what those who think apes can be taught to use language fail to understand), and it is a matter of emphasis, of predominant mode, of reigning attitude, that is the concern here. The items on the list are fairly obvious (though not in this dichotomizing arrangement), and are simply presented, with an added explanation (by letter and number) as seems necessary. The explanations are appended for those items that have particular bearing on the metonymy of Whitman's early editions. But all the items are important in showing that the metaphoric / metonymic distinction does not apply to poetry alone but to novel and drama, as well as to other arts, painting, film, music. The terms (or labels) may seem "loaded" to one side or the other, depending on the reader's acquaintance with the term in other literary or critical contexts. In such cases the explanations will make it clear that no bias is intended, that the terms mean no more than the explanation specifies, and that the terms have stylistic (not political, social, or moral) implications only.

For those already acquainted with the metaphoric/metonymic distinction, a skip to the end of the lettered and numbered explanatory paragraphs is in order.

	METAPHORIC (Similarity)	METONYMIC (Contiguity)
A. Orientation	1. thought, depth (intension) 2. past, tradition, age 3. idealism 4. culture 5. simultaneous pattern 6. auditory bias	1. sensation, surface (extension) 2. present, innovation, future 3. empiricism 4. nature 5. successive sequence 6. visual-tactile bias
B. Psychologic	1. abstract (typological) 2. general / generic (stress on laws) 3. deduction 4. analogical thought 5. dream symbolism 6. "leveling"	1. concrete (sensory) 2. particular / specific (stress on facts) 3. induction 4. circumstantial evidence 5. dream condensation-displacement 6. "sharpening"
C. Communication	1. code 2. encoder (speaker / writer) 3. autonomous ego 4. universalistic (context-free) 5. static posture 6. deliberate, slow literary composition	1. context 2. decoder (listener / reader) 3. stimulus-response 4. particularistic (context-bound) 5. dynamic action 6. spontaneous, fast literary composition

METONYMY

D. Language	1. paradigm	1. syntagm
	2. selection	2. combination
	3. substitution	3. deletion
	4. language (*langue*)	4. speech (*parole*)
	5. *in absentia*	5. *in praesentia*
	6. symbol	6. sign (*icon* and *index*)

E. Art	1. Romanticism	1. Realism
	2. poetry (verse)	2. prose (novel)
	3. lyric	3. epic
	4. drama	4. film
	5. surrealism	5. cubism
	6. harmony	6. melody

F. Literary Style	1. connotation	1. denotation
	2. hypotaxis (subordination)	2. parataxis (coordination)
	3. rhetorical figures of equivalence	3. rhetorical figures of contexture
	4. verbal style	4. nominal style
	5. montage, parallelism	5. collage, close-up
	6. disjunctive (either / or)	6. conjunctive (both / and)

To repeat for emphasis, Jakobson assures us that we are all both metaphoric and metonymic in our understanding of experience. It is not, then, a question of being one or the other (because we are both) but of which is dominant. Whether we create ourselves or respond to others' creation of certain kinds of literature (metaphoric or metonymic) because we need to confirm our own dominant choice, or because we need to maintain a balance between the two, or to restore a lack, a need, from the opposite side, is a large and fascinating question that cannot be answered here. But we certainly know enough about each side of the above dichotomy to make some distinctions about both the writer and his writing.

A 1 (intension vs. extension). The mind responds to life, to experience, by exploring it, probing it, shaping it, even in extreme cases denying it, to fit the mind's needs. A recent book, Kenneth Goldstein and Sheldon Blackman's *Cognitive Style* (1978), written more for the psychologist than the literary critic, defines the term, "*cognitive style* refers to the characteristic ways in which individuals conceptually organize the environment" (p. 2), and proceeds to review five of these characteristic ways at considerable length. But as these psychologists, as well as Cassirer, Suzanne Langer, Jean Piaget, Norman Brown, Jerome Bruner, *et al.*, assure us, the fact that the mind does not merely echo or mirror experience but transforms and reorganizes it, is accepted without question. Even when the mind refuses to turn in on itself in deep thought, investigation, analysis (*intension* is the term on the list), and rather turns outward in an attempt to copy reality "as it really is" through concern with surface and sensation (*extension*), it cannot but change that reality by what it chooses to picture or report of the "buzzing confusion" of life. Yet it is clear that the concern with sensation and surface goes toward the world as it is. The most obvious exemplification of such concern is "Song of Myself," especially the catalogs.

A2   (past, tradition, vs. present, innovation). When Jakóbson published "Two Aspects of Language" in 1956, there was no immediate and consequent reexamination of the relationship between romanticism and realism. Critics, unaware of Jakobson, were and still are, I presume, making stylistic examinations of realism (especially for the novel) that would include many of the features on the metonymy side of the dichotomy listing above. Jakobson does not in any way invalidate Ian Watt's *Rise of the Novel* (1957) but provides a linguistic framework by which realism may be seen as a by-product or one manifestation of a more inclusive world view. In "The Metaphoric and Metonymic Poles," section 5 of his essay, Jakobson writes: "The primacy of the metaphoric process in the literary schools of romanticism and symbolism has been repeatedly acknowledged, but it is still insufficiently realized that it is the predominance of metonymy which underlies and actually predetermines the so-called 'realistic' trend, which belongs to an intermediary stage between the decline of romanticism and the rise of the symbolism and is opposed to both" (pp. 77–78). This statement has little to do with Whitman as metonymist on its direct or positive side, for Whitman's early fiction was far from realistic. But the preponderance of metonymy in the early editions presupposes a mind fascinated with and glorying in the realistic details of American life. We can see this reaction even before *Leaves* in that remarkable metonymic exercise "Pictures," now available in Blodgett and Bradley as the first of the Uncollected Poems (1965: 642–49). This delight in synecdochic detail continues well up to *Drum-Taps*, where it is found at its purest (in the sense of unmixed) in such short imagistic poems as "Cavalry Crossing a Ford" or "Bivouac on a Mountain Side" (p. 300).

B5   (dream symbolism vs. dream condensation-displacement). One area where there is difference of opinion among commentators on Jakobson is the interpretation of Freud. Those who follow Jakobson explicitly accept the following statement of his and split it for the list as has been done here: "Thus in an inquiry into the structure of dreams, the decisive question is whether the symbols and temporal sequences used are based on contiguity (Freud's metonymic 'displacement' and synecdochic 'condensation') or on similarity (Freud's 'identification' and 'symbolism')" (1956: 81). Others, notably Lacan (Lemaire, 1977, pp. 195–200), put "condensation" on the metaphoric side and "displacement" on the metonymic. Of later scholars who use Jakobson's metaphor-metonymy differentiation, J. Hillis Miller (1971: 42 n. 35), Paul Ricoeur (1977: 178, 347 n. 4), and Daniel Laferrière (1978: 51–53) think Lacan may be closer to Freud's thinking than Jakobson is. The difficulty seems to be not so much with Lacan or Jakobson but with Freud, who did not go as far in clarifying this distinction as one might wish.

B5 (*cont.*). Jakobson's division does make sense, and it has been useful in examining the figurative language of many early poems. But it is possible that Jakobson, seizing on the neat opposition that suited his dichotomy, may have simplified Freud a bit. Inasmuch as dream structure (whether interpreted by Freud or by Lacan) is related to art and poetry, this matter is important, but the only way it would have any immediate relevance to Whitman would be as a clue to or mode of insight into such dream-fantasy poems as "The Sleepers." That poem, in terms of the dichotomy we are examining, is clearly structured on the metonymic-synecdochic plane, a reading unintentionally confirmed in the brilliant Freudian analysis in Chapter 4 of Edwin Miller's well-known study (1968).

B5 (*cont.*). At another level, however, Lacan's profound, and complicated, explication and application of his famous dictum "desire is metonymy" come closer to explaining certain kinds of word choice in Whitman's early poetry. The Postscript to this chapter is for those interested in an application of the Lacanian hypothesis to such lines as these: "All this I swallow, it tastes good, I like it well, it becomes mine, / I am the man, I suffer'd, I was there" ("Song of Myself," ll. 831–32). For present purposes, it is enough to acknowledge that for this particular point in the dichotomy there is no agreed interpretation.

B6 ("leveling" vs. "sharpening"). A more obvious and far-reaching distinction for *Leaves of Grass* is the "leveling"/ "sharpening" item. The two terms, for a reader-audience of literary scholars, will be something less than self-revelatory. Indeed, to be told that a poem of Whitman's, say "There Was a Child Went Forth," shows that he was not a "leveler" but a "sharpener" would arouse confusing notions of *leveling* as used by social and political commentators (Cooper's *American Democrat*, for instance) and perhaps something equally unrelated for *sharpening* (a "sharpy" is a city slicker, in nineteenth-century American slang). The two terms have quite different meanings. An early use in literary scholarship was by Ohmann in his classic analysis *Shaw* (1962). Indeed his brilliant opening chapter "Modes of Order" (with its section on "leveling" vs. "sharpening," pp. 28–39) does for Shaw, who is a "leveler," what needs to be done for Whitman, a "sharpener," who has, in this respect, no equal in American poetry. Another application of this distinction is that of the Swiss scholar, Osterwalder, who uses it in his analysis of T. S. Eliot's plays and essays (1978).

B6 (*cont.*). The terms are best understood in light of recent psychological discoveries. For this past generation there has developed (under the leadership of Bruner, George Klein, and others, and well represented in *Perception and Personality*, edited by Bruner and David Krech in 1949) a conception of personality formation that has changed much of our thinking about society, education, and human adjustment. The world out there is the same for us all, but we do not, any of us, see it the same way. To Klein and Herbert Schlesinger: "The person is a self-regulative system; though dynamic, this system is *quasi-stable* and *continuous*. It must continually bring into harmony needs, impulses, and wishes, and buffer these turbulences from within against limitations from without" (p. 36). Bruner and Leo Postman regard it in another way: "Perceiving is here regarded as regulated by the economy of personality. It operates to aid wish-fulfillment, in the reduction of tension, in reality testing, in ego defense, etc." (p. 18). Accordingly: "From the interlacing of wish and reality-press, a system of 'normalizing' mechanisms emerges, typical of the person . . . these mechanisms set the mold of experience" (p. 36). Which is to say, with Wordsworth (another "sharpener," by the way), "Of all the mighty world / Of eye, and ear—*both what they half create*, / *And what perceive*" (my italics).

Or, as Anaïs Nin has it: "We don't see things as they are, we see them as we are."

B6 (*cont.*). Klein examines these "perceptual attitudes" at some length in his *Perception, Motives, and Personality* (1970): sharpening is a "tendency to be hypersensitive to minutiae, to respond excessively to fine nuances and small differences, to exaggerate change, and to keep adjacent or successive stimuli from fusing or losing identity." And further: "Perceptual attitude imparts the flavor to an act of perceiving, the organizing theme or leitmotif of perceptual sensitivity. The 'sharpening' attitude . . . demands, in effect: 'Be alert to all shades and nuances. Let nothing slip by unnoticed'" (pp. 134, 135). This sort of perceptual attitude lies at the base of Whitman's metonymical style and is best understood in contrast to its opposite, *leveling*.

B6 (*cont.*). Ohmann uses this distinction to find the clue to Shaw's style: "The leveler is more anxious to categorize sensations and less willing to give up a category once he has established it. . . . He levels (suppresses) differences and emphasizes similarities in the interest of perceptive stability. For him the unique, unclassifiable sensation is particularly offensive, while the sharpener at least tolerates such anomalies, and may actually seek out ambiguity and variability of classification" (1962: 28–29).

B6 (*cont.*). Another psychologist of what might be called "the Bruner school" is Else Frenkel-Brunswick, who perceives the two perceptual attitudes in terms of abstract (*i.e.*, the "leveler") vs. concrete (the "sharpener"). She writes: "The concrete attitude is one of being 'bound to the immediate experience of a given thing or situation in its uniqueness.' It can easily be seen how the escape into the concrete, the 'boundness' to the specific stimulus, represents dealing with tangibles and certainties where everything opaque and complex can be avoided" (1949: 133).

B6 (*cont.*). Osterwalder finds the same dichotomy under another set of opposing terms, *disjunction* and *conjunction* (see also F6 on the list). His references to the psychological literature on this distinction are like those mentioned above, and he concludes: "The exaggerated use of either-or relationships between objects by a metaphoric 'leveler' leads to black and white thinking. In his attempt to impose a similarity pattern on reality, the 'leveler' forces the phenomena of reality into pre-

164

LANGUAGE AND STYLE IN *Leaves of Grass*

conceived categories; an object is either A or B, but it must not be part of both A and B, because this would be detrimental to perceptual stability. The 'sharpener,' on the other hand, can allow for 'conjunctive' relationships [and / and; both / and] because he is not compelled to impose a similarity pattern derived from his earlier experience of reality" (1978: 19).

B6   (final *cont.*). The importance of this distinction to *Leaves of Grass* can be seen clearly in "There Was a Child Went Forth," presented and discussed near the end of this chapter. The metonymic character of Whitman's poetry never disappears completely, but almost so in such poems as "Song of the Universal" (1874) or "Eidólons" (1876). On the disjunction / conjunction difference, it is a notable style-marker of the early editions that conjunction is predominant; disjunction rarely occurs in *Leaves* (there are only eight *eithers* given in Eby's *Concordance*) and chiefly in the late poems.

C2   (encoder vs. decoder). One of the milestones in the rapprochement of linguistics and literary criticism was the famous conference at Indiana in 1958. The proceedings were published two years later, under the editorship of Thomas Sebeok, as *Style in Language*. In that volume certainly the most far-reaching essay was Jakobson's "Closing Statement," better known by its more indicative subtitle "Linguistics and Poetics." In his remarks, Jakobson again makes use of the metaphoric-metonymic distinction, but he now puts this dichotomy in a literary context and attempts to shape a definition of poetry that would embrace his linguistic convictions.

C2   (*cont.*). The intention in his whole statement is to define, or to explain for linguistics, the poetic function possible when language is used in a certain way, which he does by selecting for attention the six separate functions in any verbal message. He presents the relationships in a chart, but what he is explaining is that: (*a*) a *message* is directed by (*b*) an *addresser* to (*c*) an *addressee*, which message must have (*d*) a *context* referred to (*e*) a *code* common to both the addresser and the addressee, and, finally, (*f*) a *contact* through which the participants can stay in communication. One of these six elements will be paramount (indeed, the ruling factor) in any message, even though few messages have only one function that alone is important. The point Jakobson is making is that even though two or three functions may be of significance to either the addresser (the encoder) or the audience (the addressees), one is predominant and establishes the character of the communication. There will always be some diversity because of "a different hierarchical order of functions" (1960: 353), in which case the relation of those different functions may permit us to group a certain class of writings under some particular label.

C2 (*cont.*). Jakobson's chart has had a decisive impact on all recent textual criticism, even in the so-called explosion of the Jakobson diagram by Jacques Derrida, Paul de Man, and other deconstructionists. The best brief survey and analysis of that exciting twenty-year sequence is by Christine Brooke-Rose in the second chapter of her brilliant new treatment, *A Rhetoric of the Unreal* (1981: 22–50). With enviable poise, she handles the often acrimonious debaters, and perhaps my own impatience deserves some explanation. From my pragmatic point of view, the merit of any of the seemingly antithetical critical positions rests in its ability to explain why and how poetry (in this instance *Leaves*, and specifically the early poems) works. I have found Jakobson's approach and terminology most valuable in capturing and labeling stylistic features of the platform poems, but I already knew they were poetry, by prior intuitive response. Jakobson does not, then, help one find the poetry in *Leaves*, but he does help one explain it.

C2 (*cont.*). Now in terms of the six elements (*a* to *f* above), Jakobson says that "the set (*Einstellung*) toward the MESSAGE as such, focus on the message for its own sake, is the POETIC function of language" (1960: 356). By contrast, any ordinary expository prose is shaped by its referential function. Its writer intends to convey information. Denotative language is accordingly appropriate, and the more successful it is, the less attention will be drawn to its language organization. In clear effective prose the language becomes almost transparent. The idea the word symbolizes comes to mind so immediately that we move on to the next word, and the next, so quickly that we are hardly conscious of our eye and mental movements or of the actual physical words. Metaphors are rare in cookbooks. The writer of expository prose consciously avoids alliteration, meter, internal rhyme, or any other prosodic device that may appear accidentally, for they would only be distracting (by drawing attention to the *message* and away from the *referential* intention).

C2 (*cont.*). *Per contra*, poetry does want to draw attention to itself.

And here we come to the most celebrated (perhaps because the most baffling to literary scholars) dictum in Jakobson's work: *"The poetic function projects the principle of equivalence from the axis of selection into the axis of combination"* (1960: 358). There have been elaborate explanations of this statement—one of the more successful is Geoffrey Leech, "Linguistics and the Figures of Rhetoric," (1966: 139–47), and also by Jakobson himself in "Poetry of Grammar and Grammar of Poetry" (1968)—but essentially what Jakobson means is that the linguistic sign of poetry is what we now call "parallelism" (*i.e.*, recurrence of stress, rhythm and rhyme, semantic equivalence, and the assorted prosodic devices). That these prosodic devices may be used in electioneering (Jakobson refers to "I like Ike"), in advertising, in mnemonic patterns (medical students remember the order of the major nerves with the traditional line "On Old Olympus' Towering Tops, A Finn and German Picked Some Hops"), is beside the point.

C2 (*cont.*). Although there have been various attempts to fit *Leaves* to the epic tradition (Roy Harvey Pearce, James Miller, Jr.), Whitman's work does not meet this epic requirement ("focused on the third person"), as he himself was quite aware. It might seem to fit Jakobson's test for the lyric, for "Myself" seems clearly overendowed with first-person usages (it obviously has the greatest percentage per line). Yet that major poem is more programmatic than lyrical (as is "Starting from Paumanok" also, with the next highest percentage of first-person uses). Jakobson, however, is not concerned with occurrences of "I" but with language "oriented toward the first person" (1960: 355), and there are indeed such poems in *Leaves*, chiefly in the Calamus section and also, later, in the Drum-Taps section, and elsewhere in the volume.

C2 (final *cont.*). But the characteristic poems of the first three editions were of the third sort, where "the second person is imbued with the conative function." There are not many of what Jakobson would call the "supplicatory" sort ("Prayer of Columbus," if we read Columbus as Whitman, parts of "Passage to India," etc.), but there are many of the "exhortative" sort. But what are exhortations? They are traditionally sermons, lectures, public speeches, political or patriotic oratory, pep talks, commencement addresses, sometimes editorials and pleas in journalism, but are rarely poetry of a very high order. Yet it is difficult to read "Song of the Open Road" and then Jakobson's further clarification without seeing the relationship or tie-in. He writes: "Orientation toward the ADDRESSEE, the CONATIVE function, finds its purest grammatical expression in the vocative and imperative, which syntactically, morphologically, and even phonemically deviate from other nominal and verbal categories. The imperative sentences cardinally differ from declarative sentences: the latter are and the former are not liable to a truth test. . . . The imperative cannot be challenged by a question 'is it true or not?'. . . In contradistinction to the imperative sentences, the declarative sentences are convertible into interrogative sentences." (1960: 355). The point at issue here is not the obvious concern with the encoder (Whitman or the persona), which we have always recognized, but the fact that through the speech acts and other devices (as rhetorical questions) Whitman involves the decoder (the listener, the reader) far more directly and intentionally than does any other poet of the nineteenth century. Since we have already discussed this matter in the chapter on speech acts, it is relevant here only in that it also puts Whitman on the metonymic side of the dichotomy.

D1 (paradigm vs. syntagm). The grid presented near the beginning of this chapter can be used to demonstrate the difference between metonymy and metaphor, but it relates also to the very structure of language. One way to grasp what Jakobson does with these earlier theories is to use the grid not just for figurative language but for all language. Almost all the commentators on Jakobson use the grid approach in some fashion or other, but the most useful for a layman in linguistics is that of Wicker (1975), although he oversimplifies some of the literary works to which he applies the grid principle.

Wicker presents the components for a simple sentence this way (p. 34):

	A	B	C	D
1	he	can	go	tomorrow
2	she	may	come	soon
3	I	will	ask	next
4	you	could	sleep	now

In column A the personal pronouns stand in a paradigmatic relationship with each other; in column B the auxiliary verbs stand also in a paradigmatic relationship; column C is a paradigm of verbs; and so on. Each vertical column contains a group of *similar* items. Going the other way, you relate *he* to *can* to *go* to *tomorrow* syntagmatically to make a sentence (a syntagmatic chain). You can also make a syntagm of A4, B1, C3, D2 (*you can ask soon*) by relating different items in a series. The point is that only through a two-dimensional matrix can you make a sentence, which you do by the *selection* of a paradigm and the *combination* into a syntagm. You make a different sentence to communicate a different meaning by substitution of one paradigmatic element for another, with a corresponding shift in your syntagmatic horizontal path.

D3 (substitution vs. deletion). In Jakobson's use of this pattern for the metaphoric-metonymic dichotomy there is one slip, which only Lodge seems to have caught. Jakobson makes an important distinction between *substitution* (under Metaphor) and *contexture* (under Metonymy), but Lodge is quite correct in pointing out that *substitution* is an operation of the mind of which *contexture* is hardly the paired opposite: "I suggest that the term we need is *deletion*: deletion is to combination as substitution is to selection. Metonymics and synecdoches are *condensations* of contexture" (1977: 76). For the newcomer to this sort of analysis, all this may be still a bit confusing. But it will be clearer a few pages farther on when metonymy and synecdoche are explained with examples from "Song of Myself," illustrating through them how condensation is achieved by the deletion of unnecessary elements.

D3 (*cont.*). If we look at the grid again, we can see the difficulty the aphasic faces when there is a block in either the vertical (similarity, paradigm) or horizontal (contiguity, syntagm) level. At the vertical row, the patient cannot make the appropriate selection from the paradigmatic elements ordinarily available, nor can he substitute the correct for the incorrect selection that has been made. A common practice is to enlarge the subject-area word—*thing* can include almost any intended subject, to the detriment of any specificity in communication. But there can also be a direct if somewhat erratic consequence. Jakobson discusses this in both "Similarity Disorder" and "Contiguity Disorder" (1956: 63–70, 71–75), and quotes (p. 80) from a Russian novelist who late in life suffered what would be called a "similarity disorder." The mild aphasia was not sufficient to prevent his writing, but it did manifest itself in a stylistic change. This novelist already had a penchant for metonymy and particularly for synecdoche, but as a consequence of his illness he carried these so far that the exorbitant piling up of details made a travesty of his realistic style.

D3 (final *cont.*). Now it is true that Whitman never had a "similarity disorder" similar to that of the Russian novelist, but somewhat like the French novelist, Jean Giono, he may seem excessively committed to the metonymic mode. Indeed, the parade of synecdochic details in many poems did seem excessive to many readers: Emerson's "inventory," Thoreau's "thousand of brick," Psmith's "including the kitchen sink," all bespeak an impatience with the catalogs that do seem to have made their point by five items, add on fifteen more to make sure, wear us down with twenty-five more, and suffocate us with fifty-five additionals. But Whitman's catalogs are not necessarily "in support" of any thesis, nor are they intended "to back up" or "to prepare for" some larger generalization. Rather, they parade one synecdochic detail after another just for the sake of the details themselves. They are most apparent, of course, in the early editions and disappear later.

D4 (*langue* vs. *parole*). It was Ferdinand de Saussure who made the initial hypothesis upon which Jakobson develops his analysis, and one distinction Saussure makes has recently been widely used in the semiotic analyses by Barthes, Genette, and other French critics. It is difficult to capture the differences they mean by *langue* and *parole* through the obvious translation to "language" and "speech," respectively, but there are no other terms available. As Wicker explains, *la langue* to Saussure was "that treasury of linguistic units and rules which exist independently of the individual speaker, and into which he is born as he learns to talk." *La parole*, on the opposite side, "refers to the individual's drawing upon this treasury [*la langue*] for the purpose of actual utterance." *Langue*, then, is the whole collection of paradigms from which the speaker (or writer) selects what he needs, and *parole* (speech) is the linking of those selected items into a syntagm, an organized chain of words to communicate a meaning. "A closely related pair of terms, used particularly by theorists such as Barthes, when speaking of non-verbal 'languages,' or communication systems, is 'code' (paradigmatic) and 'message' (syntagmatic)" (1975: 14–15). Terence Hawkes explains these terms in their larger relation to semiotics, in his most useful introductory study (1977: 20–21, 42–43, 82–85).

D5 (*in absentia* vs. *in praesentia*). It was Saussure also who in referring to language first employed the terms *in absentia* and *in praesentia*, which Jakobson uses but with some modification. Saussure was not fully aware of the paradigmatic-syntagmatic interplay in language, but he clearly saw the necessity for distinguishing between selection and combination in the language process. He uses the example of a Greek temple, pointing out that we see the column holding up the adjacent roof, a contiguous relationship of two different building items which we observe in proximity, and at one time, that is, *in praesentia*, in one actual or imaginary view. But as we look at the column, which is Doric, we may be reminded of other columns (Ionic, Corinthian) which are not in this temple and are therefore present only in the brain and are *in absentia*. Jakobson realized that these two types of association (*contiguity*, the column and the roof; *similarity*, other nonpresent columns) are parallel to the *syntagmatic* and *paradigmatic* functions, and developed this insight accordingly. Metaphors in their similarity aspect are always *in absentia*, they do not and cannot exist in reality; metonymies in their contiguous aspect are always *in praesentia*, they can or may exist in the real world (1956: 61).

E1 (Romanticism vs. Realism). In the explanatory comments at A2 above, it was noted that metonymy had its role in rejecting the veneration for the past, for traditional forms, and reference was made to Watt's *Rise of the Novel*. It seems, then, that the course of metonymy was through prose and the novel, which is true. But as all writing is both metaphoric and metonymic to some degree, there may be poetry which in comparison to other poetry of its day, or its language , seems predominantly metonymic. On any spectrum, from 1 (metaphor) to 10 (metonymy), Coleridge would be somewhere in the 3–4 range and Wordsworth in the 6–7 area, both in their theoretical observations and in the verse itself. Indeed that is one reason why it was, briefly, such a good partnership or combination. There has been no occasion for Jakobson to pursue his investigations along such lines, but Lodge makes a convincing analysis of two Wordsworth poems in such a context (1977: 118–23) and has a whole chapter on Philip Larkin (pp. 212–20), whom he rightly considers far more metonymic than metaphoric.

E1 (*cont.*). Osterwalder is more concerned with Eliot's essays and plays than with his poetry, but he notes the same range for the theater:

> Transferred to drama, Jakobson's statement has the following implications: stage properties and stage action are predominantly iconic or indexical; they are visual 'in praesentia.'. . . Language in general and the poetic function of language in particular is primarily symbolic. It is auditory and refers to 'in

absentia' relationships, especially in the case of poetic language. . . . Tentatively one could venture the following generalization: plays in which stage properties and stage action, i.e. icons and indexes, play a crucial part are rather decoder-oriented and belong to the metonymic principle. In a metaphoric end of the scale there is a static play almost devoid of stage action whose main impact is achieved by poetic language and certain symbolic actions. This type of play is encoder-oriented, because poetic language often uses a code, an imputed learned convention which is not completely shared by the whole audience (1978: 16).

Thus *Murder in the Cathedral* is nearer one end (the metaphoric) and *The Confidential Clerk* or *The Elder Statesman* at the other (metonymic), with *The Family Reunion* and *The Cocktail Party* nearer the middle.

E1 (*cont.*). Can a reverse of what Osterwalder found in Eliot be found in Whitman? Possibly so, for a quick glance at the longer poems from "Passage to India" to "Eidólons" shows a steady increase in the *in absentia* figures. There even seems to be sudden increase in such figures after his stroke in January, 1873, but whether there is a possibility of physical impairment as a contributing factor would be hard to prove.

E2 (verse vs. novel). It is true, however, that in the larger sense verse is on the metaphoric and prose on the metonymic side of any dividing line of writing. Granting as much, are we acknowledging then that all prose is metonymic? No, for metonymy and synecdoche are tropes, figures of speech, and as such belong to literature, not to prose. We are all aware of the vexation we have made for ourselves by refusing to create and use a critical vocabulary which makes distinctions between the kinds of writing. If we employ the terms available and claim that Whitman's alleged poetry is really only a blend of oratory, journalism, old and new rhetoric, personal essay, lyceum lecture, and public diary, we are immediately put on the defensive. The subject matter and manner of communication of those six kinds of communication, whether taken individually or collectively, are seen as something less (not in quantity but in quality) than the poetry we revere (even though we cannot define it). The metaphoric-metonymic distinction does help, however, perhaps because, as a new way of cutting the pie, it is freed of the prepossessions which make the approach immediately above so frustrating.

It is a critical commonplace that if we cannot define pure poetry we can, at least, point to pure prose, which is mathematics or technical writing, *i.e.*, scientific prose, which has neither metaphor nor metonymy —in fact, no figurative language at all: it is pure referential language. Accordingly, the best place to find metonymy has been in literary prose, chiefly fiction, and most uses of Jakobson's hypothesis have been by critics and commentators on novelists. It may have been because the terminology was still too mystifying that Fred See's penetrating analysis of William Dean Howells (1974) has not received the attention it deserves, for it seems to be the only application of Jakobson's dichotomy to nineteenth-century American literature. See perceived that the metaphoric falsifications of such major writers as Hawthorne and Melville, themselves reacting against a host of metaphorical-sentimental fictions, served as a negative (but none the less powerful) influence on Howells. This is a valuable insight into the method of American realism, and a larger analysis of Howells' fiction, plus an extension to Henry James and Samuel Clemens, and even to such novels as Harold Frederic's *Damnation of Theron Ware* or Theodore Dreiser's *Sister Carrie*, is clearly in order.

An even more detailed analysis of the metonymical mode is that of J. Hillis Miller in "The Fiction of Realism," (1971). The first part of this illuminating essay focuses on the *Sketches by Boz*, which "offer an excellent opportunity to test the validity of Jakobson's historical and linguistic schematizations. . . . The *Sketches*, in spite of Dickens' well-known use of metaphor, are in fact based on a brilliant and consistent exploitation of what Jakobson calls 'the metonymical texture of realistic prose.'" Miller's analysis of the *Sketches* and, less extensively, of *Oliver Twist* (which together take up the first forty-two pages of the essay) do show the relevance of metonymy to Dickens' style, but Miller also demonstrates that the metaphor still remains, that indeed for Dickens "metonymy is the foundation and support of metaphor" (p. 13).

A year earlier, in France, Genette had made the same claim for Proust in his brilliant analysis "Métonymie chez Proust," originally in *Poétique* (1970) and available in this country in *Figures III* (1972). This is not to say that Miller followed Genette in the sense of being indebted to him, for they worked independently, but I mention these well-known scholars together to demonstrate the import of Jakobson's distinction, which has, however, been directed to the analysis of fiction.

METONYMY

John Romano's *Dickens and Reality* (1978) extends the "metonymic approach" that Miller first perceived to the rest of Dickens; on his own, Frederic Jameson does so for Wyndham Lewis in *Hudson Review* (1973); Wicker (1975), for theological as well as critical reasons, does so for Lawrence, Joyce, Waugh, Beckett, Robbe-Grillet, and Mailer. There are some exceptions, as in the Lodge and Osterwalder studies previously mentioned. Also, in France, Albert Henry in *Métonymie et Métaphore* has shown in some "by the way" examples that metonymy is basic to much of the poetry of Saint-John Perse. But no one has pursued Jakobson's insight to a thorough examination of the relationship of metaphor to metonymy in poetry. It should be done, as can be seen by a look at metonymy in Whitman.

Whitman's Practice

Let us start with those last words above, "a look at metonymy in Whitman." We cannot look at metonymy in Whitman because we cannot look at Whitman, he is long dead. What is meant is Whitman's *Leaves*; but part of the full statement has been deleted (see D3 on the dichotomy list). This is one of the most common metonymic devices, the cause for the result, and we are so used to it that we are always making statements that are literally nonsense:

STUDENT: Where can I find some samples of free verse?
TEACHER: Look under Whitman.

Beyond such Mark Twain and Ring Lardner devices, there are many serious and valid uses of metonymy and synecdoche. The definitions are all about the same, and this one from J. Hillis Miller is both typical and useful: "Metonymy may be defined as a linguistic substitution in which a thing is named not directly but by way of something adjacent to it either temporally or spatially. Synecdoche, substituting part for whole, container for thing contained, attribute for substance, and so on, is an important subdivision of metonymy" (1971: 9–10). It should be remembered that both metonymy and synecdoche are traditional in classical rhetoric, are talked about by Aristotle along with metaphor, and René Wellek and Austin Warren have even acknowledged that "metonymy and metaphor may be the characterizing structures of two poetic types—poetry of association by contiguity, of movement within a single world of discourse, and poetry of association by comparison, joining a plurality of worlds" (1963: 195).

There have been a number of studies of metaphor but few of metonymy, and those few are in French. The major essays by Genette have now been translated (1982), including the key essay on metonymy (pp. 103–126). The scattered references in articles and books, beyond those previously mentioned, are Stephen Ullmann, both *Style in the French Novel* (pp. 210–13) and *Language and Style* (pp. 177–81); Jerzy Pelc, *Studies* (pp. 154–58); Leech (1974: 141, 217–18); and Stephen Brown, *The World of Imagery*, (1927). The Brown volume was written long before the new (*i.e.*, post-Jakobson) understanding, and its reprinting in 1966 does not take into account recent scholarship on figurative language of any sort. Nevertheless Brown does recognize the real distinction between metaphor, metonymy, and synecdoche, and does give a number of clear examples from traditional English poetry (pp. 149–60). He also provides a figurative explanation, which may be helpful to those for whom the terms are new:

> Let the circle A represent the main idea that would be plainly expressed if no figure were used. The *b* will stand for the notion that is brought in (imported) to take its place when a figure is employed.

In Metaphor (Fig. 1) two circles intersect (but the two are not, properly speaking, in the same plane) A and *b* [the parts of A and *b* that overlap] appearing to the mind as identical in a certain respect. In Synecdoche (Fig. 2) a segment (*b*) of the main idea (A) is emphasized and in speech takes the place of A. Thus "A fleet of twenty *sail* (i.e., ships) loomed up in the offing." In Metonymy (Fig. 3) the imported notion (*b*), though it may have various connections with A, is not part of it. "From the cradle to the grave (i.e., from birth to death)." (pp. 152–53)

The traditional explanation provided by Brown and his diagrammatic explanation are acceptable for practical, not for theoretical, reasons. The theoretical distinction between metaphor, synecdoche, and metonymy is not precise, but for the practical purposes of this book it would

be not a help but a hindrance to explore and explain the various positions taken, especially as concerns the distinguishing features of metaphor and synecdoche. Perelman seems to have been the first to question
the traditional distinctions, but a full (and necessarily complicated) explanation of this fascinating theoretical problem is that of Group μ (a
team of Belgian philologists at Liège) in *A General Rhetoric* (1970,
trans. 1981). The stunning proposal there propounded that a "metaphor is the product of two synecdoches" (p. 107) is understandable in
terms of the figures Brown provides. But Group μ's explanation is too
technical and involves too many unfamiliar terms for the general American reader of Whitman to whom this book is directed—although there
is an American treatment of metonymy and synecdoche that considers
Group μ's impact on metonymy theory, Peter Schofer and Donald Rice
(1977) in a technical discussion that has been further elaborated on by
Rice alone (1980). Nevertheless, a stylistic examination of *Leaves of
Grass* via Group μ's critical apparatus would provide an enormously
valuable and detailed explanation of Whitman's artistry in rhetoric.

Let me add a final comment on the uses of the terms *metonymy* and
synecdoche in recent literary criticism of Whitman. There is only one
critic who uses these terms in any serious sense, Harold Bloom in two
books. In *A Map of misreading* (1975) there is a brief analysis of "As I
Ebb'd with the Ocean of Life," in which the "overt synecdoche" of line
9, "The rim, the sediment that stands for all the water and all the land
of the globe," is noted. Bloom comments, "The beach for him is the
greatest of synecdoches, standing for ocean and for earth, for mother
and for father, but most of all for himself, Whitman, as human sufferer
rather than as poet" (p. 181). Later he quotes the last section of the
poem and adds these remarks: "The 'just as much' repetition is the
agency by which the metonymy of 'Me and mine, loose windrows, little
corpses' becomes the metalepsis of "We, capricious, brought hither we
know not whence.' As a metonymy of an metonymy, the 'We, capricious' triumphantly reverses the reductive pattern of the poem, for the
present time in which Whitman is cut off from his poetic self becomes a
wholly negated time, and so no time at all. The poetic past is introjected
and the images of lateness become exalted" (p. 183).

The pointing out of synecdoche and metonymy is clearly correct,
but it is embarrassing to me to applaud that recognition yet disagree

with the reading. As I read the poem, the last section is framed by the "phantom" of line 56, who is the "you" of the last three lines. That "you" is the reader. One of the startling effects of Whitman's use of the speech act is this direct address to the reader. Like the "Listener up there! what have you to confide to me?" of "Song of Myself" (l. 1321), or the "Camerado, this is no book" passage in "So Long," or the many other poems in the early editions, the "you" is *you*, the present reader of that poem as well as the present reader of this sentence. The intimacy and the immediacy of such poems are even present in the paragraph from "Nature" (and here, too, "you" is addressed directly) with which Bloom begins his chapter. In these circumstances, the "reductive pattern of the poem" is not reversed but presented to us as reader-judges (of the poet as well as the poem) with a controlled poignancy rare in the early Whitman.

In Chapter 9, "Emerson and Whitman: The American Sublime," of Bloom's *Poetry and Repression*, there is another use of these terms. The book (and this chapter) is an important discovery and announcement of an Emerson-Whitman contribution, but it is one of those dense books that sometimes eludes me. In this chapter *metonymy* and *synecdoche* are used only some half-dozen times, yet at key junctions in the presentation. But they are used in a much extended sense. "Myself" is the only poem examined, and Bloom gives this projection of the poem: "Employing my own shorthand, this is the pattern of ratios in *Song of Myself* [by sections]:

 1–6   *Clinamen*, irony of presence and absence
 7–27 *Tessera*, synecdoche of part for whole
28–30 *Kenosis*, metonymy of emptying out
31–38 *Daemonization*, hyperbole of high and low
39–49 *Askesis*, metaphor of inside vs. outside
50–52 *Apophrades*, metalepsis reversing early and late" (p. 248).

There have been many attempts to divide the fifty-two stanzas into inclusive larger groupings, and this division into six is not unusual. The italicized words are Kabbalistic terms of Bloom's devising. But to say that the first six sections of "irony of presence and absence" are followed by twenty-one sections of synecdoche, which are themselves followed by three sections of metonymy, is confusing. Synecdoche and metonymy are found here and there throughout the poem, as to a lesser extent are the other four. But to extend a term that concerns one kind of substitution to embrace the others goes against the idea of dividing the poem into six parts for purposes of clarification. In sections 7 through 27 there are a great many synecdoches, to be sure, but there are just as many (probably more) in the next twenty-one sections.

Here is a later comment of Bloom's, truly valuable for its suggestive aura, but ultimately confusing to me in its lack of specificity: "Whitman, surpassing all his descendants [poets: Hart Crane, Wallace Stevens, A. R. Ammons, John Ashbery; novelists: Ernest Hemingway, Mailer], makes of a linked sex-and-death a noble synecdoche for all of existence, which is the figurative design of sections 7–27 of *Song of Myself*. A universalizing flood tide of reversals-into-the-opposite reaches a great climax in section 24, which is an antithetical completion of the self without rival in American poetry, astonishing both for its dignity and its pathos, and transcending any other modern poet's attempt to think and to represent by synecdoche" (p. 257).

If we return to J. Hillis Miller's definitions and Stephen Brown's illustrative circles, we can make some initial applications for purposes of clarification. The examples are from "Myself," line references from the final version, and the relevant words have been italicized.

Metonymy encompasses the following five aspects:

(1) Cause for effect. An example, already noted, is that of "Whitman" for his poetry, but it is most often used in describing things as having qualities of which they are the cause: "As the *hugging and loving bed-fellow* sleeps at my side" (l. 60).

(2) Container for contained. When Whitman writes: "The *city sleeps* and the *country sleeps*" (l. 324), he means the dwellers in the city and the country. This figure is so common in everyday speech that Whitman sometimes uses the device by denying it: "I pass death with the dying and birth with the new-wash'd babe, and *am not contain'd between my hat and boots*" (l. 133).

(3) Possessor for possessed. This device is found all through the catalogs; here, for instance, except for the canal boy, the others are pictured by their tools: "The *paving-man* leans on *his two-handed rammer*, the *reporter's lead* flies swiftly over *the notebook*, the *sign-painter* is *lettering with blue and gold*, / The canal boy trots on the tow-path, the *book-*

keeper counts at *his desk*, the *shoemaker* waxes *his thread*" (ll. 296–97).

(4) Office or occupation for its sign, symbol, or significant accompaniment. This, equally as common as (3) above, is indeed much like it in its effect. For instance: "As the *fare-collector* goes through the train he gives notice *by the jingling of loose change*" (l. 312) can be shortened to "The *driver* with *his interrogating thumb*" (l. 154).

(5) Any subject for various adjuncts. This is quite as common as those above and is often extended to make a stanza. Section 12 is typical and short enough to be quoted in full:

> The butcher-boy puts off his killing-clothes, or sharpens his knife at the stall
>   in the market,
> I enjoy his repartee and his shuffle and break-down.
>
> Blacksmiths with grimed and hairy chests environ the anvil,
> Each has his main-sledge, they are all out, there is great heat in the fire.
>
> From the cinder-strew'd threshold I follow their movements,
> The lithe sheer of their waists plays even with their massive arms,
> Overhand the hammers swing, overhand so slow, overhand so sure,
> They do not hasten, each man hits in his place. (ll. 217–24)

This is the first quotation long enough for us to note the features of the last section in the dichotomy list, "Literary Style." In addition to F3, rhetorical figures of contexture, which in this passage are both metonymy and synecdoche, the passage uses denotation not connotation, parataxis (coordination) not hypotaxis (subordination), a nominal style not a verbal one, collage and close-up rather than montage and parallelism, and is conjunctive (a series taken one after the other, the use of *and*) not disjunctive (separating items by *either/or*, or comparable device).

Synecdoche is always considered in the traditional rhetorics as separate from metonymy. But after Jakobson there seems little reason to continue to speak of the three main tropes as metaphor, metonymy, and synecdoche, when the line of separation clearly belongs after metaphor to distinguish that figure (which, concerned with similarity, involves a specific mental, and perhaps emotional, operation) from metonymy and synecdoche (which involve contiguous relationships). Whether we consider synecdoche a coequal or a branch of metonymy makes little difference as far as our analysis of *Leaves* is concerned, and the distinction is useful chiefly for reasons of clarification. The most elaborate and valuable treatment, if one wishes to pursue this distinction, is that of Henry

(1971), whose opening chapter shows how metonymy works by "comprehension" and synecdoche by "extension," although he also notes that one cannot say they are different by their internal logic.

(1) Physical part for the whole. In its simplest form, this is seen in lines 374–76:

> Of every hue and caste am I, of every rank and religion,
> A farmer, mechanic, artist, gentleman, sailor, quaker,
> Prisoner, fancy-man, rowdy, lawyer, physician, priest.

Although in this case the whole (the American people) is first split into subdivisions as race and social group, and then status and faith (in line 330 at the beginning of this stanza 16, he similarly declares, "I am of old and young, of the foolish as much as the wise"), with the subdivisions then pictured through synecdochic details, farmer to priest. An even better, but longer, example of this use of synecdochic exemplification is the opening (ll. 1096–1110) of stanza 43, a vivid manifestation of his "faith," which encloses all worship "ancient and modern."

(2a) Genus for species. Using this, which is something like the above, we can suggest the genus (say, the necessities of life) by the species (bread, "Give us this day . . ."). Whitman says, for example: "Who goes there? hankering, gross, mystical, nude; / How is it I extract strength from the beef I eat?" (ll. 389–90). Or, he asks a series of rhetorical questions to convey the startling / not-so-startling "purpose" his utterance intends:

> Do you guess I have some intricate purpose?
> Well, I have, for the Fourth-month showers have, and the mica on the side of
>   the rock has,
> Do you take it I would astonish?
> Does the daylight astonish? does the early redstart twittering through the
>   woods?
> Do I astonish more than they? (ll. 382–86)

(2b) Species and genus. In rhetoric textbooks there is usually a mention of this, the reverse of (2a), that is, the genus substituted for the species. It is always mentioned that this form is rare and is used as a euphemism, the writer not wanting to be specific about death, disease, drunkenness. Euphemism was, of course, something Whitman delighted in challenging, so this sort of substitution is even more rare in *Leaves* than elsewhere in poetry. But although he may have wished to be specific about sex, he was still living in the nineteenth century. He does use "copulation" (l. 521) and can speak "of wombs and of father-stuff" (l. 512) and of "teats" (l. 250), although since this reference was to the "grunting sow," it was doubtless not seen as so offensive. But such assaults on Victorian reticence had limits. Whitman's belief that masturbation, the erotic delight in one's own body, was also a subject entitled to poetic treatment is, of course, present in the poetry, but here he does use a modified form of synecdoche. It is a very successful use, not euphemistic in any derogatory sense, but clearly substituting synec-dochic details for the direct anatomical, sensual, and psychological de-tails of an actual description of the act. The passage (stanza 28) is too long to be given here in full, but it is important to recognize the lines as a unique (for that time, at least) use of synecdoche. This section is representative:

> The sentries desert every other part of me,
> They have left me helpless to a red marauder,
> They all come to the headland to witness and assist against me,
> I am given up by traitors,
> I talk wildly, I have lost my wits, I and nobody else am the greatest traitor,
> I went first to the headland, my own hands carried me there. (ll. 633–38)

(3) Material for what is made of it. This is often merely a single word or phrase substitution. The notion that nature glorifies God ("Consider the lilies of the field") can, with Whitman's typical inten-tion to shock and to jar the reader out of his narrow complacency, be said this way: "The scent of these arm-pits aroma finer than prayer" (l. 525). But an extended version of this form of synecdoche is that vi-sion of the stunning variety of American life, the justly famous catalog near the beginning of stanza 33, lines 717–97.

(4) The use of definite number. It may seem odd to list such a prac-tice under synecdoche, but what is involved is the specification of a defi-nite in preference to an indefinite term. In the long catalog just men-tioned, line 792 reads: "Speeding amid the seven satellites and the broad ring, and the diameter of eighty thousand miles." What do the numbers add? They make it apparent that the speaker or writer knows what he's talking about. He might have dropped "seven" and said "many thousand miles" or even "many miles," and note how the line is weakened. Sometimes he intends to be indefinite or uncertain, yet

keeps the quality of definite enumeration, as in the eyewitness account of the victory of the *Bonhomme Richard*, "The husky voices of the two or three officers yet fit for duty" (l. 936). Would the line be destroyed by having "few" instead of "two or three"? No, but it would be weakened by showing us an observer-narrator willing to make shortcuts and vague estimates instead of one who is passionately involved with the human side of the conflict and gives the precise detail (or as precise as he can be in fitful light of the ship on fire). Again, what is the value of the specific and repeated number "Twenty-eight," (stanza 11, ll. 199–201) that begins the account of the twenty-ninth would-be swimmer? Of course it needs to be considered along with the other memorable virtues of the stanza (both prosodic and thematic) as Smith does very memorably (1968: 88–91).

But the emphasis here is less on the individual value of the specific number to a specific line, than on the great many times Whitman uses definite numbers. Whitman probably uses more numbers (*i.e.*, synecdoche of this sort) than any other poet in the language, on a percentage basis. The reason for thinking so is that he is much further on the metonymic side than is any other major poet (especially in the early poetry—after the Civil War the use of numbers diminishes as the metonymic verve of his poetry slackens). To set that estimate in a different perspective, there are surely many more numbers (again on a percentage basis) in Wordsworth than in Coleridge. Remember "Five years have passed . . . five summers . . . five long winters," "Three years she grew," "We are Seven," "A six years darling of a pigmy size," and there must be many more. In Coleridge, there is that shortstop joke, "He stoppeth one of three," and remember the crew that "dropped down one by one"? How many were there? "Four times fifty living men." But here is Jakobson's law at play, for Coleridge, way over on the metaphoric side here, "projects the principle of equivalence from the axis of selection into the axis of combination" (1960: 358); to wit, instead of saying "two hundred" as Whitman certainly and Wordsworth probably would have done, he must consider meter, alliteration, and line length, so he sets up his word combination with that in mind as well as the relevance of the exact numerical specification. Similarly, in "Kubla Khan" we find: "So twice five miles of fertile ground." Such lines, with their alliteration and assonance, do help create and maintain the incantatory effect of the poetry, with perhaps some minor sacrifice of exponential credibility. So, if we do not count the numbers Coleridge employed for prosodic reasons, Wordsworth would have perhaps twice as many specific numbers, for he was nearer the metonymic end of the spectrum, and, to be sure, part of the reason we put him on the metonymic side would be that he used numbers. And Whitman, of course, more metonymic still, would use even more.

(5) Nominal use of the adjective. This device is very rarely used (not at all in "Myself"), although it is listed in most rhetoric texts. It has been the practice in some formal poetry to drop the noun and make the accompanying adjective stand for the noun, *e.g.*, "the immortals" for "the gods." It fits the pattern for synecdoche, but it is not something that is found in ordinary speech. Indeed, of all the devices of metonymy and synecdoche, this is the only one that is "poetical." One can see that with the elevated language of certain poems and within the confines of adjusting what one is saying to line length, meter, and rhyme (one must agree with Jakobson that, if one grants the poetic potential of the initial emotional idea, the tension resulting from these self-imposed restraints is what makes great poetry of the metaphoric kind) this device may be a valuable aid. But Whitman, with his free line structure and absence of meter and rhyme, had no need of such aid and so had no occasion to use it. There were none in the first three editions, but, as might be guessed, there are some in that elevated, somewhat unnatural language of those pretentiously prophetic poems in 1867 and thereafter.

"The Return of the Heroes" (1867) uses this particular form of synecdoche four times without any great help to the poem that I can see. It is a confused poem to begin with, because Whitman is trying to do two things at once, to celebrate the peaceful disbanding of the armies as well as the bumper harvest of that year, but neither intention justifies the highfalutin language of many sections mixed up with the ordinary idiom of the rest. In the last stanza, where he is trying to unite the two themes, he writes: "Yet but for thee O Powerful, not a scythe might swing as now in security" (l. 120). It is not clear in the line that "O Powerful" means the country, the nation, but in the context it does follow. Also, line 117 reads: "Beneath thy look O Maternal," both of these synecdoches referring to the "Mother of All" (ll. 109, 106, 94). Earlier, at line 61, referring to the Civil War casualties, he says, "Nor do I forget you Departed," the capital letter used, no doubt, to alert the reader that what he is looking at is not a grammatical blunder but a bit of poetic license. Related to this form of synecdoche may be the unfortunate practice in his late poetry of adding the suffix *ess* to verbs or adjectives to make nouns (and thereby subjects or objects of the clause), and an example in this poem is: "Dispensatress, that by a word givest a thousand miles, a million farms, and missest nothing" (l. 34). Other late poems use the same device, as in "Thou Mother with Thy Equal Brood": "The fruit of all the Old ripening today in Thee" (l. 46), where again the context alerts us to the reference to Old World. In "Passage to India," "O Thou transcendent" (l. 194) may not even be a substitution at all but an unnecessary inversion, but what "The ostent evanescent" of "Eidólons" (l. 21) may or may not be, is hard to say.

But we do not read Whitman for the ornamental synecdoches just mentioned, and we do not *not* read him because of them either, for the force and vitality of his standard metonymic style make the late weakness no more threatening than the reckless "inkhorn" ventures with the French language in the early poetry. Related to the above form of synecdoche, in which the adjective takes the place of the noun, another device concerns the use of adjectives for which there seems to be no specific name. Leech finds that "adjectives that refer to emotional or other inner states" are "frequently used in a transferred sense" and attached to nouns to which they have no semantic connection (1974: 218). In their normal use these adjectives would be applied to a person (his examples are *sad child* and *friendly person*) but can get transferred in two ways: first, the "expressing or evincing" of the quality (as in *a sad face, a friendly greeting*); second, "causing or evoking" the quality (as in *a sad story*). There are a few of these transferred adjectives in "Myself" and many more in the late poems. Looked at literally, at their face value, these expressions are absurd, but we are so used to them in advertising, and sometimes in our own conversation, that we do not examine them closely. When Whitman talks of "the arrogant republics" (l. 107), "my prophetical screams" (l. 572), the "friendly bees, huskings, house-raisings" (l. 755), the star's "mournful shining" (l. 940), or "my barbaric yawp" (l. 1333), we accept the transferred adjective and frequently transfer it back again to the speaker, the persona.

But we need to think of metonymy in two ways: as a semantic device (which we have just examined) and as a structural device. Contiguity is the key element in both. To give a mental picture of something (building, event, person, scene is to describe the details as they appear to us so that the reader can reassemble them in his imagination. The order of presentation of the details determines the order of the language we use. This practice is so basic that we are generally unaware of it, except in situations that impose additional structures on our language organization, as in poetry. The demands of meter, rhyme, and other assorted prosodic features must inevitably force some variations in the standard syntagmatic order—generally speaking, the fewer the better. Since Whitman freed himself of many of these poetic-language demands, there is no prosodic justification for any departures from normal syntax in the language of *Leaves* (with rare and disastrous exceptions, as "O Captain! My Captain!").

But it is clear that there are variations, for Whitman could not reject all poetic features of language and still be a poet. He abjured only certain elements of the conventional verse of his day. In doing so, he retained rhythm but not meter, parallelism but not rhyme, and expressly limited the use of alliteration, assonance, onomatopoeia, and other "sound" features. At what might be called the "unit level" (individual words, phrases, clauses, sentences) he also rejected "poetic diction" (in the early editions especially), but he no more abjured poetic language than he had renounced rhythm and parallelism. Likewise, he seems to have consciously avoided the pointed use of simile and metaphor (again, primarily in the early poetry), but the larger metaphor of the poem itself was inherent in his thinking and its poetic product. What he retained was metonymy, in the individual features we have been pointing out, but also as a structural principle of considerable poetic efficacy.

We must not forget that we use metonymy all the time in daily language, as one of the idiomatic economies of speech. Strictly speaking, these metonymies are nonsensical ("His wife is expecting," "Oil is wrecking our economy," "Answer the door"), but they make no trouble for us because we contribute the missing element automatically ("... a baby," "The exorbitant price of ... ," etc.). Charles Ruhl, in "Pragmatic Metonymy" (1976), explains that we condone, cooperate with, and encourage this metonymic feature of communication by our habitual contribution. What we do for the sports broadcaster (where metonymic language is pandemic) we can also do for these lines from "Myself"—and here, too, I italicize the metonymic focus:

> This is the press of a *bashful hand*, this the float and odor of hair,
> This the touch of my lips to yours, this the murmur of yearning,
> This the far-off depth and height reflecting my own face,
> This the *thoughtful merge* of myself, and the outlet again. (ll. 378–81)

We know there is literally no such thing as a "bashful hand," but we read and accept it as the "hand of a bashful person." We do not know at first whose hand it is, or whose hair, but the next lines assure us that it is the speaker's whose hand we press, whose hair we see and smell, whose lips we kiss, whose murmur we hear, whose reflection we see. Cooperating in making the language meaningful, are we not also committing ourselves to the imaginary encounter with the speaker? If so, we can accept "thoughtful merge" not as nonsense but as the fusion of speaker and hearer (*i.e.*, poet and reader). The reader is thus drawn into imaginary participation by a skillful handling of metonymy.

Two sections farther on (again, my italics here and below), the speaker "walks with the *tender and growing night*" and calls "to the earth and sea half-held by night" in language that continues at the metonymic level but gradually shifts toward personification as he considers the earth and the sea. He begins:

> Press close *bare-bosom'd night*—press close *magnetic nourishing night*!
> Night of the south winds—night of the large few stars!
> Still *nodding night—mad naked* summer *night*. (ll. 435–37)

And then to earth:

> Smile O voluptuous *cool-breath'd earth*!
> Earth of the *slumbering and liquid trees*!
> Earth of *departed sunset*—earth of the mountains misty-topt! (ll. 438–40)
>
> *Far-swooping elbow'd earth*—rich *apple-blossom'd earth!*
> Smile for your lover comes. (ll. 444–45)

And to the sea, with similar fusion of metonymy and personification:

> I behold from the beach your crooked *inviting* fingers, (l. 449)
>
> Cushion me soft, rock me in *billowy* drowse,
> Dash me with *amorous* wet, I can repay you. (ll. 452–53)

But this giving of personal characteristics to nonpersonal things, whether via personification or not, is really part of the metaphoric attitude (indeed, some would say *is* the metaphoric attitude). That would explain why there are more of them in the late poetry. There are about a dozen of these in the 1,336 lines of "Myself" and about the same number in the first 24 lines of "Thy Mystic Trumpeter" (1872). I have no bias against the transferred adjective or the metaphoric uses of it, although Whitman's late uses, "liquid prelude," "fretting world," "noisy hours," "holy calm," "refreshing night" (ll. 14–17) seem a bit on the obvious side, the death of metaphor. I only raise the issue to point out that Whitman began essentially as a metonymic poet and ended as a metaphoric poet. If you like one, you usually don't like the other (as much, anyway).

A final caveat is needed before applying all the above to a demonstration, because there is a line of demarcation, a separation not of degree but of kind, between poetry and prose, between the most prosaic metaphoric poetry and the most poetic metonymic prose that has not been elucidated. This is a feature that Jakobson accepts but did not establish or initiate. It comes from another of the famous Prague school, the Czech critic Mukařovsky, and is called "foregrounding." It will be brought to bear in my concluding chapter to show how Whitman makes poetry out of his most elaborate, sensitive, and often daring metonymic language.

It is sufficient here to demonstrate that such language is present, and is found in all periods of Whitman's literary career, though mostly in the early period. All twelve poems of the 1855 edition are strongly metonymic with the exception of "Europe" and "A Boston Ballad," both of which had been published earlier. There is, to be sure, considerable metonymic writing in them too, but it is not central to Whitman's purpose. There are other motives in the other ten, but the one metonymic piece that is the nearest thing to being only that is "There Was a Child Went Forth." Many readers have seen it in its first-edition form, but for analytical purposes it is useful to have it handy for easy reference. If the printing of this present book cannot match the line length of the wide-paged first edition, it does not matter a great deal, for in this poem Whitman is working with smaller units (phrases mostly) and with groups of lines rather than with individual line structure and appearance. Again, there is no special contextual preparation for this poem in the sense that it is part of a group (as with the Calamus poems later) and that

METONYMY

preceding poems prepare the reader for it; it is, in fact, preceded by the two poems mentioned above.

1   THERE was a child went forth every day,
And the first object he looked upon and received with wonder or pity or love or dread, that object he became,
And that object became part of him for the day or a certain part of the day....or for many years or stretching cycles of years.

The early lilacs became part of this child,
5   And grass, and white and red morningglories, and white and red clover, and the song of the phoebe-bird,
And the March-born lambs, and the sow's pink-faint litter, and the mare's foal, and the cow's calf, and the noisy brood of the barnyard or by the mire of the pondside..and the fish suspending themselves so curiously below there..and the beautiful curious liquid..and the water-plants with their graceful flat heads..all became part of him.

And the field-sprouts of April and May became part of him.... wintergrain sprouts, and those of the light-yellow corn, and of the esculent roots of the garden,
And the appletrees covered with blossoms, and the fruit afterward.... and woodberries..and the commonest weeds by the road;
And the old drunkard staggering home from the outhouse of the tavern whence he had lately risen,
10 And the schoolmistress that passed on her way to the school..and the friendly boys that passed..and the quarrelsome boys..and the tidy and freshcheeked girls..and the barefoot negro boy and girl,
And all the changes of city and country wherever he went.

His own parents..he that had propelled the fatherstuff at night, and fathered him..and she that conceived him in her womb and birthed him....they gave this child more of themselves than that,
They gave him afterward every day....they and of them became part of him.

The mother at home quietly placing the dishes on the suppertable,
15 The mother with mild words....clean her cap and gown....a wholesome odor falling off her person and clothes as she walks by:
The father, strong, selfsufficient, manly, mean, angered, unjust,
The blow, the quick loud word, the tight bargain, the crafty lure,
The family usages, the language, the company, the furniture....the yearning and swelling heart,
Affection that will not be gainsayed....The sense of what is real....the thought if after all it should prove unreal,

20   The doubts of daytime and the doubts of nighttime...the curious
      whether and how,
    Whether that which appears so is so....Or is it all flashes and specks?
    Men and women crowding fast in the streets..if they are not flashes and
      specks what are they?
    The streets themselves, and the facades of houses....the goods in the
      windows,
    Vehicles..teams..the tiered wharves, and the huge crossing at the
      ferries;
25   The village on the highland seen from afar at sunset....the river
      between,
    Shadows..aureola and mist..light falling on roofs and gables of white or
      brown, three miles off,
    The schooner near by sleepily dropping down the tide..the little boat
      slacktowed astern,
    The hurrying tumbling waves and quickbroken crests and slapping;
    The strata of colored clouds....the long bar of maroontint away solitary
      by itself....the spread of purity it lies motionless in,
30   The horizon's edge, the flying seacrow, the fragrance of saltmarsh and
      shoremud;
    These became part of that child who went forth every day, and who
      now goes and will always go forth every day,
    And these become of him or her that peruses them now.

We are probably never consciously aware that we are reading metaphorical or metonymical language unless we focus our attention on the
words and phrases. But once we are so alerted, as here, the almost pure
metonymy stands out. Indeed the one central metaphor is clearly supported by the nearly total metonymic foundation. There is even a legitimate question whether that key metaphor is not itself metonymic: that
is, the second line, specifically "that object he became," and the particu-
larizations of it in line 4, end of line 6, opening of line 7, end of line 13,
opening of line 31, and line 32. Since, in actuality, the child cannot
be his experience (therefore *in absentia*), we should read the figure as
metaphorical, even while acknowledging the contiguity that seems to
govern Whitman's presentation. There is also one "limited metaphor"
in line 27, "The schooner . . . sleepily dropping down," but otherwise
we find a straight metonymic presentation, excluding the introductory
three and concluding two lines. There is a controlling metaphor, to
be sure, but it does not abrogate the point this chapter is trying to

establish—*i.e.*, the insufficient attention given to metonymy as Whitman's essential mode in the early poetry.

There are important features that may be overlooked in our delight with the carefully delimited details. First, if this were truly metonymic writing and nothing more, the division into thirty-two lines would be unnecessary; the five, long, compound sentences presented seriatim in one long paragraph would do. Yet spacing out the descriptive details is necessary, for it slows us down enough to provide opportunity for an image to be formed. The use of dots, two, three, and four dots, is found throughout the first edition, including the prose preface, and, as mentioned elsewhere, seems to be a carry-over from a script prepared for oral delivery. They clearly are not ellipses, and if we think of them as indicating breath pauses in oral reading we can capture a spacing between the items to help give each one its momentary individual emphasis.

The capitalizing of the first word is not of any special import—Whitman did not title the poems of the first edition but put the opening word or words in capital letters. Subsequently untitled poems became known by the first line or a segment of it. Lines 2 and 3 establish the direction of the poem and they also establish the paratactic (*i.e.*, coordinate rather than subordinate) presentation. The shaping effect of our earliest experiences with the outside world is acknowledged, but whether it will create a "leveler" or a "sharpener" is not at this stage apparent. The absence of subordination may foretell that nothing the "child" experiences has already been noted and categorized, and certainly the second stanza establishes or corroborates such a reading. It might be thought that the details to follow will be grouped by the qualifiers in the second line, that the poet will group the childhood experiences in terms of the kind of reception they have received (wonder, pity, love, dread), but even that structuring is absent. The third line has one of those metonymic deletions, "stretching cycles of years" for "cycles of years which stretch on through many years."

The second stanza begins the series of exposures to the variety of events in the child's daily life. The paratactic, conjunctive, much extended sentence maintains the parity of the incidents and events. We give appropriate credit to Clemens for the famous paratactic passage in which Huck tells of the spell of the great river, we applaud Hemingway for his recognition and imitation of this feature of Clemens' style—the style for democratic prose—but we should also recognize Whitman's parallel and much earlier use. That it is not in "prose" is beside the point, for it is not in "poetry" either, to the extent that line six is neither or both. This seems to be the first, conscious, artistic use of the paratactic style not only in this poem but in the whole first edition, including the Preface, although it had been present in oratory (and daily conversation) for many years.

The apparent typographical error in line five, "morningglories," was intentional. There are fusions in the later lines, and also in other poems of the first edition, as "Shipcarpentering," "Ironworks or whiteleadworks" (ll. 134, 136) of "Occupations," all of which became hyphenated words in subsequent editions. There are a fair number of other linguistic experiments, some of which remained—as the apostrophe plus *d* endings for past participles—but the two, three, or four dots to suggest voice pauses, and the uniting of certain nouns and their adjectives by dropping the hyphen, disappeared after the first edition.

The eye-catching length of line six was certainly intentional, and the ordering of its elements was probably not as casual or as accidental as it appears. Note that "lilacs" of line four would be no shock to the reader of conventional poetry of the 1850s, nor would "grass" in the next line. The apparent typographical error, already mentioned, would draw attention to the use of the very common flower, and the "phoebe" is hardly a glamorous bird, and so we are moving toward realistic description. In line six, "the March-born lambs" (later the "third-month") are different as an element in a poetic series only because of the specific, metonymic "March-born" rather than a conventional "spring." But what is to us the lovely surprise of the "sow's pink-faint litter" is the first intentional shocker to the reader of conventional poetry of that day. If "sow" had appeared in any previous American poetry, I am unaware of it; the coinage "pink-faint" is not only new but beautifully graphic; the homely word *litter* seemed common and coarse to Victorian America, which might have anticipated a less exact *brood*. Perhaps we might even say that Whitman himself gave way to Victorian America when in 1872 at Dartmouth he did not celebrate this country's fertility with the ode "Thou Mother with Thy Equal Litter."

The next stanza (ll. 7–11) continues the enumeration, adding over a dozen new items to the thirteen already mentioned. Two questions need to be answered here: Why a separate stanza? What is the *raison d'être* for this structuring of a brief catalog? Both can be answered by the subtly controlled "random juxtaposition" employed by the metonymic poet. Note how the uses of "became" organize this poem, for although the first use may be a metaphor, it is developed by metonymic examples. In announcing the theme, the doubleness of experience, in the first stanza, the poet responds to his milieu, "that object he *became*" (l. 2; and let me italicize to draw attention), but he also ingests, indeed, is not only nurtured by but is molded by that environment. "That object *became* part of him" (l. 3). This passive, malleable, sentient, curious, solemnly observant child (the child we all were) silently stores up the free, unstructured, unevaluated encounters of early experience: "The early lilacs *became* part of this child" (l. 4) and "all *became* part of him" (l. 6).

In stanza 3, we find that these many equally valued, seen and experienced *natural* events "*became* part of him" (l. 7), and that *human* events ("the old drunkard," "the schoolmistress," "the barefoot negro boy and girl") were accepted by the growing child in the same placid, uncategorized fashion. Let me point out a small, perhaps almost unnoticed, linguistic stratagem here: the carefully placed semicolon at the end of line 8 separates the earlier series of this single-sentence stanza (ll. 7–8, natural—*i.e.*, nonhuman—occurrences) from the second series (ll. 9–10, human encounters), to show that even though the objects are later found to be of a different order, they are there (in childhood) not differentiated; they are separate but subsumed in the same level of perception; they do, indeed, belong to the same sentence.

For the two-line fourth stanza, I suppose it may be said that Whitman accepts the truism of environment over heredity in the formation of character. But there are a couple of points of interest. The father who "propelled the fatherstuff at night" was another bit of realistic description, like "sow" (l. 6) and the strange nonjudgmental description of the drunkard (l. 9), meant to shock the circumspect reader. If so, Whitman apparently decided (correctly, in this case) that it did not work, so he dropped it in later editions, perhaps because he recognized that, shock or not, it was a bit of a distraction and because (unlike Tristram Shandy) the child would not have known. Another novelty, the metonymic reduction of "gave him birth" to "birthed him" (l. 12) to parallel the earlier "conceived him" was a brilliant tactic and was fortunately retained in all later printings. But the point in these two lines is to separate from the child's earlier observations of life the even more formative events of his family involvement. The parents gave him not only inherited characteristics but in a certain sense themselves, for if we are creatures of our environment, they gave him their own environment, "they and of them *became* part of him" (l. 13). The inclusion "and of them" in the first edition, which I read as a reference not to mother and father individually but to their relationship as senior members, along with the other children, in forming the home environment, was valuable to the poem, and I am sorry Whitman dropped it after 1860, when he was revising this poem to make of it a personal lyric (see Golden's facsimile of the Blue Book, 222)—the other consequences of which revising will be apparent below.

Section 5 begins as an exemplification of these home influences by the same use of synecdoche (the part for the whole) that is the method of this poem. The mother's contribution (ll. 14–15), the father's (ll. 16–17), and the family's (ll. 18–19) are followed by the boy's puzzled acceptance and his attempts to fathom this gift of perceived life (ll. 19–22). As a grown man (l. 31), he treasures the formative experiences that "*became* part of that child" that he was and still is ("who now goes and will always go forth every day"). The final series, lines 23–30, explains the questions his participation in the family has occasioned, "if they are not flashes and specks what are they?" (l. 22). But even more, they reveal this poem as the exemplification and clarification of Emerson's famous question in "Nature" (in section 6, "Idealism"): "A noble doubt perpetually suggests itself,—whether this end be not the Final Cause of The Universe; and whether nature outwardly exists. It is sufficient account of that Appearance we call the World, that God will teach a human mind, and so makes it the receiver of a certain number of congruent sensations, which we call sun and moon, man and woman, house and trade. In my utter impotence to test the authenticity of the report of my senses, to know whether the impressions they make on me correspond with outlying objects, what difference does it make, whether Orion is up there in heaven, or some god paints the image in the firmament of the soul?"

Whitman's series (really a small catalog) answers the "noble doubt" with a parade of specifics, not the generalities of "sun and moon, man and woman, house and trade" but the observed details of experience. In the spectrum, idealism to empiricism, romanticism to realism, metaphoric to metonymic, Emerson may be no closer to one end of the spectrum than Whitman is to the other, but there is a clear difference between them. It may not have made much difference to Emerson "whether Orion is up there in heaven [sky]," but it meant literally all the difference in the world to Whitman. Emerson did not so much love nature for itself as admire it as a pathway to the Over-Soul. Later in "Nature," in the section called "Spirit," Emerson can say, "The world proceeds from the same spirit as the body of man. It is a remoter and inferior incarnation of God, a projection of God in the unconscious." Those adjectives, "remoter," "inferior," cannot describe Whitman's view. He does not use nature to transcend nature; rather, he loves, embraces, swallows nature to incarnate God in himself.

He also does more: what has happened to him can also happen to us (as decoder, audience, reader). Since our own childhood will have passed, he will re-create the experience for us in his lines. "These," the shaping encounters with nature, "*became* part of that child," that is, Whitman and/or narrator, but now (and note the shift to present tense) "these *become* of him or her that peruses them now." This last line was improved in 1860 to read: "All these *become* part of him or her who peruses them here." What we have is the direction of the poem from the first section now brought to focus not on the child or the narrator, but on us, the readers. In the poem Whitman has been calling up out of memory or making up a series of encounters with the world not only to celebrate his own experience with nature, as the lyric poet would do, but to present an imaginative experience to which we can react with a response parallel to his. Rather than a conventional nature poem, we have a pouring out of synecdochic details (standing for the outpouring of nature), no more blatantly patterned than is nature itself, but carefully and subtly organized by six *becames* and a *become*. The metonymist (the realist) customarily does not interpret life (at least not in any obvious sense) but presents it.

That he dropped this whole last line in 1867 is beside the point. The late change was part of a gradual shift that had been going on for some years; he was moving toward the metaphoric side of the spectrum. It is startling, however, and something of a rarity, that a lyric (a self-reflective poem) can be made by the omission of one line. The explanation seems to be that in writing the poem with the conscious decoder-directed intent, he got so caught up in remembered early experience that the lines reflect the poet's inner self more fully than the didactic purpose warranted.

Be that as it may, the poem is a model of the metonymic style with its predominance of synecdochic detail. As readers we may grant as much but still ask why there seems to be so little regard for order, cohesion, structure in much metonymic writing—to wit, lines 24–30 might be read in reverse order without destroying the poem. Although those lines cannot really be read that way, there would be so slight a loss that the query is valid. The point is that the use of random juxtaposition is just as intentional as are the quietly inserted *became*s and *become*. If we are made aware of order, cohesion, structure, whether in art or nature, they have been imposed ("I placed a jar in Tennessee"). They imply that the buzzing confusion of life has been subjected to the confines of categories, systems, pigeonholes, to which the details of experience are made to conform. This is not to say that art, by its nature, is a Procrustean bed, but that to some poets in the middle of the nineteenth century conventional poetry may have seemed that way. And that is just what the metonymic poet rejects. Nature, or life, is falsified when it is categorized—that is what a "leveler" does (as Shaw, says Ohmann) but Whitman is a "sharpener." His poem rejoices in the enormous variety of life's manifestations, which are best presented by multiple synecdoches, upon which any obvious structuring would be an imposition, a falsification. There have been many attempts to find an order, a meaningful sequence, in the long catalogs in "Song of Myself," but they are no more subject to imposed logical structure than is the present poem.

What is true of "There Was a Child Went Forth" is true also of practically all of the poems of the first and second editions, most of the third (1860), and many in *Drum-Taps and Sequel* of 1865. Even in poems of clear lyric intent the metonymic attitude remains Whitman's characteristic mode, for example, stanza 6 of "When Lilacs Last," beginning "Coffin that passes through lanes and streets," has a clear metonymic base. Whitman was at his confident best, in the years from 1855 to 1860, when writing in the metonymic mode. With the Civil War and his sympathies, with a need to write the kind of poetry called for in *Democratic Vistas*, with a concession to what he thought his new English audience expected of the American prophet, with a strange compunction to write "good gray poetry" to match his new title, he turned away from metonymy. There are faults in many of the metonymic poems, to be sure, but they are the faults of excess. The faults of the subsequent almost officially prophetic poems ("Equal Brood," etc.) are not too painful to enumerate, but not in this chapter.

Postscript

A perceptive reader of this manuscript in its early stages was perturbed at the inclusion of this Postscript. My presentation, and therefore implied acceptance, of Lacan's theory of the origin of metonymy seemed to him to engage me in the consequent acceptance of Lacan's hypothesis of man's destructive search for a lost and unattainable paradise. I respect the real concern and appreciate the well-intended warning, but let me explain why I still include this Postscript. To the extent that I understand Lacan, I do not agree with the psychological and political implications he extrapolates from "desire is metonymy," and that is why I have made Jakobson and not Lacan the central authority in the chapter. But there seems no way one can investigate the current discussion of metonymy (particularly among French critics) without acknowledging Lacan. Accordingly, although Lacan cannot be ignored, he can be put in a postscript. The intricacies of the distinctions between the Lacanian and the Jakobsonian positions are too complicated for a "practical" study of Whitman's style, as is the intention here. For those interested in going beyond the simplified presentation here, I suggest Maria Ruegg's impressive analysis in *Glyph* (1979).

In the discussion of B5 on the dichotomy list, I promised to add this section to show how Lacan's hypothesis helps explain some of Whitman's poetic language. The lines I start with are from "Myself":

> All this I swallow, it tastes good, I like it well, it becomes mine,
> I am the man, I suffer'd, I was there. (ll. 831–32)

They are the concluding lines to a section of stanza 33 in which Whitman rewrites a newspaper account of the shipwreck of the *San Francisco* and the rescue of the survivors. The imaginative re-creation of the scene with its vivid details of the "lank loose-gown'd women" and "the silent old-faced infants and the lifted sick, and the sharp-lipp'd un-shaved men" (ll. 829–30) is justly famous, but for the moment I want to question the origin, the classification, and the efficacy of their conse-quent: "All this I swallow." Is it a metaphor? Clearly not, for there is nothing for the *tenor* and *vehicle* of any implied comparison to attach to. It is, in fact, metonymy, or so Lacan would name it, although it does not exactly fit the "cause for effect," "container for contained," or any of the other conventional rhetorical rules listed above.

Lacan contends that an infant in its earliest stage of life, pre-Oedipal, is guided by the causal chain "lack→need→instinct→desire." The *lack* is the just-born baby's incompleteness because of the separa-tion from the mother at birth; the *need* is the bodily hunger related to its metabolism; the *instinct* occurs as the need is answered by the mother (nursing) and received with erotic satisfaction (suckling); *desire* is the response to repeat the sequence when the need recurs. In Lacan's fa-mous phrase, "desire is metonymy," he means that we are led through a horizontal exploration (thus the grid at the beginning of this chapter) and primitive evaluation of experience by this initial four-part causal se-quence. Accordingly: "All the objects of the subject's desire will always be a reminder of some primal experience of pleasure, of a scene which was lived passively and will always refer back through associative links which become more complex and subtle with the passage of time, to that lived experience" (Lemaire, *Lacan*, 164). Lacan, with his singular view that "the unconscious is structured like a language," puts this four-part causal chain early enough in experience to be pre-Oedipal and claims that the formation of the unconscious follows the principle "de-sire is metonymy" in the same four-part sequence. He then goes on to explain how the Oedipal experience seems to modify (and complicate) the infant's psychological and language development, leading him to his other famous phrase, "the symptom is metaphor."

Our concern here, however, is with metonymy and Lacan's insis-tence that it shapes our language even as it forms our unconscious. It is not always clear just what section of Freud is being explained or cor-rected by this theory of Lacan's but it seems to be Freud's contention that one of the earliest of the "pregenital sexual organizations is the *oral*, or if one will the cannibalistic. Here the sexual activity is not yet separated from the taking of nourishment and the contrasts within it are not yet differentiated. The object of the one activity is also that of the other, the sexual aim then consists in the incorporation of the object into one's own body, the prototype of identification, which later plays such an important role" (1938: 597). Psychoanalyst Charles Brenner, speaking of introjection, adds that when the ego uses this identification defensively "it is often unconsciously modeled after the physical action of eating or swallowing. This means that the person using this mechanism of identification unconsciously imagines that he is eating or being eaten by the person with whom he becomes identified" (1974: 94).

Metonymy is a crucial element not only in the structuring of our own experience but also in our attempts to convey to others our response to that experience. As such it is part of our daily experience and conversation. We may be hungry for dinner, but also hungry for approval. We may eat honey because it is so sweet, but we may also say, "Honey, you're so sweet I could eat you up." At the everyday level of writing and conversation, metonymy is the most common sort of figurative language. Whitman's practice would be to use metonymy in a fashion that we easily recognize and readily interpret without having heard it so many times elsewhere that it no longer stirs the imagination.

Whitman acknowledged that a key word could only be used once, and he does use *swallow* only the one time, but *swallowing* once also. At line 800, somewhat as a preparation for the second occasion some thirty lines later, he says, "I fly those flights of a fluid and swallowing soul." In Lacan's interpretation of Freud, "swallowing soul" is figurative not in the metaphoric but in the metonymic sense (contiguous, associative, related), for his first (and *our* first) experiential knowledge was nursing. And the second use of *swallow*, as he recalls the rescue of the survivors of the shipwreck, is also far less metaphoric than metonymic: "All this I swallow, it tastes good, I like it well, it becomes mine, / I am the man, I suffer'd, I was there."

Presumably most of us add so many other ways of knowing, build up so many manners of receiving experience, that the primitive mode of knowing by incorporation, in Freud's sense, is more or less forgotten. But it is never completely superimposed or overlaid for Whitman, and never completely lost for the rest of us, for the lines still occasion the emotive response he intended. Whitman's word choice was not neurotically motivated at all, nor was he craftily selecting words and phrases to remind us of our infant satisfactions. Rather, he seems to be speaking from nearly subconscious yet deeply felt personal responses in his own self-education. There are many other words that function in this same metonymic fashion. These—devour, eat, feed, hunger, mouth, nourish, taste—are among the hundreds of such uses in *Leaves*:

> And who has made hymns fit for this earth? for I am mad with *devouring* ecstasy to make hymns for the whole earth. ("Excelsior," l. 12)

> From the hungry gnaw that *eats* me night and day, ("Pent-Up Aching Rivers," l. 11)

> You shall no longer take things at second hand or third hand, nor look through the eyes of the dead, nor *feed* on the spectres in books, ("Myself," l. 35)

> Not in many a *hungry* wish told to the skies only, ("Not Heaving from My Ribb'd Breast Only," l. 9)

> Open *mouth* of my soul uttering gladness, ("Song at Sunset," l. 5)

> Press close bare-bosom'd night—press close magnetic *nourishing* night, ("Myself," l. 435)

> I am willing to wait to be understood by the growth of the *taste* of myself. ("By Blue Ontario's Shore," l. 246)

It is difficult to read that final quotation with a straight face when we recall line 544 in "Myself," "I dote on myself, there is a lot of me and all so luscious."

But aside from such occasional overstatements of Whitman's, it is important to an understanding of his style to recognize this metonymic as distinct from metaphoric vocabulary. It is not that this figurative use of the digestive functions is unique with him, for examples are readily found in the Bible, in the classics, in Chaucer, Shakespeare, Milton, etc. Even in prose, in Francis Bacon's essay "Of Studies," for example, there is the well-known comment on reading: "Some books are to be tasted, others to be swallowed, and some few to be chewed and digested; that is, some books are to be read only in parts; others to be read, but not curiously; and some few to be read wholly and with diligence and attention." Bacon's explanation is not necessary, and certainly not memorable, but the aphoristic opening is a clear example of the device Whitman uses so frequently. But the distinctive feature of Whitman's use is that it frequently and regularly relates to himself or, strictly speaking, to the persona who professedly utters these assorted metonymies. Bacon's sentence tells us something valuable about reading but not much about Bacon himself; Walter Whitman's lines tell us not so much about the world as about Walt Whitman and how he sees that world.

Mark Van Doren once remarked that Whitman was one of the most "erethistic" poets of whom he knew, that is, excessively and inordinately responsive to sensory stimuli. Literally speaking, that could hardly be true, for *erethism* is a physiological term that would not fit any of the real experiences in Whitman's life. From all the biographical evidence (outside the poetry) he seems more phlegmatic than erethistic. But in the poetry, it is a different situation altogether. Not only *taste* but all the other senses, especially *touch* (with such correlates as ache, caress, feel, graze, itch, press, quiver, rub, soft, sting, throb), are of signal importance to Whitman's poetic vocabulary. But it has not been previously noticed that most of these uses are metonymic and are used by the persona to suggest a way of knowing and understanding and evaluating some level or aspect of experience. In the instance of the shipwreck, Whitman uses metonymy as a means of communicating the persona's full empathy with the survivors, their horrors and fears, their pain, the numbness or strain of the rescue; and he thus invites our own empathy by identification with the persona.

If we examine *Leaves* through Eby's *Concordance*, using the five senses (and all correlated terms) as guides, we will find hundreds of these metonymies, with those that are most striking and personal in their boldness in the early editions. There are, indeed, many more metonymies than there are for any other English or American poet of the nineteenth century for whom concordances are available, and not unsurprisingly there are fewer metaphors. Such a comparison raises a number of questions, only one of which needs mention here. Does Whitman use so many metonymies to make up for the absence of metaphors? The answer must be yes, although not at all at any conscious level on Whitman's part. Rather, Whitman uses metonymy because, as understood in Lacanian terms, in his psychological bent he was metonymic—or, better, because he created a persona who is such.

To Gay Wilson Allen I am indebted (as in so many other areas of Whitman scholarship) for my discovery of the only critic who had even a glimmer of the tremendous import of this situation. "Many years ago," Allen writes, "Count Mirsky identified 'metonymy' as Whitman's characteristic figure of speech" (1977: 281). The reference was to D. Mirsky's "Poet of American Democracy," originally published as the Introduction to Chukovsky's Russian translation of *Leaves* in 1935. The only English translation of part of Mirsky's essay is that in Allen (ed.), *Walt Whitman Abroad* (1955), where this crucial definition of the persona is made: "The 'Walt Whitman' whom Whitman 'celebrated' was not an individual endowed with a definite biography, a definite personality differentiating him from others; *he was a metonymical type, the average man, the average American, bringing out from the American masses the sum and substance of the contemporary scene*" (p. 177; my italics). Later in his essay, Mirsky details what, from his Marxian viewpoint, he considers Whitman's failure to comprehend the inherent contradictions in American bourgeois democracy. He thus provides another means by which the weakness of the late consciously prophetic poetry (seen at its weak-best in "Passage to India" and at its near-worst in "Song of the Universal") can be measured. But if Mirsky is right for the wrong reasons as far as the late poetry is concerned, it is the insight into the metonymic intent and mode of the early poems (up to and including *Drum Taps*) that makes his essay a pioneer study of metonymy in Whitman.

But to create the metonymic hero, the persona of "Song of Myself," the poet himself must at least grasp imaginatively or otherwise comprehend the role he imagines. And we must remember that Whitman lived in a "green" period that can never be found again. Yet if our first native poet did not fully intuit the danger of such a role as his in a much stronger state than anything America has even yet attained, other poets certainly did. It would be interesting to know whether another metonymic poet Osip Mandelstam knew this translation of *Leaves* and Mirsky's introductory essay, for much of the best work of that martyred poet relates to the inevitable trap and fate (both poetically and personally) of any current Whitman poet in an aggressively defensive totalitarian state. (See particularly Jane Gray Harris, Introduction to *Mandelstam*, 19–22.) One pertinent aspect of this crucial contemporary crisis of the poet in an enforced socialistic state, of which Mandelstam was a notable victim, is clearly explained by Czeslaw Milosz, *The Captive Mind*

(1955), especially in Chapter 3, "Ketman," with its disturbing analysis of totalitarian culture. But even there, there is a brilliant insight into the metonymic Whitman. The book is long out of print (although another edition will obviously follow the awarding of the Nobel Prize), so here is the passage in its entirety, for it is a remarkable explanation of the effect Whitman's metonymic passages (in this instance, about the city) can create:

> Never has there been a close study of how necessary to man are the experiences which we clumsily call aesthetic. Such experiences are associated with works of art for only an insignificant number of individuals. The majority find pleasure of an aesthetic nature in the mere fact of their existence within the stream of life. In the cities, the eye meets colorful store displays, the diversity of human types. Looking at passers-by, one can guess from their faces the story of their lives. This movement of the imagination when a man is walking through a crowd has an erotic tinge, his emotions are very close to physiological sensations. He rejoices in dresses, in the flash of lights; while, for instance, Parisian markets with their heaps of vegetables and flowers, fish of every shape and hue, fruits, sides of meat dripping with every shade of red offer delights, he need not go seeking them in Dutch or Impressionist painting. He hears snatches of arias, the throbbing of motors mixed with the warble of birds, called greetings, laughter. His nose is assailed by changing odors: coffee, gasoline, oranges, ozone, roasting nuts, perfumes.
>
> Those who have sung of the large cities have consecrated many pages to the description of this joyous immersion in the reservoir of universal life. The swimmer who trusts himself to the wave, and senses the immensity of the element that surrounds him lives through a like emotion. I am thinking of such great singers of the city as Balzac, Baudelaire, and Whitman. It would seem that the exciting and invigorating power of this participation in mass life springs from the feeling of *potentiality*, of constant unexpectedness, of a mystery one ever pursues. (pp. 61–62)

Milosz' grasp of Freud's "oceanic sense" as found in the mixed participation in and response to city living does capture, as none of us critics has before, the occasion of Whitman's metonymic writing and the rationale for its paratactic, nominal, and conjunctive style.

But biography (outside the poetry) has not prepared us for or provided us with any awareness of this side in Whitman's life. He even seems more phlegmatic about than responsive to the excitements of life around him. But there are occasional insights in the record if one is looking for them. If Whitman can write as he does, then we should pay more attention to comments like the following in order to find out what his life (as poet) was like. Here is a quotation from a long letter of Helen Price (a good, practical, commonsense person and longtime Whitman family friend) to Bucke. He quotes the letter in his *Walt Whitman*, the work Whitman helped with and wanted to be the official and authorized (if not the definitive) biography:

> One day I called on his mother in Brooklyn and found him there. When I was going home he said he would cross the ferry with me. On our journey we had to pass through one of the great markets of New York in order to reach the cars running to the upper part of the city. I was hurrying through, according to my usual custom, but he kept constantly stopping me to point out the beautiful combinations of colors at the butcher's stalls, and other stands; but above all the fish excited in him quite an enthusiasm. He made me admire their beautiful shapes and delicate tints, and I learned from him that day a lesson I have never forgotten. (p. 31)

But if Whitman is metonymic in person and style, is he then less a poet? Perhaps so. Certainly if metaphor is the hallmark of poetry, and if metaphors in *Leaves* are notable chiefly for their rarity, we must acknowledge the implications. Most important is to recognize the intensity with which metaphor is championed, by critics and by poets. Aristotle does group metonymy, synecdoche, metaphor, and simile together as figures of speech, but he also made it clear in *Poetics* that "the most important thing by far is to have command of metaphor; this alone cannot be imparted to another; it is the sign of genius." The primacy of metaphor, especially in the nineteenth century, is seen at its most extreme in the scorn of simile as too elementary, too plebian, leading to Stéphane Mallarmé's famous dictum, "I have expunged the word *like* from the dictionary." But why should Mallarmé or any other defender of the poetic faith at its most pure wish to reject *simile*, which is after all on the same side as metaphor in any opposition to metonymy? The reason is that even *simile*, with its *like* or *as*, acknowledges by those words that it is only a mental comparison, not the identification of true metaphor. And, as might be surmised, there are a great many more similes than metaphors in *Leaves*.

The apotheosis of metaphor in the nineteenth century and even today has been widely and variously discussed, but my concern here is with the stylistic implications. Compared with metonymy, metaphor is more original, more creative in the full sense, clearly more surprising (even to the extent of jolting the mind into a new awareness), and recognizably more powerful in its intellectual and emotional impact. Metonymy tends to remind us of what we already know; metaphor of what we do not know or had not thought of until that moment of apperception. Occasionally, metonymy may appear suddenly, and in our surprise we may react as to a metaphor (one's first reaction to "Camerado, this is no book, / Who touches this touches a man" would be of this sort), but that response comes from our surprise, not from the figure itself. To the extent, then, that newly created metaphor must dominate poetic expression, *Leaves* is not poetry of the first rank. Yet since no poetry can be 100 percent metaphor, and since there is no other available name for what Whitman's writing represents, perhaps we can say he is not a great metaphoric poet but is the best metonymic poet in the business.

ᐬ VI ᐬ

THE JOURNALISTIC BACKGROUND

Emerson once cleverly described *Leaves of Grass* as a "mixture of the New York *Herald* and the *Bhagavad-Gita*," perhaps meaning to suggest that behind the flamboyant style (reminiscent of James Gordon Bennett's popular paper) of the first two editions one might find the profound speculation on the here and hereafter (reminiscent of the Hindu classic). One may doubt the *Bhagavad-Gita* part, but on the *Herald* reference (whether slighting or not) Emerson was certainly correct. It was not the only such reference, for Charles Eliot Norton and Edward Everett Hale had both briefly alluded to the newspaper language of the first edition. Indeed, of the early reviews, the only ones that seem consciously to avoid talking about Whitman's journalistic background are by that anonymous critic who wrote the poetry.

In subsequent generations of Whitman criticism, Emerson's bright remark has often been quoted, chiefly to show that our wisest American was not taken in quite as much as his first famous letter might imply. But no one has seriously examined *Leaves* to show the New York *Herald* features Emerson recognized. There has been considerable discussion of Whitman's journalism, but chiefly for the ideas (political, social, and literary) his editorials, features, and reviews reveal: for its content, not its style; for what he said, not for how he said it. Yet before *Leaves*, Whitman's first and only training in language use was as a journalist. This chapter will explore some of the implications of Emerson's insight.

It was mentioned earlier that the motive, the initial impulse, to create that new style of language for the first edition was Whitman's intense desire "to go about the country spouting my pieces, proclaiming my faith." But whether he was actually going to say these pieces, or whether he was only using the stance of the prophet, the wander-teacher, he still had to use the language he knew. It was not the language of his family, as any examination of the family correspondence would make obvious; or that of the Bible, which he seems to have venerated or even studied only in old age, when he touted the Bible to pick up a little credit for *Leaves* by a sort of cultural back-formation; or that from any language study of printed versions of speeches he had heard and admired (Elias Hicks, for instance, or Emerson or Henry Ward Beecher).

Rather, he used the language of the profession he had trained himself for, journalism. Our concern here is not with words alone, although like any journalist he used the dictionaries of his time (Webster and Worcester), but the way words were joined and ordered. If there truly was any "long foreground" for *Leaves*, as Emerson surmised there must have been, it was Whitman's long engagement with newspaper and magazine writing. That long foreground is also to be found in such different Americans as Benjamin Franklin, Orestes Brownson, Howells, and Clemens; Whitman was the only one for whom it led to the making of a new sort of poetry. He did so by a shrewd blend of platform speaking and journalistic prose, and what held them together was his new use of the old rhetorical rules.

A useful pragmatic term that describes the writing in the 1855 Preface and the poems it introduces is *persuasive functional style*, a term explained by Alexandr Stich, a Czech critic. His article in the *Journal of Literary Semantics* (1973), attempts to redefine and rename the Czech term *publicistic style*. That term had been regularly used by the famous Prague school to apply to a higher artistic form of journalism-essay as practiced by such nineteenth-century figures as Heinrich Heine, Aleksandr Herzen, George Sand, Victor Hugo, and by such poets as Pierre Jean de Béranger, Nikolai Nekrasov, Heine, William Morris, Vladimir Mayakovsky. Stich reports that he had examined these writers to determine the stylistic features they had in common and found a style that is "relatively stable" with its own "type of stylistic organization . . . generally referred to as hortatory or persuasive" (p. 67).

Such high-level journalism will, of course, influence the reader by

LANGUAGE AND STYLE IN *Leaves of Grass*

its subject matter, but Stich explains that "the influencing is due not only to the context of the text but to the linguistic make-up as well" (p. 67). And it is that, the linguistic makeup, which is the concern here. The "semantic structure characteristic" of journalism depends on the linguistic stratagems necessary to establish "(1) direct contact between author and audience, (2) convey appeal to the addressee . . . (3) evaluate the facts communicated" (p. 71). Stich then demonstrates their use in a speech of E. M. Forster, found in *Two Cheers for Democracy* (1951), for which he italicizes "all the linguistic devices that give this text its persuasive background" (p. 76). Rather than follow him through a text of remote interest to Whitman scholars, let me pick out the pertinent stylistic features, paraphrase Stich's reasoning by selective quotation, and make the application to "Myself" (using the final version unless otherwise noted).

Presentation of information may "highlight the author of the utterance (the creator of the evaluation) and challenge the addressee to adopt his own attitude" (p. 72). Whitman has many such challenges, especially near the end of the poem when he is directly speaking to the audience:

> I teach straying from me, yet who can stray from me?
> I follow you whoever you are from the present hour,
> My words itch at your ears till you understand them. (ll. 1244–46)

or

> And I say to mankind, Be not curious about God,
> For I who am curious about each am not curious about God,
> (No array of terms can say how much I am at peace about God and about death.) (ll. 1278–80)

In certain "semantic features of grammatical devices" in journalism, there may be some variation: for instance, the "use of person in verbs and pronouns may or may not play a predominant role" (p. 73). There is no question that the first person is predominant in "Myself":

> I know I am august,
> I do not trouble my spirit to vindicate itself or be understood,
> I see that the elementary laws never apologize,
> I reckon I behave no prouder than the level I plant my house by after all.
> (ll. 409–412)

Indeed, the self-assertiveness is strong enough to offend some, perhaps because he waited until so late in the poem to explain specifically that "(It is you talking just as much as myself, I act as the tongue of you, / Tied in your mouth, in mine it begins to be loosen'd)" (ll. 1248–49).

Stich goes on to point out journalistic uses of *we*, *you* (singular and plural), and *they*, matters previously discussed in Chapter III. But it is important to note that Whitman, even as a journalist, recognized that some devices would need to be modified for the prophetic poetry he wished to utter. An early note to himself is in the Feinberg Collection (now at the Library of Congress): "In lectures the sense of directly addressing people—you a live audience of men and women—as distinct from a tame literary statement to be read." A second note is similar: "Lectures. Ego-Style. First-person-style. Style of composition an animated ego-style—'I do not think'—'I perceive'—or something involving self-esteem, decision, authority—as opposed to the current *third-person-style*, essayism, didactic, removed from animation, stating general truths in a didactic well-smoothed—" (*NF*: 131–32). He stopped there in mid-sentence, having written enough to remind himself of what he was up to. Whitman's perception that there was a midway point between journalism and oratory, on which a new kind of prophetic poetry might be based, was exactly right. As editor, for instance, he had used the editorial *we* (which Stich, following the Continental tradition, calls "pluralis modestiae") for the same reason that editors have always used that pronoun, to remove the ego and to give the impression of editorial staff consensus. But if you want to destroy a most characteristic element in Whitman's style, just put in *we* instead of *I* and see what happens:

> We celebrate ourselves, and sing ourselves,
> And what we assume you shall assume,

is truly to assume nonsense.

An additional feature of journalism is that it "may create persuasive neologisms," which are "born not only from a need to designate new objects, relationships, or actions; they are also essential to affix new emotional and evaluative attitudes to denotata for which appellatives already exist" (p. 73). This is perhaps an excessively formal definition for what we recognize in *Leaves* in practice as: en masse, ensemble, camerado, adhesiveness, libertad, eleves, imperturbe, even such special use of idiomatic expressions as Open Road or So Long. Further on, Stich points out: "Popular terms of speech attest to the author's linguistic ties with broad sections of the public, while more esoteric and especially foreign quotations bring the author closer to a more erudite social stratum" (p. 74). It would also include Whitman's use of slang, colloquial phrasing, or made-up or borrowed expressions not found in the poetry of his day. We must always remember that these words were not used to make his poetry compatible with working-class taste. Rather, he was writing for the educated, if somewhat disaffected, middle-class reader, for whom the somewhat outré language would demonstrate the speaker's engagement with "the people." In "Myself" we find: pert, woolly-pates, darkey, tipsy, sponger, snivel, a suck and a sell, sticks, cock, barleycorn, carlacue, kelson, reckon, tenoned, ducking, about enough, cushion me soft, foofoos, roughs, dung, coulter, tilth, dote, stoop, heave'e'yo, whirr, love-grip, dab, it *sails* me, fakes, omnific, chef-d'oevre, hinge, stucco'd, evince, amies, speed, scalloped scum, hummer, buzzer, hindways, pic-nics, jigs, base-ball, he-festivals, sqush, hot (in the sense of angry), plummets, knuckled tight, flags (weary), ambulanza, jetblack sunrise, spirting, gums, cuffed, bask, topknot, scarfed, grit, drudge, privies, babes, middling, and so on, up to "yawp" in the last section. These should be separated from those neologisms, if that is what they are, of the late poems, when Whitman tried to give certain words "officially poetic" meaning by adding fake archaic endings: ancientest, originatress, pasturages, matest, masterest, doest, goest, hadst, sat'st, etc. There are over a hundred of these, none of them manifesting any neologistic talent or nerve. In the early poems he often showed more nerve than talent in some of his French borrowings, the made-up words (as admirant, diminute, philosophs), the slang; even so, no important section or passage is seriously damaged by their use, chiefly because the key passages, the crucial lines, are always in straight idiomatic English of serious intent. Only in the late poetry does the inflated language so dominate what should be significant passages that one cannot but wonder if it is a cover for insufficient poetic grasp of his subject.

Stich continues: "Another [journalistic] characteristic is that it formulates evaluative attitudes to denotata in its own textual realizations." He points out that philosophical, social, and cultural language is neutral ("primarily unmarked for emotional and evaluative connotation") in technical style, but in journalism, "much of this technology acquires emotional and evaluative overtones, which are deliberately and often systematically sought after" (p. 73). He makes reference to Harold Lasswell's well-known *Language of Politics*, and it is, in fact, surprising that Whitman does use many of the key terms listed in that study: the Revolution, Declaration, Constitution, Washington; the many abstractions, equality, democracy, freedom; favorable group terms, the West, Alamo, Pioneers, the army, farmers, workmen. More interesting are the many scenes in "Song of Myself" which would by their subject matter alone occasion an initial favorable response: the harvest (ll. 160–67), the marriage of the trapper (ll. 178–82), the runaway slave (ll. 183–92), the rescue of the shipwrecked passengers (ll. 818–27), the saving of "the mashed fireman" (ll. 843–50), the Goliad massacre (ll. 864–89), John Paul Jones's famous victory (ll. 890–932). In the opposite sense (but still evaluative), when he presents in the first edition a thirty-line catalog in which he appraises all previous religions (ll. 1020–1049), he begins with a clear evaluative comment: "Outbidding at the start the old cautious hucksters, / The most they offer for mankind and eternity less than a spirt of my own seminal wet" (ll. 1021–1022). In the Blue Book and thereafter in the general so-called refinement of his late career, he dropped the second line but left in the earlier "hucksters," for clearly some such orientation was essential to the passage.

Developing the viewpoint illustrated above, Stich points out that journalism "may also be viewed as an independent stylistic phenomenon from the point of view of the general structure of the text. . . . Seldom does an author addressing a public audience confine himself to . . . a mere linear sequence of items whose interdependence remains obscure until placed in a definite context" (p. 74). This is the clue to the well-known "hop, skip, and a jump" organization of "Myself" (and most of the other platform poems). "Often whole sequences of lexical units—sequences that exist as ready-made complex units prior to the actual act of communication—are incorporated into the text," as, for example, all the little scenes noted just above. Again, journalistic "texts often incorporate texts from outside sources without separating them from the author's text proper" (p. 74). Thus, the saving of the shipwrecked passengers (ll. 818–27) was drawn from the New York newspaper account, the marriage of the trapper (ll. 178–82) was a verbal account of Alfred Joseph Miller's painting *The Trapper's Bride*, the naval battle of the *Bonhomme Richard* and the *Serapis* was perhaps family legend but was certainly indebted to the written account (Blodgett and Bradley edition, [1965], 66n., 36n., 69n.). But these are incorporated into the long poem, as are the other such units, whether their origin is discovered or not; admittedly it is sometimes difficult to ignore altogether the dread cry of "plagiarism" when the borrowed item is so central, as in "To the Man-of-War Bird," but on this as on so many Whitman problems Gay Wilson Allen is our wisest guide in his two articles on Whitman and Jules Michelet.

A last point Stich makes he draws from Forster's *Two Cheers*: "Our text also contains clearly appellative elements—if not direct, undisguised form (the imperative, for example), then indirectly. To this end it uses modal devices ('to have to,' 'must not') and assertory statements ('most of us will agree,' 'we have faith')" (p. 77). This feature is also found in "Myself," from the directive of line 2, "you shall assume," through the question of line 24, "Have you felt so proud to get at the meanings of poems?," to the invitation and promise of the next line, "Stop this day and night with me and you shall possess the origin of all poems," to the final encouragement and commitment:

> Failing to fetch me at first keep encouraged,
> Missing me one place search another,
> I stop somewhere waiting for you. (ll. 1334–36)

There are also what Stich calls "assertory statements" throughout "Myself," many of them indicated by classification in the speech-act chapter above, but few of them are as mild and tentative as those of Forster noted in Stich's quotation. There are also many modals, although on these one must be careful to distinguish those directed to "you," the audience and/or reader, from those that refer to the subject of the particular sentence. For instance, the *must* in these two lines "I believe in you my soul, the other I am must not abase itself to you, / And you must not be abased to the other" (ll. 82–83) is not specifically a persuasive construction, for it is not directed to the reader except in the larger sense in which the whole poem is for the reader. Only near the end of the poem will the modal be used in the sense that Stich means, "Not I, not any one else can travel that road for you, / You *must* travel it for your-self" (ll. 1210–11) and "You are also asking me questions, and I hear you, / I answer that I cannot answer, you *must* find out for yourself" (ll. 1223–24; my italics). Perhaps, here, it is appropriate to remind ourselves that "persuasive functional style" is not the language of the drill sergeant on the parade ground. Although in "Myself" there is near-continual maneuvering in scene and style to gain and maintain rapport with the audience, it is not until the last sections (when pre-sumably the rapport has been built and sustained) that directives of the *must* sort appear. Behind the flamboyant language and actions of the persona throughout the poem, the poet manages the persona carefully, even discreetly, so as not to endanger his rapport by leaning on the au-dience too soon.

Stich finishes his article with comments on particular devices that he points out in the Forster example, few of which pertain to *Leaves*. But let me stop to make a point here about "persuasive functional style" and to use this paragraph as a transition to a more detailed analysis of journalistic and promotional prose. Stich's refinement of the Czech critical term *publicistic style* provides a space, an area, in the spectrum from prose to poetry, or, better, from technical style to artistic style, in which to place Whitman's language experiment. It would be silly to claim there was no persuasive function in Carlyle, Emerson, or *Walden*, but of course that is prose not poetry. But what needs to be pointed out is that *Leaves* originated as a specimen of "publicistic style," rooted in oratory and journalism, but presented in a form that lifted it above any parallel journalistic venture. Its reputation is now such that we are no longer forced to defend its right to be treated as literature, as po-etry, but we should explain what kind of poetry it is. At that level, valu-able as Stich's presentation is, we are still short of defining, of ex-plaining, the organization of language, the way words are used, that separates Whitman's writing (in the first three editions) from that of his contemporaries.

JOURNALISTIC STYLE AND SYNTAX

What is striking is the bafflement of early critics to find a name, a label, a category for *Leaves*. Hortatory poetry, to use Jakobson's term, has a programmatic tone and journalistic style that Jakobson himself does not discuss. But something of what needs to be done for Whitman has been done in two studies of two very different twentieth-century poets: Christine Brooke-Rose for Ezra Pound's Usura Canto (canto 45), and Marie Borroff's two chapters on Marianne Moore in *Language and the Poet*. Brooke-Rose finds the programmatic tone (the term is mine, not hers) in the canto she dissects, the indictment of usury. She accepts the "rhetorical litany" as the overt form of the canto, but finds that in practice it turns out to be "an anti-litany, on a certain level, an exorcism" (1976: 16). She also recognizes similarities to Aristotle's epideictic style and to Emile Benveniste's *discours* (pp. 20, 21). But most notable is her full and elaborate analysis of the language of the canto, with complete attention to its rhetorical, semantic, phonic, and prosodic interplay. In spite of the obvious differences between the Usura Canto and any of Whitman's poems, there is a didactic sameness, with many common rhetorical figures. The closest approximation in Whitman would be the caustic "Respondez!," a very good poem of its sort which he kept in print for twenty-five years and then, truly unfortunately, dropped as the final version of his vision of himself, and the poetry he wanted to be known for, changed.

Borroff's remarkable book compares and contrasts the poetry of Robert Frost, Wallace Stevens, and Marianne Moore, through one of the more notable recent examinations of poetic language. Her analysis of the artful simplicity of Frost and range of diction in Stevens has been helpful, but I am especially indebted to her discussion of Moore, as the remainder of this chapter will make obvious. Chapter 5 of *Language and the Poet*, entitled "Marianne Moore's Promotional Prose: The Uses of Syntax," is of particular value here for two different though related reasons. First is her report and comparison of the Finite Verb Elements and the Romance-Latin vocabulary derivation of the three poets, Frost, Stevens, Moore. The second is her careful and detailed analysis of certain characteristics of journalistic, advertising, and promotional prose which she found as a feature of Moore's poetic style. Both of these can be extremely valuable in dealing with Whitman, though in a fashion obviously unintended by the critic. Although she uses the tabulations of Finite Verb Elements and Romance-Latin words as part of her comparison of those three poets, her distinction between and contrast of these two stylistic hallmarks can serve to demonstrate the difference in poetic style between Whitman's early (1855–1860, the first three editions) and late (1865–1881) work.

For each of the three poets, Borroff examines a large selection of poems and, for comparative purposes, presents in the Appendix tables enumerating the Finite Verb Element count and the Romance-Latin origins. Those tables provided the basis for such a valuable comparative analysis that I compiled a representative number of words from the early and the late poems in *Leaves* and made a similar count (using Ernest Klein's *Comprehensive Etymological Dictionary of the English Language*) to see whether a comparison would reveal any notable difference. We are all aware, impressionistically at least, of the difference between Frost's poetic style and that of Stevens, and of Moore's style as distinct from the other two, but it is almost impossible to devise a measure as clear, direct, and decisive as that which Borroff provides. Similarly we are all aware of the change in Whitman's style after the Civil War, but few of us have an objective standard to measure how complete that change was.

But before presenting the results of my own investigation, let me explain what the two headings, Finite Verb Elements and Romance-Latin origins, mean and their relation to each other in language usage. I shall paraphrase Borroff's explanation, acknowledging that her searching investigation uses these and other analytic techniques in a far more profound and discriminating analysis than anything attempted here.

In the early chapters of her study, particularly in Chapter 2 (1979: 23–41) and in the specific and detailed notes to that chapter (pp. 159–65), she provides the critical apparatus for examining the range of diction in English and American poetry. The distinctions made among the levels of diction are "distinctively formal," in Greek, Latin, and Romance-language borrowings and in various archaisms; "common," words of native (Teutonic) origin; and "distinctively colloquial." These three levels apply to all English use, not just poetry, but analysis of the work of Frost, Stevens, and Moore may reveal comparative differences in the language they employ. Such analysis would show that a high Romance-Latin count and use of archaic words and forms relate to the high formal tradition in English (and American) poetry.

Once a style is achieved or established, the poet normally stays with it (as happens with the three she analyzes), although variations will occur depending on the subject or mood of some particular poem. "But subject matter aside, the proportions of the parts of speech can be seen to vary in accordance with the level of formality, in accordance with genre at the formal level, and, within this double constraint, *in accordance with the imaginative bias of the individual speaker or writer*" (p. 92). I italicize the final phrase of Borroff's statement, for I believe my tabulation will show that whatever "imaginative bias" dominated Whitman's style for the first three editions, a very different (indeed, radically different) bias is exemplified in the poetry thereafter.

The tables on Romance-Latin origins must, however, be seen in relation to the other, contrasting tables on Finite Verb Elements (tables are in the Appendix). The Finite Verb Element "(the part of the verb having person, number, tense, and mood) . . . provides the single best index of syntactic elaboration" and "is therefore the single most significant statistical variable in comparative studies of style" (pp. 91, 92). Valuable as the count may be when considered alone, it is even more revealing when seen in combination. It is, indeed, this double approach that is critically most important. In a significant statement, she explains this major clue to stylistic analysis: "Statistically, this tendency manifests itself in an inverse correlation which seems to hold true for English texts across the board: the higher the consecutive Romance-Latinate percentiles, the lower the consecutive percentiles of finite verbs" (p. 93).

Why this should be cannot be answered simply, but essentially it does relate to the state of mind of the poet (or any speaker or writer), his attitude to life and the world around him, the workings of his imagination. But true as that statement may be, it is too unspecific to mean very much. What we need is a tie-in to the use of language. Borroff makes this specific by "an examination of the expressive value of particular words," invoking "the important grammatical distinction between 'stative' and 'dynamic'" (p. 96). She analyzes this distinction for verbs, nouns, adjectives, and adverbs, but I will summarize what she says about verbs, for the tables on Finite Verb Elements focus on them. Basically any word may be stative or dynamic, depending on whether the concept it signifies is "stable or changing, permanent or temporary, absolute or variable" (p. 96). For instance, there is the well-known catalog in stanza 15 of "Song of Myself":

The pure contralto sings in the organ loft,
The carpenter dresses his plank, the tongue of his foreplane
    whistles its wild ascending lisp,
The married and unmarried children ride home to their Thanksgiving
    dinner, (ll. 264–66)

The catalog continues with over fifty more items, all presented in this same simple present. But what would happen if these and the rest of the catalog were changed to the progressive?

> The pure contralto is singing in the organ loft,
> The carpenter is dressing his plank . . .

Note how the situation has been altered from a timeless present freed of change (the pure contralto's singing, as Whitman wrote it, is affirmed as if forever; it is constant, never changing) to a description of something that is happening in a historical present, taking place at that time, and inevitably then to change, to cease. The catalog as found in the first edition uses stative verbs. When we change the verb to the progressive we make the situation dynamic and so change the meaning of the lines. "When language attempts to hold its subject matter constant, its grammar inevitably takes on stative characteristics. We can expect such language to contain few finite verbs; of the verbs it does contain, many, if not most, will be stative" (p. 97).

Lynen, in his *Design of the Present*, comes at this point in a different way:

> This immediacy depends on the illusion that the experience is now transpiring, that the words are addressed directly to the reader, and that the things and events of 1860 [1855] are immediately before the reader's eyes. To achieve this effect, the poem's natural progression must be arrested or concealed so that the present will seem to remain the same throughout. If the passage of time is at all noticeable, the whole character of the poem changes. The poet and his day slide into the past, for the things he names are not identical with the things the reader is now perceiving. (pp. 285–86)

This special concern of Whitman's of speaking from and maintaining the present is a feature of the speech-act organization of many of the early poems. Lynen is not concerned with speech acts, but he sees clearly that the insistence on the present is essential to the poetic illusion Whitman creates. He does this, Lynen contends, by concealing the forward movement of literary time, so that it might appear that the present at every point in the poem is the same present. But in fact time does pass in the poem, and there is no way of stopping it. Not only do words and statements follow chronologically, but the reader too must move forward. . . . To make the whole poem seem to be but one present moment is therefore to create a fiction—an illusion, if you will. And despite Whitman's intention to present things themselves, rather than images and interpretations, it is far less unreasonable to recognize his fiction-making than to suppose that there can be poetry without illusion. (p. 290)

This stative aspect of the timeless present has also been discussed in a different way, in connection with Wright's "lyric present," but here it is necessary to understand not *how* but *why* it is so predominant in Whitman's early poetry. The temptation is to think of Whitman and his poetry as dynamic, as attuned to the driving energy of an always growing, expanding, changing America. Indeed, nine out of ten readers of *Leaves*, if asked to pick the more appropriate of the two words (*static* vs. *dynamic*) would surely pick *dynamic*. Whitman does acknowledge growth, of course, indeed welcomes it, but always in terms of his faith in the permanence of democratic ideals, in the Revolution, in the moral power of liberty, in the large sanity of the people, which is seen all through the early poetry and is essential to his prophetic utterance. If he scolds the people, as he sometimes does, it is to remind them of their inherited democratic creed. A good example is the poem originally called "Poem of Remembrances for a Girl or Boy of These States," which underwent various deletions before it was finally dropped in 1881. It is an effective presentation of Whitman's democratic faith and fortunately is now available in Blodgett and Bradley (1965: 588–90), where one may note the predominance of stative verbs, without which, indeed, there could be no poem. Admittedly the poem is programmatic, but why Whitman would drop it and keep "Song of the Exposition" or "Song of the Universal" is difficult to understand.

Stative verbs are not only the *sings*, *dresses*, *whistles*, *ride* of the catalog. Indeed many are "forms of *to be*, which can link any subject with any attribute in logical definition or factual statement," sometimes "with obtrusive frequency" (p. 97). And so these characteristic lines in "Myself" (again, notice the paralleling in the first two lines):

> And I know that the hand of God *is* the elderhand of my own,
> And I know that the spirit of God *is* the eldest brother of my own,

And that all the men ever born *are* also my brothers....and the women my
  sisters and lovers,
And that a kelson of creation *is* love; (1855 ed., ll. 83–85; my italics here
  and below)

or

I believe a leaf of grass *is* no less than the journeywork of the stars,
And the pismire *is* equally perfect, and a grain of sand, and the egg of the
  wren, (ll. 663–64)

And a mouse *is* miracle enough to stagger sextillions of infidels. (l. 669)

Less frequent but quite typical is "the use of *have* as a stative verb
meaning 'to be endowed with, to be characterized by having'" (p. 98).
One example will suffice: "Do you guess I *have* some intricate purpose? / Well I *have*....for the April rain *has*, and the mica on the side of
a rock *has*" (1855 ed., ll. 381–82). Related to the stative verbs used in
description of characteristic behavior are the "two modal auxiliaries,
can (signifying an innate capacity) and *will* (signifying habitual and
hence predictable action)" (p. 98), both of which are used often in
"Myself" and elsewhere: "I *can* cheerfully take it now, or with equal
cheerfulness I *can* wait" (l. 418). They are also used with the negative
for emphasis, "No guard *can* shut me off, no law prevent me" (l. 803),
or as applied to nature, "There is no stoppage, and never *can* be stoppage" (l. 1190). Many of the uses of *will*, along with *shall*, relate primarily to the future, but the stative uses are found also. In relation to
himself, when the persona says, "I will not have a single person slighted
or left away" (l. 374), he is talking not about some future action but
about his insistence in the practice of democracy. In "To Think of
Time" there is a line which, when we mentally insert the proper punctuation, presents in practice this stative meaning:

What will be will be well, for what is is well, (l. 64)

Borroff goes beyond the verb in her treatment of the stative, for, as
she makes clear, "it is the noun, as signifier of entities, that is most in-
trinsically stative" (p. 97). Here is a statement quoted in full, not because of any intended comparison of Moore's poetry with *Leaves of
Grass*, but only because what Borroff finds in Moore can be used for
Whitman, different as their poetry is. "In view of the stative character of
Moore's grammar, strikingly apparent in her treatment of the finite

verb, we ought not to be surprised by the importance and dramatic saliency in her language of the most stative of the parts of speech, the noun. Squadrons of nouns in series, virtually devoid of modification, march through *The Complete Poems*" (p. 99). They do not march right through *Leaves* because Whitman mixed up the chronological sequence in terms of some other arrangement, of which Crawley has the most cogent explanation. But if *Leaves* were a chronological arrangement, the march would have gone through the first three editions, faltered in 1865, and slowed to a walk thereafter. The most notable example of a squadron of nouns is the catalog-conclusion to "I Sing the Body Electric," added in 1856 and kept pretty much the same thereafter. It has always seemed a bit histrionic, something of a flourish to back up his boast to Emerson in the epilogue of that volume. Be that as it may, the catalog, much of which is an anatomical listing of parts of the body, is not alone in the novelty of providing a plain list of names, for there was an even longer catalog of trades in "Occupations." Still, the preponderance of nouns in *Leaves* has been long recognized, and it is mentioned here again only because, in the new context of Whitman's journalism and the stative concept of his world view, the noun dominance and the catalog take on a much more profound stylistic significance.

But our focus here is on the stative verbs (not the nouns) because they relate to the tabulation of Finite Verb Elements. Let me explain how those tables in the Appendix have been organized. In order to give a fair representation of the poem, and in consideration of the fact that the beginning and the end of some poems are not always representative of the whole poem (for instance, the opening of "Proto-Leaf," later called "Starting from Paumanok," begins with a series of premodifiers, 136 words in all, with only one Finite Verb Element), I have used the first and last 200 words, along with 200 words near the middle of the poem. For "Myself," the first poem on the list, the table reads this way: there were 22 Finite Verb Elements in the first 200 words, 26 in the 200 words near the middle, 29 in the final 200 words. The total of 77 was then divided by the number of words in the sample to give a percentage of 12.8. Perhaps some younger scholar with computer training will do the whole of *Leaves* (with the Romance-Latin count also) to refine my tabulation and help us all in making accurate judgments on our first truly native poet.

Some oddities in the tables can be explained. In "Out of the Cradle Endlessly Rocking" there is a long series of predominantly prepositional phrases before the "I" of the poem (the persona) announces himself. This series of premodifiers, as in "Starting from Paumanok," occasions an odd-looking tally for that particular word block, but the unusual structure of many openings and closings in *Leaves* is intentional, and not to consider them would be to give a false picture. Also included is a selection of lines from Calamus of 1860, a cluster of short poems and an intentional departure from the pattern of the two earlier editions. To parallel this feature for the late poetry, there is a similar sampling from Drum-Taps. To adjust my counting to the others, four poems were tabulated at the beginning, at the middle, and at the end of each group, and Finite Verb Elements in the first or last fifty words were counted. For the poems after 1860, there was another problem, in that there were not enough longer poems to match those of earlier editions. Accordingly, for the years after 1873 ("Song of the Redwood Tree" was the last poem over 600 lines) complete poems were used. I selected those best known, up to the appropriate number to balance the early poems. Of these complete poems checked, the only surprise was the high number of Finite Verb Elements in "Prayer of Columbus." But when we remember that the poem is something of a dramatic monologue, the count is not so surprising (for traditionally, Finite Verb Elements are always dominant in conversation or speaking). Another oddity is their absence in "The Dalliance of Eagles." It is one of the most effective of the late poems, and it is something of a surprise to realize that it is not a complete sentence.

Here is a summary of the tables given in the Appendix:

	Early Poetry (1855–1860)	Late Poetry (After 1865)
Finite Verb Elements	12.0% (1,083 uses in 9,000 ll.)	5.5% (496 uses in 9,000 ll.)
Romance-Latin Words	12.6% (1,138 words in 9,000 ll.)	21.5% (1,935 words in 9,000 ll.)

Now there is no objective standard, no ideal proportion of Finite Verb Elements to Romance-Latin vocabulary. Rather, that proportion grows out of and is dependent on the poet's personality, his subject, and his style. Nevertheless, a proportion once established is one of the hall-marks by which we distinguish a poet's work. Admitting some variation from poem to poem, we are still able, by representative sampling, to characterize a poet's language, for the proportion remains relatively constant. That is true for *Leaves* through the first three editions. Note that through 1860 the Finite Verb Elements maintain the same proportion as do the number of words of Romance-Latin origin. This is a key characteristic of Whitman's style, and, remember, style is the man. But then, from 1865 on, the poetic language takes on an altogether different character, with less than half as many Finite Verb Elements and almost twice as many words of Romance-Latin origin.

This change in Whitman's diction, in his poetic language, is truly astounding. There is no way here of justifying a claim that no other major English or American has so completely reversed himself or, more specifically, has dropped an earlier style to replace it with another completely different style. But I cannot believe that a change comparable to that in Whitman's diction can ever be found. We have seen some of the reasons, the disappearance of the speech act, the shift away from the strong metonymic style with its catalogs and realistic treatment of detail, the cessation of the assertive antithetical style with its many negatives. These might have much to do with the early emphasis on common (sometimes colloquial) language of our Anglo-Saxon inheritance, but there should also be something in their place.

The Romance-Latin tabulation used the same word blocks as the Finite Verb Elements count. However, one feature of the late poetry, which the tables do not show, is the increasing use of archaism, archaic forms, and false archaisms that in many of the late poems parallel the increasing use of words of Romance-Latin etymology. Together they seem to be used to disguise his fading poetic powers, yet they do seem to have been accepted without murmur by his growing band of disciples. The real question is whether this was a conscious cover-up or whether he really believed some of those late efforts were significant poetry. Sometimes the only way to resolve a query of this sort is to force an answer from the evidence. Let me be specific. Here are the opening lines from section 14 of "Myself":

> The wild gander leads his flock through the cool night,
> Ya-honk! he says, and *sounds* it down to me like an *invitation*;

THE JOURNALISTIC BACKGROUND

> The *pert* may *suppose* it meaningless, but I listen *closer*,
> I find its *purpose* and *place* up there toward the wintry sky.

In these forty-four words from the 1860 edition there are six Finite Verb Elements (leads, says, sounds, may, listen, find) and seven that can be considered of Romance-Latin derivation (italicized). Two words, *sounds* as a verb and *pert* as a noun, are remotely of Romance-Latin origin and so are here listed, even though they seem to be taken from American colloquial language. So, six divided by forty-four is 13.6 percent for Finite Verb Elements, and seven divided by forty-four is 15.9 percent for the Romance-Latin tabulation, only slightly above the average for each of the early editions.

There is no gander in the late poetry but there is a trumpeter swan. The opening lines of "The Mystic Trumpeter" are the nearest parallel in the late poetry. It takes twice as many lines to cover the parallel (but by no means identical) thought:

> Hark, some wild *trumpeter*, some *strange musician*,
> Hovering *unseen* in *air*, *vibrates capricious tunes* to-night.

> I hear thee *trumpeter*, listening *alert* I *catch* thy *notes*,
> Now pouring, whirling like a *tempest* round me,
> Now low, *subdued*, now in the *distance* lost.

> Come nearer bodiless one, haply in thee *resounds*
> Some dead *composer*, haply thy *pensive* life
> Was fill'd with *aspirations* high, *unform'd ideals*,

Here there are seven Finite Verb Elements (Hark, vibrates, hear, catch, come, resounds, was), but in a sixty-three-word passage, and there are now twenty-one words of Romance-Latin origin (and italicized here, also). A sensitive reader of this chapter in its early stages remarked, "How beautifully the difference between *sounds* and *resounds* epitomizes the difference between the two poems!" The percentages are, then, 11.1 percent for the Finite Verb Elements and a startling 33.3 percent for the Romance-Latin tabulation.

If the early style is a Whitman contribution to the world's poetry, these lines are a near-travesty. *Hark!* Who ever says or writes *hark*? We say *listen*, but for Whitman at this stage in his career *listen* was apparently too common a word. Indeed, for other poems he even went back to change "listen to "list"! And what was Whitman listening to? Earlier he tells us "Ya-honk!" But the trumpeter swan cries no ya-honk or any comparable onomatopoeic sound, rather the "strange musician . . . Hovering unseen . . . vibrates capricious tunes to-night." There is none of the direct concrete language of the early style, but only abstract description, such as "mystic" (meaning what?) in the title. What is added by calling the musician in the first line "strange"? A "hovering" swan is not only "unseen" but quite impossible, for a swan is much too heavy to stay aloft without steady and strong beating of the wings to keep it moving. Why is "vibrates" chosen instead of *sings* or *cries*, or even better, *hoots* or *honks*, which is what the trumpeter swan does? Not only does the trumpeter's honk not *vibrate*, it also follows the swan's instinctive nature (as Whitman tells us the gander does), so is certainly not *capricious*.

As for the last three lines of the excerpt, "haply in thee" and "haply thy pensive" are ludicrous when compared with Whitman's blunt idiomatic style of a dozen years earlier. There is a "haply" in Keats's "Ode to a Nightingale" (l. 36), but a comparison of the two will illustrate the effective and ineffective use of archaisms. And why *thee* and *thy*? Whittier used these pronouns in his poetry (and in his prose and correspondence) with complete consistency, but had Whitman and the swan suddenly become Quakers? This is what I meant by suggesting that this too-obvious archaism was a contrivance to give the account an air of high solemnity which the subject could not carry by itself.

Note, too, the real surprise of the run-on lines, unheard of earlier, for the whole point of this line length was to finish the thought. In terms of his thought structure, this stanza should have begun:

> Come nearer bodiless one,
> Haply in thee resounds some dead composer,
> Haply thy pensive life was fill'd with aspirations high,
> Unform'd ideals, waves, oceans musical, chaotically singing.

But Borroff is right—the key and the sign are the excess of Romance-Latinate words. In filling out the rest of the fourth line just above, I drew from the next line in the poem as it stands, and four of the last five words are of Romance-Latin origin. The use of such a vocabulary (and of archaisms) need not lead to vagueness, thinness of imagery, abstraction. Borroff shows that it is not so in Marianne Moore, with her specialized use of scientific terminology, and particularly not in Wallace Stevens, the master of the high formal diction in recent American poetry. But what is the justification of the late *Leaves* when it tries to invade the high formality of English traditional poetry? Pound and Eliot, as young poets and students of poetry, could not stand Whitman (Pound recanted a bit in later years), yet both imitated his early style— but never the late.

If Whitman really was not counterfeiting English high formal style, he revealed a naïveté that is almost as difficult to understand. If all this had happened after his stroke, we could posit that as a far-reaching physical explanation. But the stroke did not come until 1873. A somewhat tentative explanation is that the hiatus occasioned by the Civil War was much more drastic than we have realized. When he suddenly had attention drawn to himself by the publicity of the Harlan dismissal and, an unrelated event, quite as suddenly found a new important audience in England, he happened to be at a standstill poetically. He could not get back to the mood, the state of mind, of the 1854–1859 burst, yet he felt he could not be silent in response to the public attention that at last was coming his way.

Walt Whitman was a secretive person. He had no real confidants, except the Peter Doyles of his other career, in whom such confiding as here suggested would be pointless. He had condoned, and perhaps contrived, all the brouhaha over the Harlan dismissal (to think that he did not know of O'Connor's *Good Gray Poet* before it was published is nonsense; to think that O'Connor would have published it if Whitman had seriously asked him not to is also nonsense). How he felt about the situation he was in we really do not know. In any event, he seems to have been unable to wait until inspiration returned. Feeling compelled to respond to the pressure around him to live up to his calling, he did what he did. As the self-proclaimed national poet, he had accepted the ideal occasion for a public poem (the disbanding of the armies, and nature's response in the bountiful harvest). Thus, in 1867, he started a new poem "The Return of the Heroes," in the old style of 1856 (see Blodgett and Bradley, [1965], p. 359 n.) but could not maintain it, and finally (in 1881) dropped the opening to leave the present beginning: a stanza of solemn, overelevated pretentiousness that he would have scorned ten years earlier.

During this time Whitman also let himself be occupied writing prose, *Democratic Vistas* (originally articles for *Galaxy*, which not unsurprisingly turned down the last article in the series). If we compare that piece of journalism either with the early poetry or with his own actual newspaper and magazine articles (for *Life Illustrated*, or the lighthearted promotional prose of the first edition), we see the same entrapment in an elaborate, nonconversational, heavily Latinate, intentionally complicated style. Once in a while he forgets the new role he has adopted, as when he lashes out at the hypocrisy and corruption of life in Washington, in the most vigorous paragraphs in the essay. But the only good American prose of the late years is *Specimen Days*, something he did not take as seriously as his so-called answer to Carlyle.

To repeat, he was under great pressure (self-imposed in large part) to live up to what he thought was expected of him. Whether he ever could have willed himself back into the frame of mind out of which the early poems came is doubtful, for his view of himself and the world had changed. In any case there is no record, no indication that he even tried. Instead he tried to become for the first time the Poet—the American Singer of Songs. If there was a psychological as well as a physical cause for his stroke six months later, it might well have been the tension in the new role he was trying to play.

The truth, however, is that we do not really know why Whitman's poetry changed. All we do know is that it did—drastically, fatally—and that not enough of us have been willing to acknowledge as much. There does seem to be something of a bridge in *Drum-Taps and Sequel*, as the tables indicate (see Appendix). But that transition, if it exists, would be best exhibited through a much more detailed examination than can be attempted here. My specific intention and purpose are to draw attention to the drastic division, almost a split, in Whitman's poetic style, and I trust the tables demonstrate as much.

Journalism in the middle of the last century provided an excellent schooling in effective use of language, particularly when one was involved in regular journalistic practice as Whitman was. A check through the feature columns he did for the New Orleans *Crescent* in 1848 shows many of the stylistic mannerisms Borroff lists, although Whitman's use of them is hardly noteworthy. In his journalism, from the *Aurora* (via Joseph Jay Rubin's discovery) to the *Crescent*, Whitman always seems a little diffident, a little self-conscious. In the poetry in 1855 there is a certain zest or dash, an easy confidence, sometimes even boldness—especially, of course, in "Song of Myself"—that is not in the previous journalism (it comes from the creation of that remarkable persona), so that the journalistic devices and practices are more eye-catching or attention-getting.

One of the features Borroff notes relates to Marianne Moore's limited use of finite verbs, a matter already noted in the discussion of the tables. But the further point she makes is that when "one grammatical element is lacking [the finite verb], others must be present in its place," which "in Moore's syntax, is the present or past participial phrase" (p. 95). This is also a feature of Whitman's poetry throughout his career, but is especially notable in the early poetry. The beginning of stanza 43, "I do not despise you priests; / My faith is the greatest of faiths and the least of faiths," is followed by thirteen lines with twenty-three present participial phrases to complete the sentence. In the 1856 poem, "Song of the Broad-Axe," the poet speaks of how the axe has served mankind. The second section of the stanza begins: "Than this nothing has better served, it has served all" (l. 151). Then follow fourteen past participial phrases, each beginning "Served." The beautiful use of the clustered present participles in "Out of the Cradle" (ll. 130–43), beginning: "The aria sinking, / All else continuing, the stars shining, / The winds blowing" is only one of the best known of many such uses.

Another journalistic feature which Borroff analyzes with care is the "complex noun phrase." She writes: "The complex noun phrase is clearly an information-compacting device. As is to be expected, it has been developed to extremes of elaboration in promotional prose and other genres in which language is characteristically loaded with descriptive detail. Each such phrase takes advantage, one might say, of an explicit reference to something in the descriptive content of the passage to add one or more facts about it to the sentence in which the reference is made. In styles of lower density, such facts would be stated in individual sentences, each with its own finite verb" (p. 103). The basic noun phrase will have a noun (or pronoun) serving as head and will contain what are called "closed-system items" (determiners, quantifiers, possessive pronouns, numerals). The *complex* noun phrase, which is the concern here, goes beyond the basic in containing not only "closed-system items" but at least one "open-class item." The extended complex noun phrase is always eye-catching by its length but also, it seems to me, provides suspense, something like the good old periodic sentence. The length comes from the inclusion of open-class premodifiers and/or postmodifiers. The premodifiers "include adjectives, present and past participles, nouns converted to adjectival use, and nouns in the inflected genitive." The postmodifiers may include these as well, but also "prepositional phrases, present and past participial phrases, infinitive phrases, and relative clauses" (p. 102). If all of these were used at once, an enormous sentence would follow. It seems unlikely anyone has ever done so. But Whitman came close.

An example of beautifully controlled premodifiers is the opening section of "As I Ebb'd," with the beginning three *as* clauses, shifting to the three *where* clauses, shifting again to present and past participles before reaching the principal verb, "was seized." Similarly, the opening nineteen lines of "Out of the Cradle" present an accumulation of premodifiers but here controlled by initial reiteration in the memorable list of prepositional phrases. Anaphora does provide an easy grouping, and the spell of the "Out of the . . . / Out of the . . . / Out of the . . .," or later, the eight lines beginning "From . . .," may draw attention away from what is really taking place, *i.e.*, the accumulation of premodifiers that so shape our perception and sensitivity that we are quite prepared for the reminiscence that follows. Postmodifiers are used with equal effectiveness all through the early poetry. Note stanza 3 of "Ferry," which is made up of only two sentences. The first begins, "It avails not, time nor place—distance avails not," and continues in a series of postmodifiers, again connected by anaphora, to show the unity of the poet and the audience in their common experience. The second part begins, "I too many and many a time cross'd the river of old," and then describes in twenty-one postmodifiers the events of the crossing we share with him. An extreme example would be "Our Old Feuillage," which follows its titular first line with over a hundred postmodifiers that make up the poem. In a valuable (and amusing) note, Blodgett and Bradley (1965: 170—71) provide Whitman's rationale for this startling display.

A feature of Whitman's use of pre- and postmodifiers is that for prosodic reasons he groups his modifying words, phrases, or clauses according to semantic structure. For instance, in the extensive use in the poems just mentioned he does not have occasion to employ any infinitive phrases. Yet they are used elsewhere, as in "A Song of Joys," where he writes of what was apparently a personal dream. In the original version of 1860, the poem is divided into numbered sentences, of which there are forty-one in the poem. Numbers 39 and 40, which are in the climactic position at the end of the poem, were separated in later versions of the poem, to no notable advancement. But to the example: the infinitive phrase, in both instances, fulfills the postmodifying function:

39. O the orator's joys!
    To inflate the chest—to roll the thunder of the voice out from the ribs
        and throat,
    To make the people rage, weep, hate, desire, with yourself,
    To lead America—to quell America with a great tongue.

40. O the joy of a manly self-hood!
    Personality—to be servile to none—to defer to none—not to any
        tyrant, known or unknown,
    To walk with erect carriage, a step springy and elastic,
    To look with calm gaze, or with flashing eye,
    To speak with a full and sonorous voice out of a broad chest,
    To confront with your personality all the other personalities of the earth.

Whitman wanted to be that sort of figure but did not have the character for it. Yet out of that wish, the imagining of himself in the role, he created the persona that dominates the first three editions. He could write out the message that he could not speak, and thus make a new kind of literature. Oratory was the dream, and writing and printing were the actual production—journalism, promotional writing, even self-promotional writing, in rhetorical garments.

Indeed, all the variations Borroff details in her careful and expert analysis of journalistic and promotional prose in Marianne Moore are found *in extenso* in the first three editions of *Leaves*. But the difference between Whitman's use and Moore's is very real, even though the semantic and syntactic features may be the same. She is subtle, deft, witty, has perfect control, can achieve startling poetic effects from seemingly grossly unpoetic material, can give a line an ironic, humorous, light, or wholly serious bent with very delicate, almost infinitesimal prosodic gestures, such as word placement, syllabication, variations in line length, etc. Compared to her, in cultural perception, in poetic sophistication, in prosodic finesse, Whitman is an innocent.

Moore used the syntactical features of journalistic and promotional prose, not because she was a journalist or a promoter, but because she found a way of using those language features for poetic reasons that few journalists, advertisers, or promoters could have understood. Whitman used the language of journalism because he was a journalist. He was not even a very good one, as were his friends John Swinton and William Swinton, James Redpath, and Richard Hinton, but it was the only training in language he had. And what will be apparent to anyone who reads much Whitman is that not only the items previously discussed but further characteristics of stative language are found all through the early *Leaves*, especially in the catalogs. Borroff points out four of these:

(1) Nouns used as modifiers in a compound word. An example in the 1855 "Myself" seems self-explanatory: "The big doors of the *country-barn* stand open and ready / The dried grass of *harvest-time* loads the slow-drawn wagon" (ll. 160–61; my italics here and below), as do these lines in "Occupations," "*Ironworks* or *whiteleadworks..sugarhouse..steam-saws*, and the great mills and factories, / The *cotton-bale*..the stevedore's hook..the saw and buck of the sawyer..the screen of the *coalscreener*..the mould of the moulder..the *workingknife* of the butcher" (ll. 136–37). Whitman's trick of running the compound words together is found only in the first edition; after that he used the hyphen.

(2) The predominance of nouns over verbs. Some catalogs, like the above, are without verbs altogether, but more typical are those with strings of clauses, as the famous stanza 33 of "Myself." I took the first twenty-one lines (three hundred words) for a noun and verb comparison, and I ignored adjectives, adverbs, articles, prepositions, and even pronouns and gerunds, which, if included, would make the noun count even higher. In this sample there were eighty-five nouns and eighteen verbs (almost five to one). A representative passage from the noncatalog part of the rest of the poem would be the first and last two hundred words, which together have seventy-six nouns and sixty-four verbs. We are all aware of the predominance of nouns in the early editions, but it is probably the catalogs that emphasize this difference.

(3) The adjectival compound. This form is of course found in all

kinds of writing, but what Borroff finds is that "the improvisational compounding of premodifiers is a regular practice among writers of promotional prose" (p. 105), and this too is a feature of the early editions. Here are a few that Whitman compounded in "Myself." He is watching the blacksmiths as he stands on "the cinder-strewed threshold" (l. 215); in the catalog in section 15, he notes that "The groups of newly-come immigrants cover the wharf or levee" (l. 278). In the notorious section 24, on his delight in his own body (ll. 530–44), many of the adjectival compounds are figurative, chiefly to avoid the blunt frankness, which, even at this boldest time in his career, he knew might offend. The sexual exploration is there, to be sure, but the adjectival compound is elaborately yet very carefully contrived. One might also note the use of epistrophe (final repetition: the opposite of anaphora), which unites these lines and others not quoted. Here the words are "it shall be you" at the end of most lines:

> . . . *firm masculine* coulter, it shall be you (l. 532)

> . . . your *milky stream pale strippings* of my life; (l. 534)

> Root of *washed* sweet-flag, *timorous pond*-snipe, nest of *guarded duplicate*
> eggs, it shall be you, (l. 536)

> *Trickling* sap of maple, fibre of *manly* wheat, it shall be you; (l. 540)

> Winds whose *soft-tickling* genitals rub against me, it shall be you,
> (l. 542; my italics here and below)

Such adjectival compounding is a form of what Borroff means when she points out another feature of promotional prose, the condensed simile, although Whitman seems to be even closer to metaphor in the usage here. In similar fashion the adjectival compounding in the second half of section 21 is occasioned by the personification of night and the earth as lovers:

> Press close *bare-bosomed* night! Press close *magnetic nourishing* night
> (l. 436)

> Still *nodding* night! *Mad naked summer* night!
> Smile O *voluptuous coolbreathed* earth, (ll. 438–39)

> *Far-swooping elbowed* earth! Rich *apple-blossomed* earth! (l. 455)

One particular form of the condensed simile that Borroff notes "at its simplest is formed by adding the suffix *-like* to a noun" (p. 106), so *snake-like*, etc. There may be some of these in *Leaves* but unfortunately

Eby's *Concordance* is organized by the beginnings of words only. Perhaps such practice, which she finds as fairly common in advertising and I note regularly in sportswriting, is only of this century.

(4) The inflected genitive of the noun. This is not common in *Leaves*. The well-known line, "The scent of these arm-pits aroma finer than prayer" ought to have the apostrophe after "arm-pits," if that is the way to read the line. But the line in the 1855 edition was "The scent of these arm-pits is aroma finer than prayer" (l. 528). In 1860 he dropped the *is* and replaced it with a comma, which successfully blocks any attempts to find a genitive construction. But the inflected genitive is used mostly in the catalogs. Thus in the catalog from "Occupations," from which "the stevedore's hook" quoted above was taken, preceding lines have "the pilot's wheel and bell" (l. 121), "the lady's wristlet" and "the druggist's vials and jars" (l. 131), "the etui of oculist's or aurist's instruments, or dentist's instruments" (l. 132), but these are not quite as startling in their construction or in their replacement as those Borroff finds in Moore.

About the only well-known pieces of journalism and/or promotional prose of Whitman's that we have are the 1855 Preface, the 1856 Epilogue, and "The Eighteenth Presidency!" It is not difficult to find parallels in the poetry to certain lines or passages in this prose. Notable, of course, is the 1855 Preface, which Whitman could not use as a preface after he made a good part of two major poems out of it in 1856—poems we now know as "By Blue Ontario's Shore" and "Song of Prudence." Many of the features to which Borroff has drawn attention are understandably found in the prose as well as in the poetry. Parts of the 1855 Preface were not transferred to the poetry because the subject matter, rather than the style, was not appropriate. Here is a poetically unused sentence from the 1855 Preface in which he is writing about the daily beauty around us (with my italics for certain of the features we have been discussing): "Each precise object or condition or combination or process exhibits a beauty....the multiplication table its—old age its—the *carpenter's trade* its—the *grand-opera* its....the *hugehulled clean-shaped* New-York clipper at sea under steam or full sail gleams with unmatched beauty....the American circles and large harmonies of government gleam with theirs....and the commonest definite intentions and actions with theirs." Is that passage a midway stage between prose and poetry? Perhaps so, for it could be transferred, with a five-line division, to look like this:

Each precise object or condition or combination or process exhibits a beauty,
The multiplication table its—old age its—the carpenter's trade its—
    the grand opera its,
The hugehulled cleanshaped New-York clipper at sea under steam or full sail
    gleams with unmatched beauty,
The American circles and large harmonies of government gleam with theirs,
And the commonest definite intentions and actions with theirs.

This study was beyond possibility of revision when I found out about the poetic arrangement of the 1855 Preface by William Everson. His is a remarkable venture, and I am truly sorry not to have been able to refer to it at numerous places in this book, for it confirms and corroborates many of the points made here. His presentation of this particular sentence (*American Bard*, 26) has a slight difference in punctuation.

But does journalistic prose become poetry by cutting it up in uneven lines? Yes and no. Yes, to the extent that the five-unit structure or division was already inherent in the original sentence. No, to the extent that the lines themselves are meaningless, for poetry is oral, not print; even though we may never pronounce the words, we always read to the inner ear. To say this another way, if the 1855 Preface was poetry, it was and still is so in its discourse form. The value of the line arrangement is to alert us to or remind us of extra values in the words and their arrangement above and beyond the straight "communication of ideas" function of conventional prose. If there are no extra values, if nothing would be gained by focusing on the message itself (in Jakobson's terms), then clearly the presentation in lines traditionally reserved for poetry would be an irritation.

There is, in fact, no clear demarcation between journalistic prose and poetry, as both Whitman and Marianne Moore might demonstrate. Many of the features of journalism we have been examining are present in significant fashion in Whitman's poetry, but they alone are not enough. Indeed if we were to take a good, fairly short Whitman poem, say "To Think of Time," and write it out in discourse form in five or six paragraphs and slip it into a Freshman Reader, how many (even with careful reading) would recognize it as something more than an essay on death? Or, to reverse the example, many of the features we have been discussing are, indeed, present in greater proportion in "Our Old Feuillage" than in "Myself," "Occupations," or even "Prudence" and "Ontario's Shore" (so indebted to the 1855 Preface). There is no single explanation of why "Our Old Feuillage" is not one of Whitman's successes, for there is clearly a sufficiency of the journalistic devices we have been examining. It seems, indeed, that it is not those features but what is done with them that is the issue. Instead of showing why "Our Old Feuillage" is not one of Whitman's successes, it would be more useful to show how he made successes, made poetry, out of similar material but in a different form or with a different manner of presentation. And that is the purpose of the final chapter.

~ VII ~
THE RHETORICAL-ORATORICAL COMBINATION

Leaves of Grass is not promotional or journalistic prose in uneven lines, nor is it a collection of *cursus*, speech acts, rhetorical questions, metonymic descriptions, or a series of negations. But all of these can contribute to its poetic effect if some way can be found to bring them together for their mutual support. To do that, the traditional, and indeed mandatory, way for a would-be poet was through the traditional and mandatory prosody of English verse practice. As a young man he had tried that way and had even found some small support in newspaper and magazine publication. But it is clear that he had rejected traditional verse in the experimental period before *Leaves*. The pre-1855 notebooks are not very clear or orderly and there are certainly many false starts, but none of them are in any conventional verse form.

In a brilliant and penetrating sentence, the Thomist scholar Etienne Gilson once said: "Verse is there to keep the poet from speaking." The sentence is quoted (pp. 12–13) and its context provided (p. 218) by Group µ (1981), but the implications to help us understand Whitman's situation are not explored. But what is the implication? Essentially that, if one insists on speaking, a medium outside of verse must be found. Whitman did that, and the great gain, *Leaves*, was achieved—but at a consequent great price. Did he reject verse because the prosodic discipline was too difficult? Many thought so. W. H. Auden, at a symposium in Toronto, in one of the shrewdest comments on this question on record, spoke of the uneasiness of the traditional poet for writers of free verse: "There are some people who, like D. H. Lawrence, you feel have to write in free verse, but I think it's the exception because anyone who has ever played a game knows that to play you have to have certain rules. Rules can vary from one game to another. But your whole excitement and freedom comes out of working inside these. Why the hell should poetry be any different? I don't understand it. It's enormous fun. As Valéry said, a poet is somebody whose imagination is stimulated by artificial restrictions. And this seems to be because it is a game, solemn if you like, but a game. All arts are a game. And therefore rules apply" (1981: 7).

There is no easy way to defend Whitman against this implied charge, for *he did* proclaim himself the American Poet, in the 1855 Preface and elsewhere, and *he did not* follow the rules of that solemn game. Late in his career he foolishly spoke out against the rules, claiming they had no relevance in this modern age—proving only that he was more on the defensive than any poet pictured in that 1855 Preface should have been. Indeed there is little in his comments about traditional poetry or about his own poetry to show that he had much understanding of the necessity, the challenge, and the rewards of poetic discipline. Valéry's statement may not be the whole truth about poetry, but it is true.

Someone may someday find a better, a clearer explanation of the way in which Whitman united the various elements discussed in the earlier chapters, but, for the time being, the best explanation is that he used the old rhetorics for poetic (that is, nonrhetorical) ends. It is possible that he may have happened on this method by accident, in the early pursuit of some fantasy of becoming literally the voice of America; if so, that dream remained only a dream while he shaped his imagination, his thinking, his writing to the transfer of oral rhetoric to the printed page.

It seems incredible that an uneducated (that is, in any formal sense —the self-education, I acknowledge) misfit, thirty years old, could produce within six years a volume that changed the history of American poetry. Such early notebooks as we have show the tremendous impediment occasioned by the absence of any formal education. He is completely without system, wastes time and paper on countless false leads, clips an amazing number of articles, many of which, with their pointing fingers, show his momentary convictions. But out of or through this welter of lecture drafts and notes and fragments (as Bucke calls them), the form developed. With no social confidence, with no literary friends to ask for counsel, with no family support, but with startling inner confidence, he found how to put in print that self-creation of himself as democratic prophet which he had conjured up in those six years. And in the form he adopted and adapted he was completely and absolutely right. There are faults in the early *Leaves*, to be sure, but they are almost entirely the faults of excess—the faults of genius.

It so happens that the faults of excess are almost always the faults of *young* genius, which Whitman certainly was not. It is something of an anomaly that he is the oldest of all the late starters in poetry. Possibly Shakespeare was older, but we do not know enough to be sure. But in the nature of things we think of any great poet as already testing himself in and with language in his teens or soon after. Be that as it may, Whitman worked alone and without any literary models (Esther Shephard's claims for George Sand's influence or T. R. Rajasekharaiah's belief that in the Lenox Library's holdings of Hindu writings Whitman found the key are ingenious but not convincing) because there were none, with the possible exception of Tupper, who might have provided a negative influence, as suggested. Even could he have known of Christopher Smart or William Blake, there is nothing in our knowledge of Whitman to indicate that he would have had any grasp at all of what they were up to.

Possibly Whitman was not completely aware of what he himself was up to, in the sense that he possessed any literary sophistication to talk about his method. He knew he was right, but it was an inner conviction, not something he could justify by parallels in literary history. But before demonstrating Whitman's method of making poetry out of imagined prophetic utterances, let me state the rationale in literary terms he would not have understood. Whitman used journalistic language, performed speech acts, used the *cursus*, though he could not know what the term meant, even as he employed a metonymic style without knowing that he was doing so (like Molière's Monsieur Jourdain), but he did so in terms of a foregrounding device of which he was enormously conscious and in which he was remarkably skilled.

Foregrounding is the distinction Mukařovsky proposes to separate literature from other writing. His well-known essay "Standard Language and Poetic Language" (1970) goes on to other matters, but specific to the present issue foregrounding is "the aesthetically intentional distortion of linguistic components" by which the message draws attention to itself. In conventional referential writing, the purpose of which is to convey information only, language becomes so habitual that we do not even notice it; it becomes what Mukařovsky calls "automatized." This "automatized" language must be present as a background; in the literal sense, *fore*grounding brings language out of its *back*ground by whatever devices the writer chooses to use. In the previous sentence, if I had made every word, or even every major word, begin with the same letter, or the same syllable, or had them all rhyme, it would have drawn attention away from what the words were symbolizing to the words themselves. To have accidental alliteration or rhyming is actually a real blunder in serious expository prose, for it is a distraction that interrupts the developing flow of information.

Background can also apply to any type or form of writing against which the writer wishes his creation to be placed. For Wordsworth, in his Preface to and earlier practice in *Lyrical Ballads*, the background was eighteenth-century poetry. Whitman was not quite so clear and forthright in his preface and practice in 1855, partly because his preface belonged to the act itself, and partly because he was working out his "foregrounding" as he went along and was still experimenting. The two, three, and four dots to indicate the length of pauses between word groups in speaking the lines, the occasional lack of punctuation or its use for rhetorical rather than grammatical reasons, the near-complete lack of parentheses even though parenthetical remarks are present, the failure to signify (by either italics or quotation marks) what is quoted material, all such reminders of the original oratorical impulse are still found in the 1855 edition, but most were gone in 1856, and all had vanished by the 1860 edition.

In Wordsworth, the "foregrounding" devices sharply differentiated his writing from that of his traditional eighteenth-century predecessors and contemporaries, but it was still recognized as poetry. Whitman's foregrounding was even more drastic, so much so that many readers rejected *Leaves* as poetry altogether. Verse and verse forms might undergo various internal changes, but to reject verse altogether was to challenge not just one generation's literary fashion but what many considered the nature of poetry itself. Indeed, what is the proper response to the cutting up of Bartolomeo Vanzetti's final speech into lines presumably like Whitman's and putting it into a poetry anthology? A somewhat comparable situation is used by Winfried Nöth, "The Semiotic Framework of Textlinguistics" (1978), to show the difference between poetry and everyday language. He quotes a recipe for North Indian lamb curry, reminds us that we would consider the recipe obviously nonpoetic, and then tells us that he found it in Bern Porter's *Found Poems* (1972: 90). Nöth comments: "Since the textual structures do not change when the recipe is considered as a poem, the framework of textlinguistics has to be abandoned in favor of a situational or semiotic framework in order to describe the poeticalness of the above text [the recipe]. Within this semiotic framework we can observe that the poeticalness of this text depends on the *focus*. . . . It is not the text but the situational framework that changes when the author / reader takes a different attitude toward the text" (1978: 30).

Nöth's example is extreme; indeed, that is why it was chosen (to take something as far beyond Whitman as Whitman was beyond Longfellow) in order to make clear his point about focus alone as a form of foregrounding. But a clarification is necessary. Vanzetti is no great poet any more than is the originator of the North Indian lamb curry recipe, for in *created* art, not accidental art, the focus is controlled by the artist, is indeed intentionally shaped or formed or made by him. There is nothing adventitious about the poetry in *Leaves*. It may or may not be the kind of poetry you admire, but there is no doubt that what is on the page is what Whitman intended.

Whitman is the first major poet to put into practice this linkage, this joining of the kind of focus he established to foregrounding. The focus is on Whitman himself as native bard, and the "foregrounding" is the rhetorical language of prophetic utterance. We do not know enough about the great mystery period (1848–1855) to trace the birth and growth of the persona, its role, its language, its message, its form, but we do know the end result, the first edition and its development through the next two editions. The persona is the native bard (a prophet, seer, *vates*—but of the American variety). His role is that of the wander-teacher. His language, journalistic in its origins, is first-personal, present-tense, performative (in the speech-act sense), oral-rhetorical utterance in the metonymic mode. The message is individual fulfillment through democratic participation. Its form (through 1860) is the print-

238

LANGUAGE AND STYLE IN *Leaves of Grass*

ing by the bard of his utterance. As Berryman observes: "For Whitman the poet is a *voice*. Not solely his—let us settle this problem quickly. . . . A voice, then, for himself and others; for others *as himself*—this is the intention clearly (an underlying exhibitionism and narcissism we take for granted)" (1976: 230).

It is, indeed, the voice of the prophet (the bard, the seer) that occasions the performative language (the speech act) which dominates most of these early poems. Of course, there are the immediate qualifications that each of us works out for himself. The seer was a child before he went forth. As wander-teacher he spoke to individuals ("Song of Myself") as well as to groups ("Occupations"), even about himself ("Sleepers") and to himself ("As I Ebb'd"). In addition to the "I," the speaker, the language has the all-inclusive metonymy of the book which is more than a book. The message of fulfillment through en masse involvement ("Salut au Monde," "Prudence," "Open Road") must also encounter the thought of death ("To Think of Time," "This Compost," "Assurances," "Out of the Cradle"), full and even excessive love (Children of Adam, Calamus groups), communion with nature and, through nature, with future persons ("Ferry"). The form is affirmed only tentatively in the first edition (Preface, "Song of the Answerer," "Who Learns My Lesson Complete," "Great Are the Myths"), clarified in the second (the selection of key parts of the 1855 Preface for "Ontario's Shore," the letter to Emerson), and reaches its complete manifestation in the 1860 edition, so that the bard starts out from Paumanok, journeys through the states, distributes messenger leaves along the way, departs with a "So Long," bequeaths himself in his book.

But can it be taken seriously that *Leaves* is a record of orations, lectures, harangues, soliloquies, sermons, oral musings, exhortations, which Whitman apparently never gave? Yes, but only in the sense defined by Barbara Herrnstein Smith. Her major study, *Poetic Closure* (1968), goes considerably beyond the limits of her title and discusses the oral element in poetry in all of its aspects. She writes wisely and well: "It should be recognized, furthermore, that a poem is not merely the record of an utterance that occurred in the past, as would be the transcription of a text or an oration. For the poem, as an utterance, had no initial historical occurrence. It is, was, and always will be the script for its own performance; like a play, it 'occurs' only when it is enacted" (pp. 16–17). By extension, this statement would include what we call "closet dramas," so that form would not be an exception. Similarly in Whitman, those three late long poems that he gave (or, for "Song of the Universal," planned to give) publicly were written out beforehand. Ironically, these may not be his three worst poems, but one cannot blame their ineptness on the platform orientation or lack thereof.

But with the native prophet as the focus, what was needed was a way of presenting his imagined utterances. As they were more openly, professedly utterances, the spoken words of the seer, they could not be in rhymed metrical lines, for no prophet that he knew of had ever done so (he did not know of Blake or Smart). What was also needed was a way to overcome that enormous barrier of indifference which the appearance of his utterances as printed orations would encounter. What he needed, in short, was some way of getting poetic values, but not through verse. He did so by finding in language a poetic feature, *recurrence* or *parallelism*, that was present long before verse, and this feature he exploited in a great burst of creative energy. And it is this great breakthrough—the first and perhaps only American contribution to the world's poetry—that has not been adequately explained. So here is another explanation.

In two articles that have rarely been cited by those who use his earlier studies, Jakobson expands on his statement of the "poetic function" in his famous contribution to *Style in Language* (1960). Perhaps the reason that "Grammatical Parallelism and Its Russian Facet" (1966) and "Poetry of Grammar and Grammar of Poetry" (1968) have received so little attention is that the examples he uses are largely from Russian poetry or folklore. But he does provide translations, and the principles illustrated do have a universal applicability. In the first article he takes as his starting point a quotation from the "juvenile Gerard Manley Hopkins," whose brilliance as a student of poetry Jakobson extols. Hopkins proclaimed the primacy of parallelism: "The artificial part of poetry, perhaps we shall be right to say all artifice, reduces itself to the principle of parallelism. The structure of poetry is that of a continuous parallelism" (Jakobson's quotation, 1966: 399). He develops this statement to make his own claim "that of every level of language the essence of poetic artifice consists in recurrent returns" (p. 399). He then traces parallelism through the more recent oral poetry to the earliest folklore available, to show that rhyme and meter are latter-day overlays on a basic characteristic of language that uses parallelism in "phonological, grammatical, and semantic structures in their multiform interplay," which is why "the grammar of parallelistic pieces becomes particularly significant" (p. 423).

Years ago Herbert Read recognized this feature of Whitman's style in "The Figure of Grammar: Whitman and Lawrence," a chapter in *The True Voice of Feeling*. He, too, notes Hopkins' reference to Whitman's use of the "figure of grammar" and quotes this pertinent explanation from Hopkins:

> A figure of grammar can be shifted to other words with a change of specific meaning but keeping some general agreement, as of noun over against noun, verb against verb, assertion against assertion, etc., e.g. Foxes (A) have (B) holes (C) and birds of air (A′) and (B—not B′ here) nests (C′) or more widely even than this / with a change of words but keeping the grammatical and logical meaning—as / Foxes have holes and birds of air have nests (that is / Beasts have homes to live in) but the Son of Man has not where to lay His head (that is / Man has not a home to live in): the subjects of the clauses being changed, the one does no more than say yes, the other no. (p. 95)

Read recognizes that Whitman's "figures of grammar are not so simple as this biblical example, but grammatical they are," and he goes on to demonstrate with the opening section of "As I Ebb'd." He points out that it is a single sentence, "depending for its structure, not on any inherent rhythm or spoken sound, but on a statement with its qualifying and dependent clauses." He then quotes much of the second stanza, which "repeats the same structure," and concludes: "I have no desire to deny to Whitman his special virtues, but in so far as they are technical, they belong to the art of rhetoric rather than to the art of poetry" (pp. 95–96).

A few pages farther on, Read corrects Lawrence, who had fervently maintained that for Whitman to "reject the superinduced shape of metrical laws" meant that "what proceeds, spontaneously, has no recognizable or discoverable form. It is naked utterance, unformed." But, claims Read, Whitman "has a very positive structure, the figure of grammar, as Hopkins called it." And further: "Apart from this basic structure, Whitman's verse is full of rhetorical devices which are anything but spontaneous—deliberate inversions such as 'Vigil strange I kept on the field one night'; artificial invocations, such as: 'O a strange hand writes for our dear son, O stricken mother's soul!' and, further, all the deliberate antiphonal structure of poems like 'When Lilacs last in the Dooryard bloom'd' and 'Out of the Cradle endlessly rocking.' One could elaborate a treatise on rhetoric from Whitman's practice" (pp. 98–99). Amen!

Jakobson's 1968 article expands on the Hopkins' insight in a different fashion: "The recurrent figure of grammar . . . is particularly palpable in those poetic forms, where contiguous metrical units are more or less consistently combined through a grammatical parallelism into pairs or, optionally, triplets" (pp. 599–600). Which, of course, might be readily applied to Whitman's practice, except that he would abjure the meter and frequently use more than two or three parallel grammatical phrases. But again Jakobson goes beyond Hopkins' position: "Here any noticeable reiteration of the same grammatical concept becomes an effective poetic device. . . . Let us insist on the strikingness of these devices; any sensitive reader, as [Edward] Sapir would say, feels instinctively the poetic effect and the semantic load of these grammatical appliances, 'without the slightest attempt at conscious analysis,' and in many cases the poet himself in this respect is similar to such a reader" (pp. 602–603).

And that is really what I want to do here. Not to make the elaborate analysis of the grammatical and syntactic structures of the various word units exhibiting parallelism, nor to enumerate and classify the various rhetorical "schemes" found in *Leaves*, but merely alert the reader that they are there and trust to Jakobson's (and Sapir's) conviction that the effect can be felt without conscious analysis.

The best way to alert the reader, it seems to me, is to take one poem and show the use of recurrence and parallelism in it. A good choice is "Who Learns My Lesson Complete" from the first edition because it is the shortest poem there. It does not have all the forms of parallelism, but no poem has them all. The poem underwent later changes, some good, some not, but my intention here is to get at Whitman's original and early use of recurrence. Recurrence is the means and manner of foregrounding, the factor at the beginning that separated the prose of his lectures from the poetry of the first edition. Here is the poem as found in the first edition. It has no title, but the first word is capitalized.

1   WHO learns my lesson complete?
Boss and journeyman and apprentice?....churchman and atheist?
The stupid and the wise thinker....parents and offspring....merchant and clerk and porter and customer....editor, author, artist and schoolboy?

Draw nigh and commence,
5   It is no lesson....it lets down the bars to a good lesson,
And that to another....and every one to another still.

The great laws take and effuse without argument,
I am of the same style, for I am their friend,
I love them quits and quits....I do not halt and make salaams.

10   I lie abstracted and hear beautiful tales of things and the reason of things,
They are so beautiful I nudge myself to listen.

I cannot say to any person what I hear....I cannot say it to myself....it is very wonderful.

It is no little matter, this round and delicious globe, moving so exactly in its orbit forever and ever, without one jolt or the untruth of a single second;
I do not think it was made in six days, nor in ten thousand years, nor ten decillions of years,
15   Nor planned and built one thing after another, as an architect plans and builds a house.

I do not think seventy years is the time of a man or woman,
Nor that seventy millions of years is the time of a man or woman,
Nor that years will ever stop the existence of me or any one else.

Is it wonderful that I should be immortal? as every one is immortal,
20   I know it is wonderful....but my eyesight is equally wonderful....and how I was conceived in my mother's womb is equally wonderful,
And how I was not palpable once but am now....and was born on the last day of May 1819....and passed from a babe in a creeping trance of three summers and three winters to articulate and walk....are all equally wonderful.

And that I grew six feet high....and that I have become a man thirty-six years old in 1855....and that I am here anyhow—are all equally wonderful;
And that my soul embraces you this hour, and we affect each other

without ever seeing each other, and never perhaps to see each
other, is every bit as wonderful:
And that I can think such thoughts as these is just as wonderful,
25   And that I can remind you, and you think them and know them to be
true is just as wonderful,
And that the moon spins around the earth and on with the earth is
equally wonderful,
And that they balance themselves with the sun and stars is equally
wonderful.

Come I should like to hear you tell me what there is in yourself that is
not just as wonderful,
And I should like to hear the name of anything between Sunday
morning and Saturday night that is not just as wonderful.

The poem underwent considerable revision, as Blodgett and Bradley indicate, although the adjusting of the dates in lines 21 and 22 to fit
Whitman's patriotic calendar was done for the 1856 and the 1860 editions. Since the poem is short, it has been easy to slide by it in the attention to the other major (and much longer) poems of the first edition. At
one stage in his great shift from the 1860 to the 1867 edition, Whitman
was tempted to transfer parts of the poem to other poems, but apparently realized the impossibility of that, and eventually, as the Blue Book
reminds us, decided to "leave out" the poem entirely. He did not do so,
but finally put it in the middle of Autumn Rivulets, where it successfully avoided any major critical commentary until recently. In 1979,
Don Bogen explored the changes in the text (contrasting the 1855 and
1892 versions) in an important article in *Walt Whitman Review*, especially in his detailing of the drastic shift in the relationship between the
poet (the "I" of the poem) and "you," the reader. I regret that Bogen did
not examine the Blue Book, which would have further verified his fine
analysis, but he is certainly correct on the change in this poem—a part
of the wholesale change that I have been discussing. His analysis of the
poem, its central thought and development, is such that there is no reason for me to go further, but rather I turn to recurrence and parallelism,
which are not his concern.

Let me first use a device to draw attention to the use of recurrent
words, phrases, and clauses. What follows is a code to the poem so that
only the repetitions stand out. The dash stands for a word that is used
only once, as "who," "learns," and "complete" of the first line. The signs

LANGUAGE AND STYLE IN *Leaves of Grass*

are as follows: *p* means pronoun; the *?* is carried over from the text; *1* (one) stands for a word that is repeated (both singular and plural included in the same sign), as "lesson" in the first and twice in the fifth line; *+* is for "and"; *t* is for the definite article (the indefinite articles "a" and "an" are not frequent and are not so important in their specificity, so they are written out); *C* stands for "command," of which there are only three, two in line 4 and one in line 28 (they are as much invitations as commands, but as imperatives "you" is implied, an important feature in this first version, as Bogen points out); *N* stands for a negative (no, not, nor, never); at line 8 and frequently thereafter, *I* stands for the persona of the poem; *x* means an auxiliary (do, have, can—but not the forms of "to be," which are *3s*), as in line 9 for "do"; *d* is the demonstrative pronoun (this, that) as in line 13 (the relative "that" has a number sign *4*); *b* stands for "but," distinguished from "and" intentionally; *n* stands for a number, as in line 14 and elsewhere; sign *3* is for "is" but also for the other forms of "to be" (am, are, was, etc.). The slash marks indicate the strong caesura, marked in the original with four dots.

1   — — p 1 —?
— + — + —? / — + —?
t — + t — — / — + — / — + — + — + — / —, —, — + —?
C — + C,

5   2 3 N 1 / 2 — — t — to a — 1,
+ 4 to 5 / + 6 n to 5 —.

t — — — + — 30 —,
I 3 of t — —, — I 3 p —,
I — p 8 + 8 / I x N — + 31 —.

10   I — — + 9 10 — of 11 + t — of 11,
p 3 32 10 I — p to —.

I x N 13 to 32 — p I 9 / I x N 13 2 to p / 2 3 — W.

2 3 N — —, d — + — —, — 32 — in p — — + —, 30 n — or t — of
a — —;

I x N 15 p 3 31 — n —, N in n n 16, N n n of 16,

15   N 17 + 18 n 11 — 5, 7 an — 17 + 18 a —.

I x N 15 n 16 3 t 19 of a 20 or 21,
N 4 n n of 16 3 t 19 of a 20 or 21,
N 4 16 — — — t — of p or 32 n —.

3 2 W 4 I 27 3 22? 7 6 n 3 22,

THE RHETORICAL-ORATORICAL COMBINATION

20   I 25 2 3 W / b p — 3 E W / + 23 I 3 — in p — — 3 E W,
    + 23 I 3 N — — b 3 — / + 3 — on t — — of — n / + — — a — in a
    — — of n — + n — to — + — / 3 14 E W.
    + 4 I — n — — / + 4 I x — a — n n 16 — in n / + 4 I 3 — — / 3 14
    E W;
    + 4 p — — p d —, + p — 24 25 — — 12 24 25, + N — to 12 24
    25, 3 6 — 7 W:
    + 4 I x 15 — — 7 p 3 J 7 W,
25   + 4 I x — p, + p 15 p + 25 p to 3 — 3 J 7 W,
    + 4 t — — — t 26 + on 29 t 26 3 E W,
    + 4 p — p 29 t — + — 3 E W.
    C I 27 28 to 9 p — p — — 3 in p 4 3 N J 7 W,
    + I 27 28 to 9 t — of — — — — + — — 4 3 N J 7 W.

What may look like military secret code was worked out to apply to a number of poems (Whitman's and others) to check syntactic recurrence. No one anywhere uses as much recurrence for foregrounding as Whitman does, and even Whitman moves away from it after the 1860 edition. What it demonstrates, almost visually, is the way in which much of the poem is devoted to the oratorical-rhetorical devices that in themselves highlight the parallelism. If we look at the dashes (for words used only once) we can see without counting that there are about as many dashes as signs. There are, in fact, 128 words (dashes) used only once, as contrasted with 156 words used more than once (some many more) in the 284-word poem. In a somewhat loose or offhand sense, it might be said that less than half of the words (and of the poem) are devoted to the informational, and more than half to embellishment (the foregrounding).

The value of a syntactic chart like this is that many of the very shrewd prosodic ventures are immediately apparent, and do not need the sometimes self-defeating line-by-line analysis, which can never show the linking of lines, the shifting emphases as the poem advances, the key positioning of the fifth question after the early beginning four, the increase in the use of negatives as the poem develops, the slight shifting of words in the parallel beginnings and ends of lines in the last three stanzas, so that complete repetition (which, when we know it is coming, we do not read fully) is avoided. But the most important thing to note about the use of recurrence and parallelism is Whitman's way of maintaining his focus as native prophet and at the same time achieving a means of foregrounding. There is a certain amount of parallelism in all good writing, as Mary Hiatt in *Artful Balance* shows in full detail. Even the most technical and purely expository article will have some, and there will be more as one moves from technical writing to what Stich calls "persuasive functional style." Mukařovsky's "Standard Language and Poetic Language" acknowledges as much: "Foregrounding is, of course, common in the standard language, for instance, in journalistic style, even more in essays. But here it is always subordinate to communication: its purpose is to attract the reader's (listener's) attention more closely to the subject matter expressed by the foregrounded means of expression" (p. 43). That is not true of Whitman. Foregrounding is rarely "subordinate to communication" and never in the major poems. It is true that he used most of the features of journalistic style, but over and above them he used the repetitive and paralleling devices of the oratorical rhetorics as a means of foregrounding.

Mukařovsky continues: "In poetic language foregrounding achieves maximum intensity . . . [by] being used for its own sake; it is not used in the services of communication, but in order to place in the foreground the act of expression, the act of speech itself" (1970: 43–44). But there is the question of how much foregrounding is possible and whether there is such a thing as an excess. Theoretically it is impossible to have any poem made up of 100 percent foregrounded language, for an item becomes foregrounded by comparison with other items which make up the background. In practice, however, Whitman seems to have reached some sort of upper limit in poems like "Who Learns My Lesson Complete." But it is not the number of foregrounded items so much as the placement of them that is of chief importance in Whitman's early style. The paralleling cannot be only at the beginning and end of lines, for such an invariable insistence would be self-defeating. So Whitman spaces a few repetitions of words and phrases within the lines also.

Still, most of the parallels are found at the beginnings and ends of lines—but why? Because that is the reason for the line in the first place. This is a new approach to Whitman's poetic structure, so let me explain. It is not difficult to see in the notes for those early lectures that he was working toward a rhythmic expression of his ideas, even having some of the paralleling at the beginning and end of such lines as we might make by splitting a ten-line paragraph into a fifteen- to eighteeen-line pre-poem. By no means all but many of those lectures do have word groupings for lines of poetry (his kind, that is). It is not that the word group is the whole line, for they are usually much shorter than that, but one can almost always piece together the correct word groups. Here is a passage out of which the famous section 45 of "Myself" was developed:

> Amelioration is the blood that runs through the body of the universe—I do not lag—I do not hasten—I bide my hour over billions of billions of years— I exist in the void that takes uncounted time and coheres to a nebula, and in further time cohering to an orb, marches gladly round, a beautiful tangible creature, in his place in the processions of God, where new comers have been falling in the ranks for ever, and will be so always—I could be balked no how, not if all the worlds and living beings were this minute reduced back into the impalpable film of chaos—I should surely bring up again where we now stand and go on as much further and thence on and on—my right hand is time, and my left hand is space—both are ample—a few quintillions of cycles, a few sextillions of cubic leagues, are not of importance to me—what I shall attain to I can never tell, for there is something that underlies me, of whom I am a part and instrument (*UPP*: 79–80)

What we are doing, in such practice as that indicated above, is using our own sense of rhythmic appropriateness in reshaping the prose passage to bring out, in fact to *foreground*, that extra value we sense beyond the denotative meaning of the words. We are helped, even guided sometimes, in that task by the parallelism Whitman has already subconsciously (or intuitively) put in the passage. Indeed, to get help in understanding the rhythm of *Leaves* we need to go, not to the prosodic scholars of traditional poetry, but to the students of prose. Jonathan Bishop in his sensitive study, *Emerson on the Soul*, has a fine section on prose rhythm in Emerson, much of which could apply equally to Whitman. Even such a lively, if basic, text as Virginia Tufte's *Grammar as Style*, especially her final section, "Syntactical Symbolism," provides valuable clues for determining the syntactic and semantic reasons behind the efficacy of any prose passage.

But most valuable to me has been D. W. Harding's *Words into Rhythm* (1976) echoes of which are scattered throughout this study. In his fifth chapter, Harding does trace variations in English verse, starting with Thomas Wyatt but moving quickly to Hopkins, the first to defend his departure from conventional prosodic meter with that elaborate defense of sprung rhythm. Harding accepts Hopkins' departure from prosodic meter but thinks the defense unduly complicated and somewhat unnecessary: "Instead of prosodic ingenuities, we can start from the simpler conception of rhythmical units in speech and written prose which sometimes flow into each other . . . and sometimes stand relatively isolated and salient on account of speech pauses" (p. 66). Even more important is the relation of these rhythmical speech units to the poetic line. In rebutting Graham Hough, who claims that a free-verse line is a line only because it is a rhythmical unit, Harding makes this valuable elucidation: "The converse is nearer the truth, that a phrase or part of a phrase or a succession of phrases is given a special rhythmic unity—or that its rhythmic form made more salient—by being set apart as a line. *The line invites us to find in the succession of words a rhythmical unity beyond what they would have had in a passage of prose*; or, in a very short line, to experience more saliently the speech rhythm of the word or phrase" (p. 68; my italics). It is these rhythmical units, these word groups, which are found in speech, show up to the perceiving eye in literary prose, and can be highlighted by appropriate line structure, that seem to me the key to Whitman's poetic organization.

My earliest awareness that this was so came from Benjamin Hrushovski's "On Free Rhythms in Modern Poetry" (1960). The free-rhythmic system he speaks of is found in much oral literature, in the Hebrew Bible, and some contemporary poets. The principle he finds is that a poetic line "consists of two (or seldom three) simple groups, usually parallel, or partially parallel, in their syntactic and semantic structure. These basic units are not equal . . . [but] the rhythmic impression persists in spite of all 'irregularities.' The basic units almost never consist of one or more than four stresses, that is, they are simple groups of two, three, or four stresses" (p. 189). He goes on to explain that the stresses are strong and are supported by syntactic repetition. Now this notion is a clue to the structure of the Whitman line. If we check the lines in "Who Learns My Lesson Complete," we notice how each line breaks up into one, two, three, or four short units. Even the longest line (l. 21) fits the formula Hrushovski provides, although his further explanation helps. He is answering critics of free-rhythmic poetry who claim that long

THE RHETORICAL-ORATORICAL COMBINATION

lines "are incapable of being perceived as single units," by assuring them that they do not need to read the line as a single unit but as a series of shorter word groups. Thus even the poems notable for "long lines, as Marianne Moore's or Whitman's (with a few 'explicable' exceptions) do not exceed a simple group of simple groups" (p. 189).

The long line and Whitman's attempt to handle it provide an interesting by-product of the sort of investigation this book is pursuing. In the present poem, the longest lines are 20, 21, 22, and 23, for which the four-dot caesuras are of considerable help in spotting the word groups. However, in line 20 I also make a break between "womb" and "is"; in line 21, I would make a brief pause after "trance" and after "winters" to put those prepositional phrases together in a semiparenthetical situation; in line 22, the dash after "anyhow" is much like the four dots in indicating a caesura, and, indeed, after the first edition the dots were replaced usually by dashes and later by commas; in line 23 the caesuras would come where the commas are.

In other poems there seems to be a curious uncertainty in how to handle the long line. He wanted to have them, and perhaps even to flaunt them, as a part of the foregrounding to show the educated reader (educated enough, that is, to know what the acceptable limits of a line of acceptable poetry were supposed to be) that this prophet-poet was not to be prevented from saying what he had to say by some unnatural limitation imposed by aesthetes who did not and could not speak for the people or for America.

Here are three examples from the first edition, beginning with "Occupations": "Because you are greasy or pimpled—or that you was once drunk, or a thief, or diseased, or rheumatic, or a prostitute—or are so now—or from frivolity or impotence—or that you are no scholar, and never saw your name in print....do you give in that you are any less immortal?" (l. 27). In 1860, he printed the same line, changing the dashes and four dots to commas. For the Blue Book he made editorial signals for the four-line division of the later versions. And as part of his growing squeamishness about his audience, he put parentheses around the four-line sentence.

The major down-to-earth example in "To Think of Time" was the funeral of the stage driver. These lines of section 4 are about him:

He was a goodfellow,
Freemouthed, quicktempered, not badlooking, able to take his own part,
Witty, sensitive to a slight, ready with life or death for a friend,
Fond of women,..played some..eat hearty and drank hearty,
Had known what it was to be flush..grew lowspirited toward the
    last..sickened..was helped by a contribution,
Died aged forty-one years..and that was his funeral. (ll. 42–47)

In 1860 this sentence is all one line, the dots replaced by commas and a dash for the last pair. The four compound words in the first two lines are now separated by hyphens, and there are a couple of word changes: "played some" was not intended as a dialectical double entendre in reference to the women, and so that there would be no misunderstanding he dropped "played some" and put in "gambled." In the same line he also corrects the grammatical (or is it dialetical?) error by changing "eat" to "ate." In the Blue Book he makes five signals for a division into six lines, but actually it appears as four lines in the final version.

There is an interesting problem here (and in the previous poem and all through the first edition), in that the same sentence can be presented as six lines, then all one line, then as signaled and planned for a quite different set of six lines, and finally, after a small excision of "able to take his own part, / Witty, sensitive to a slight," put in a still different four-line arrangement. Is Whitman so inept that he does not know what he is doing? Not at all; the point is that line length is not sacrosanct. Unless there is anaphora or epistrophe (or both, symploce), line length is flexible. The two-, three-, or four-word groups that Hrushovski posits are present, to be sure, but there is no reason why, for many lines, the last grouping of a line could not just as readily be the first group of the next line. The major consequence of this realization is that all attempts to scan Whitman's lines should now be called into question. Harvey Gross in his very sensible book *Sound and Form in Modern Poetry* told us some years ago that Whitman's rhythm was based on syntax, not meter (pp. 83–85), but the further observation that there is nothing stable about line length demonstrates even more dramatically that Whitman's poetry cannot be approached through traditional prosody.

The third passage is from "There Was a Child Went Forth," and in this instance he went from the 1855 three-line stanza (ll. 4–6, of which

THE RHETORICAL-ORATORICAL COMBINATION

line 6 has sixty-one words) to a six-line stanza in 1860 and in the final version (ll. 5–10). There is no need to quote the passage to make an additional point that covers all three examples. These sentences, and there are many others like them, are long not because of any complex structure (elaborate subordination, etc.) but because of his felt need to add additional metonymic details. In a very true sense the Whitman of the early editions seems inordinately convinced of the need for and the poetic efficacy of metonymy. It is, in fact, one area where his prophetic role cannot support or justify his lines. Prophetic writing is full of warnings chiefly, and also some predictions, but nothing remotely comparable to Whitman's catalogs or to lines like those just quoted. The long line, especially the one loaded with metonymic specification, gradually disappears from the long poems after 1860, but Whitman seems never to have lost his delight in the variety of nature. Accordingly such metonymy and synecdoche as are featured in the late poetry are not part of some larger purpose, as they are in the early poetry and up through "When Lilacs Last in the Dooryard Bloom'd." It is rare to get too much, but it can happen, perhaps because it may not be skillfully enough presented. Adding seven lines of personal comment after seventy-five lines of unfocused metonymic detail cannot make a great poem out of "Our Old Feuillage."

But blunders of excess aside, a great debt we owe to Whitman is for his finding of a rhythm and style through which he could bring metonymy and synecdoche to a rightful place in poetry. Daniel Laferrière in his *Sign and Subject* (1978) has a provocative concluding chapter, "The Writing Perversion." He does not mention Whitman but does quote from Edna St. Vincent Millay:

> Stranger, pause and look;
> From the dust of ages
> Lift this little book,
> Turn the tattered pages,
> Read me, do not let me die!

Her lines call for this comment: "But what precisely is the trick whereby the writer's subjectivity is shifted from his mortal self into the allegedly immortal text? In what sense are we justified in saying that writing is

'. . . a consuming of the self . . . in order to escape that annihilation of the self that is the inevitable outcome of physical generation.' It is the duty of the semiotician not to be taken in by the trick, not to collaborate with the writer's fetishization of writing, but to lay bare the signifying processes behind the trick. The trick is metonymy" (p. 81).

Laferrière is correct, of course, for metonymy is a trick, but only as metaphor and personification are only tricks, as indeed is poetry itself. But it is a trick we ask for. It is even a trick that we do not want to be reminded of at the time it is being tried on us, for we enjoy the momentary illusion, that old "willing suspension of disbelief." So, when Whitman pulls the most successful metonymic trick in poetic history, we balk at calling it a trick and think somewhere back in our minds that there are some ways in which it may possibly be true:

> Camerado, this is no book,
> Who touches this touches a man.

Appendix

FINITE VERB ELEMENTS: EARLY POETRY

Poem	First 200 Lines	Middle 200 Lines	Last 200 Lines	Total Occurrences	Percentage
Myself	22	26	29	77	12.8%
Occupations	23	18	16	57	9.5%
Think of Time	22	29	36	87	14.5%
Sleepers	14	21	30	65	10.8%
Electric	23	30	28	81	13.5%
		Total, 1855 edition		367	12.2%
Ontario	35	21	32	88	14.7%
Rolling Earth	22	20	36	78	13.0%
Ferry	14	32	29	75	12.5%
Salut	24	25	25	74	12.3%
Open Road	31	35	36	102	17.0%
		Total, 1856 edition		417	13.9%
Paumanok	5	13	18	36	6.0%
Calamus	21	24	30	75	12.5%
Cradle	6	23	13	42	7.0%
Ebb'd	22	27	16	65	10.8%
So Long	26	19	36	81	13.5%
		Total, 1860 edition		299	10.0%
		Early Poetry (9,000 lines)		1,083	12.0%

APPENDIX

FINITE VERB ELEMENTS: LATE POETRY

Poem	First 200 Lines	Middle 200 Lines	Last 200 Lines	Total Occurrences	Percentage
Drum-Taps (1865)	16	15	20	51	8.5%
Lilacs (1865)	10	11	6	27	4.5%
Pioneers (1865)	8	19	16	43	7.2%
Return of the Heroes (1867)	5	18	13	36	6.0%
Proud Music (1869)	12	12	8	32	5.3%
Passage (1871)	3	4	16	23	3.8%
Exposition (1871)	11	7	9	27	4.5%
Mystic Trumpeter (1872)	17	23	14	54	9.0%
Equal Brood (1872)	18	9	16	43	7.2%
Redwood (1874)	6	15	2	23	3.8%
Universal (1874; 467 ll.)				22	4.7%
Eidólons (1876; 505 ll.)				11	2.1%
Columbus (1876; 576 ll.)				55	9.5%
Locomotive (1881; 255 ll.)				5	2.0%
Dalliance of Eagles (1881; 95 ll.)				—	—
As Consequent (1881; 298 ll.)				7	2.3%
Italian Music in Dakota (1881; 128 ll.)				1	0.8%
Orb Aloft Full Dazzling (1881; 250 ll.)				16	6.4%
Riddle Song (1881; 328 ll.)				15	4.5%
Spirit That Form'd This Scene (1881; 98 ll.)				5	5.1%
Late Poetry (9,000 lines)				496	5.5%

APPENDIX

ROMANCE-LATIN TABULATION: EARLY POETRY

Poem	First 200 Lines	Middle 200 Lines	Last 200 Lines	Total Occurrences	Percentage
Myself	23	31	13	67	11.2%
Occupations	31	29	22	82	13.7%
Think of Time	14	35	36	85	14.2%
Sleepers	27	19	18	64	10.7%
Electric	19	18	22	59	9.8%
		Total, 1855 edition		357	11.9%
Ontario	37	38	20	95	15.8%
Rolling Earth	21	29	27	77	12.8%
Ferry	25	20	36	81	13.5%
Salut	21	30	24	75	12.5%
Open Road	25	39	29	93	15.5%
		Total, 1856 edition		421	14.0%
Paumanok	35	30	37	102	17.0%
Calamus	28	18	21	67	11.2%
Cradle	15	19	14	48	8.0%
Ebb'd	13	13	15	41	6.8%
So Long	32	43	27	102	17.0%
		Total, 1860 edition		360	12.0%
		Early Poetry (9,000 lines)		1,138	12.6%

APPENDIX

ROMANCE-LATIN TABULATION: LATE POETRY

Poem	First 200 Lines	Middle 200 Lines	Last 200 Lines	Total Occurrences	Percentage
Drum-Taps (1865)	28	27	37	92	15.3%
Lilacs (1865)	26	35	24	85	14.2%
Pioneers (1865)	44	38	43	125	20.8%
Return of the Heroes (1867)	41	49	12	102	17.0%
Proud Music (1869)	57	49	47	153	25.5%
Passage (1871)	54	43	19	116	19.3%
Exposition (1871)	36	47	31	114	19.0%
Mystic Trumpeter (1872)	54	32	61	147	24.5%
Equal Brood (1872)	38	58	53	149	24.8%
Redwood (1873)	42	57	43	142	23.7%
Universal (1874; 467 ll.)				107	22.9%
Eidólons (1876; 505 ll.)				164	32.5%
Columbus (1876; 576 ll.)				101	17.5%
Locomotive (1881; 255 ll.)				62	24.3%
Dalliance of Eagles (1881; 95 ll.)				30	31.6%
As Consequent (1881; 298 ll.)				53	17.8%
Italian Music in Dakota (1881; 128 ll.)				44	34.4%
Orb Aloft Full Dazzling (1881; 250 ll.)				41	16.4%
Riddle Song (1881; 328 ll.)				72	22.0%
Spirit That Form'd This Scene (1881; 98 ll.)				36	36.7%
Late Poetry (9,000 lines)				1,935	21.5%

Bibliography

Abrams, M. H. *The Mirror and the Lamp*. New York, 1953.

Adams, Jon-K. "The Prophetic Intent of 'Passage to India.'" *Walt Whitman Review*, XXVI (1980), 26–29.

Allen, Gay Wilson. *Aspects of Walt Whitman*. New York, 1977.

———. "Biblical Analogies for Walt Whitman's Prosody." *Revue Anglo-Americaine*, X (1933), 490–507.

———. *The New Walt Whitman Handbook*. New York, 1975.

———. *The Solitary Singer*. New York, 1955.

———. "Walt Whitman and Jules Michelet." *Etudes Anglaises*, I (1937), 230–37.

———. "Whitman and Michelet—Continued." *American Literature*, XLV (1973), 428–32.

Altieri, Charles. "What Grice Offers Literary Theory: A Proposal for 'Expressive Implicature.'" *Centrum*, VI (1978), 90–103.

Amyot, Gerald F. "Walt Whitman's 'Language Experiment.'" *Walt Whitman Review*, XX (1974), 97–103.

Anderson, Quentin. *The Imperial Self*. New York, 1971.

———. "Whitman's New Man." In *Walt Whitman's Autograph Revision of the Analysis of Leaves of Grass (for Dr. R. M. Bucke's Walt Whitman)*. New York, 1974.

Aspiz, Harold. *Walt Whitman and the Body Beautiful*. Urbana, 1980.

Asselineau, Roger. *The Evolution of Walt Whitman: The Creation of a Book*. Cambridge, 1962.

———. *The Evolution of Walt Whitman: The Creation of a Personality*. Cambridge, 1960.

———. *The Transcendentalist Constant in American Literature*. New York, 1980.

Auden, W. H. "Marshall McLuhan / W. H. Auden: Duel or Duet," edited by Robert O'Driscoll. *Canadian Forum*, LXI (May, 1981), 5–7, 15.

Austin, J. L. *How to Do Things with Words*. Cambridge, 1962.

Bach, Kent, and Robert Harnisch. *Linguistic Communication and Speech Acts*. Cambridge, 1979.

BIBLIOGRAPHY

Banfield, Ann. "The Nature of Evidence in a Falsifiable Literary Theory." In *The Concept of Style*, edited by Berel Lang. Philadelphia, 1979.

———. *Unspeakable sentences: Narration and representation in the language of fiction*. Boston, 1982.

Baron, Dennis. "Role Structure and the Language of Literature." *Journal of Literary Semantics*, IV (1975), 41–51.

Barthes, Roland. *Elements of Semiology*. Translated by Annette Lavers and Colin Smith. Boston, 1970.

Baskerville, Barnet. *The People's Voice: The Orator in American Society*. Lexington, Ky., 1979.

Beardsley, Monroe. "Verbal Style and Illocutionary Action." In *The Concept of Style*, edited by Berel Lang. Philadelphia, 1979.

Becker, John. "The Law, the Prophets, and Wisdom: On the Functions of Literature." *College English*, XXXVII (1975), 254–64.

Bergson, Henri. *Creative Evolution*. New York, 1944.

Berryman, John. "'Song of Myself': Intention and Substance." In *The Freedom of the Poet*. New York, 1976. Written in 1957 but published here for the first time.

Bickman, Martin. *The Unsounded Centre: Jungian Studies in American Romanticism*. Chapel Hill, 1980.

Bishop, Jonathan. *Emerson on the Soul*. Cambridge, 1964.

Blankenship, Jane. "The Influence of Mode, Sub-Mode, and Speaker Predilection on Style." *Speech Monographs*, XLI (1974), 85–118.

Bloom, Harold. *The Anxiety of Influence*. New York, 1973.

———. *A Map of misreading*. New York, 1975.

———. *Poetry and Repression: Revisionism from Blake to Stevens*. New Haven, 1976.

Bloomfield, Morton. "Jakobsonian Poetics and Evaluative Criticism." *University Review*, XXXVII (1971), 165–73.

———. "The Syncategorematic in Poetry: From Semantics to Syntactics." In *To Honor Roman Jakobson*, I. The Hague, 1967.

Bogen, Don. "'I' and 'You' in 'Who Learns My Lesson Complete?': Some Aspects of Whitman's Poetic Evolution." *Walt Whitman Review*, XXV (1979), 87–98.

Bolinger, Dwight. *Degree Words*. The Hague, 1972.

Borges, Jorge Luis. "The Achievements of Walt Whitman." *Texas Quarterly*, V (1962), 43–48.

Borroff, Marie. *Language and the Poet*. Chicago, 1979.

Bové, Paul. *Destructive Poetics: Heidegger and Modern Poetry*. New York, 1980.

Bowers, Fredson. "The Walt Whitman Manuscripts of 'Leaves of Grass' (1860)." In *Textual & Literary Criticism*. Cambridge, Eng., 1959.

———. *Whitman's Manuscripts: Leaves of Grass, 1860*. Chicago, 1955.

Boyd, Julian, and Zelda Boyd. "Shall and Will." In *The State of the Language*, edited by Leonard Michaels and Christopher Ricks. Berkeley, 1980.

259

Bradley, Sculley. "The Fundamental Metrical Principle in Whitman's Poetry." *American Literature*, X (1939), 437–59.

Brenner, Charles. *An Elementary Textbook of Psychoanalysis*. New York, 1974.

Bridgman, Richard. *The Colloquial Style in America*. New York, 1966.

Brooke-Rose, Christine. "The Readerhood of Man." In *The Reader in the Text*, edited by Susan Suleiman and Inge Crosman. Princeton, 1980.

———. *A Rhetoric of the Unreal: Studies in narrative and structure, especially of the fantastic*. Cambridge, Eng., 1981.

———. *A Structural Analysis of Pound's Usura Canto: Jakobson's Method Extended and Applied to Free Verse*. The Hague, 1976.

Brookes, Gerry. *The Rhetorical Form of Carlyle's Sartor Resartus*. Berkeley, 1972.

Brown, Robert, and Martin Steinmann. "Native Readers of Fiction: A Speech-Act and Genre-Rule Approach to Defining Literature." In *What Is Literature?*, edited by Paul Hernadi. Bloomington, 1978.

Brown, Roger, and Albert Gilman. "The Pronouns of Power and Solidarity." In *Style in Language*, edited by Thomas A. Sebeok. Cambridge, 1960.

Brown, Stephen. *The World of Imagery*. 1927; rpr. New York, 1966.

Bruner, Jerome, and Leo Postman. "Perception, Cognition, and Behavior." In *Perception and Personality: A Symposium*, edited by Jerome Bruner and David Krech. Durham, 1949.

Bruner, Jerome, Jacqueline Goodnow, and George Austin. *A Study of Thinking*. New York, 1956.

Bruss, Elizabeth. *Autobiographical Acts: The Changing Situation of a Literary Genre*. Baltimore, 1977.

Bucke, Richard M. *Walt Whitman*. 1883; rpr. New York, 1970.

Buell, Lawrence. *Literary Transcendentalism*. Ithaca, 1973.

Burke, Kenneth. *A Grammar of Motives*. New York, 1945.

———. *Language as Symbolic Action*. Berkeley, 1966.

———. *The Philosophy of Literary Form*. Baton Rouge, 1941.

———. "Policy Made Personal: Whitman's Verse and Prose-Salient Traits." In *Leaves of Grass: One Hundred After*, edited by Milton Hindus. Stanford, 1955.

———. *A Rhetoric of Motives*. 1950; rpr. Berkeley, 1969.

Burroughs, John. *Notes on Walt Whitman as Poet and Person*. 1867; rpr. New York, 1971.

Campbell, B. G. "Toward a Workable Taxonomy of Illocutionary Forces and Its Implication to Works of Imaginative Literature." *Language and Style*, VIII (1975), 3–20.

Campbell, Paul. "Poetic-Rhetorical, Philosophical, and Scientific Discourse." *Philosophy & Rhetoric*, VI (1973), 1–29.

Carpenter, Ronald. "The Essential Schemes of Syntax: An Analysis of Rhetorical Theory's Recommendations for Uncommon Word Orders." *Quarterly Journal of Speech*, LV (1969), 161–68.

BIBLIOGRAPHY

Cassirer, Ernst. *The Philosophy of Symbolic Forms.* Translated by Ralph Manheim. Vol. I. New Haven, 1953.

Catel, Jean. *Rhythme et Langage dans la l^r Edition Des "Leaves of Grass."* Paris, 1930.

Chase, Richard. *Walt Whitman Reconsidered.* New York, 1955.

Corman, Cid. *Word for Word: Essays on the Arts of Language.* Santa Barbara, 1977.

Coy, Rebecca. "A Study of Whitman's Diction." *Texas Studies in English,* XVI (1936), 115–24.

Crawley, Thomas Edward. *The Structure of Leaves of Grass.* Austin, 1970.

Croll, Morris. "The Cadence of English Oratorical Prose." In *Style, Rhetoric, and Rhythm: Essays by Morris Croll,* edited by Max Patrick and Robert Evans. Princeton, 1966.

Crystal, David. *The English Tone of Voice: Essays in Intonation, Prosody, and Para-Language.* London, 1975.

Crystal, David, and Derek Davy. *Investigating English Style.* Bloomington, 1969.

Culler, Jonathan. "On Trope and Persuasion." *New Literary History,* IX (1978), 607–618.

———. *Structuralist Poetics.* Ithaca, 1975.

Daiches, David. "Walt Whitman: Impressionist Prophet." In *Leaves of Grass: One Hundred Years After,* edited by Milton Hindus. Stanford, 1955.

DeMan, Paul. "The Rhetoric of Temporality." In *Interpretation: Theory and Practice,* edited by Charles Singleton. Baltimore, 1969.

DeVito, Joseph. "Levels of Abstraction in Spoken and Written Language." *Journal of Communication,* XVII (1967), 354–61.

Dillon, George. *Language Processing and the Reading of Literature.* Bloomington, 1978.

Eaves, Morris. "Romantic Expressive Theory and Blake's Idea of the Audience." *Publications of the Modern Language Association of America,* XCV (1980), 784–801.

Eby, Edwin. *A Concordance of Walt Whitman's "Leaves of Grass" and Selected Prose Writings.* Seattle, 1949–1955.

Eco, Umberto. *The Role of the Reader: Explorations in the Semiotics of Texts.* Bloomington, 1979.

Emerson, Ralph Waldo. *The Journal and Miscellaneous Notebooks of Ralph Waldo Emerson.* Vol. I, edited by William Gilman, *et al.* Cambridge, 1960.

———. "Poetry and Imagination" and "Eloquence." In *Letters and Social Aims.* Boston, 1877.

Enkvist, Nils. *Linguistics and Style.* London, 1964.

Erkkila, Betsy. *Walt Whitman Among the French.* Princeton, 1980.

Everson, William. *American Bard: By Walt Whitman. The Original Preface to Leaves of Grass Arranged in Verse by William Everson.* New York, 1982.

261

BIBLIOGRAPHY

Fanto, James. "Speech Act Theory and Its Applications to the Study of Literature." In *The Sign: Semiotics Around the World*, edited by R. W. Bailey, L. Matejka, and P. Steiner. Michigan Slavic Publications, No. 9. Ann Arbor, 1978.
Fiedler, Leslie. *No! In Thunder: Essays on Myth and Literature*. Boston, 1960.
———. "The Unbroken Tradition." In *Theories of American Literature*, edited by Donald Kartiganer and Malcolm Griffith. New York, 1972.
Finkel, William. "Walt Whitman's Manuscript Notes on Oratory." *American Literature*, XXII (1950), 29–53.
Fish, Stanley. "How to Do Things with Austin and Searle: Speech Act Theory and Literary Criticism." *Modern Language Notes*, XCI (1976), 983–1025.
———. "What Is Stylistics and Why Are They Saying Such Terrible Things About It?" In *Approaches to Poetics*, edited by Seymour Chatman. New York, 1973.
Forrey, Robert. "Whitman's 'Real Grammar': A Structuralist Approach." *Walt Whitman Review*, XXVII (1981), 14–24.
Foucault, Michel. *The Archaeology of Knowledge*. New York, 1972.
———. *Language, Counter-Memory, Practice*. Ithaca, 1977.
———. *The Order of Things: An Archaeology of the Human Sciences*. London, 1970.
Fowler, Roger. "Literature as Discourse." In *Communication and Understanding*, edited by Godfrey Vesey. Royal Institute of Philosophy Lectures, No. 10. Sussex, 1977.
Fowler, Roger, et al. *Language and Control*. London, 1979.
Fraser, Bruce. "Hedged Performatives." In *Syntax and Semantics, III: Speech Acts*, edited by P. Cole and J. Morgan. New York, 1975.
Frenkel-Brunswick, Else. "Intolerance of Ambiguity as an Emotional and Perceptual Personality Variable." In *Perception and Personality: A Symposium*, edited by Jerome Bruner and David Krech. Durham, 1949.
Freud, Sigmund. *The Basic Writings of Sigmund Freud*. Translated by A. A. Brill. New York, 1938.
Frye, Northrop. *Anatomy of Criticism: Four Essays*. Princeton, 1957.
———. *The Well-Tempered Critic*. Bloomington, 1963.
Gelley, Alexander. "Metonymy, Schematism, and the Space of Literature." *New Literary History*, XI (1980), 469–87.
Gelpi, Albert. *The Tenth Muse: The Psyche of the American Poet*. Cambridge, 1975.
Genette, Gérard. *Figures of Literary Discourse*. Translated by Alan Sheridan. Introduction by Marie-Rose Logan. New York, 1982.
———. "La Rhetorique Restreinte" and "Metonymie chez Proust." In *Figures III*. Paris, 1972.
Gilman, Albert, and Roger Brown. "Personality and Style in Concord." In

262

BIBLIOGRAPHY

Transcendentalism and Its Legacy, edited by Myron Simon and Thornton Parsons. Ann Arbor, 1966.

Ginsberg, Allen. "Interviewed by Allen Young." In *Gay Sunshine Interviews*, Vol. I, edited by Winston Leyland. San Francisco, 1978.

Givón, Talmy. "Negation in Language: Pragmatics, Function, Ontology." In *Syntax and Semantics, IX: Pragmatics*, edited by Peter Cole. New York, 1978.

Goldstein, Kenneth, and Sheldon Blackman. *Cognitive Style*. New York, 1978.

Gross, Harvey. *Sound and Form in Modern Poetry*. Ann Arbor, 1964.

Group μ. *A General Rhetoric*. Translated by Paul Burrell and Edgar Slotkin. Baltimore, 1981.

Hale, Edward Everett. "Edward Everett Hale's Review." In *Walt Whitman: The Critical Heritage*, edited by Milton Hindus. New York, 1971.

Hall, Robert. "Literature as Speech-Event." *Dieciocho*, III (1980), 87–96.

Hancher, Michael. "Beyond a Speech-Act Theory of Literary Discourse." *Modern Language Notes*, XCII (1977), 1081–1098.

———. "The Classification of Cooperative Illocutionary Acts." *Language and Society*, VIII (1979), 1–14.

———. "Understanding Poetic Speech Acts." *College English*, XXXVI (1975), 632–39.

———, ed. "Speech Acts and Literature." Papers and recorded discussion of a forum: panelists Stanley Fish, Barbara Herrnstein Smith, Martin Steinmann, E. D. Hirsch. *Centrum*, III (1975).

Harding, D. W. *Words into Rhythm: English Speech Rhythm in Verse and Prose*. The Clark Lectures. Cambridge, Eng., 1976.

Hawkes, Terence. *Structuralism and Semiotics*. Berkeley, 1977.

Heidegger, Martin. *On the Way to Language*. New York, 1971.

Henry, Albert. *Métonymie et Métaphore*. Paris, 1971.

Hiatt, Mary. *Artful Balance: The Parallel Structures in Style*. New York, 1975.

Hirsch, E. D. *The Philosophy of Composition*. Chiago, 1977.

Holloway, John. "Appendix 2: Logic, feeling, and structure in nineteenth century political oratory; a primer of analysis." In *Narrative and Structure*. Cambridge, Eng., 1979.

Holzman, Philip, and George Klein. "Cognitive System—Principles of Leveling and Sharpening." *Journal of Psychology*, XXXVII (1954), 105–122.

Hosek, Chaviva. "The Rhetoric of Whitman's 1855 Preface to *Leaves of Grass*." *Walt Whitman Review*, XXV (1979), 163–73.

Hrushovski, Benjamin. "On Free Rhythms in Modern Poetry." In *Style in Language*, edited by Thomas Sebeok. Cambridge, 1960.

Hudson, Derek. *Martin Tupper: His Rise and Fall*. London, 1949.

Hunt, Russell. "Whitman's Poetics and the Unity of 'Calamus.'" *American Literature*, XLVI (1975), 482–94.

263

BIBLIOGRAPHY

Hyde, Michael. "Jacques Lacan's Psychoanalytic Theory of Speech and Language." *Quarterly Journal of Speech*, LXVI (1980), 96–108.
Jakobson, Roman. "Closing Statement: Linguistics and Poetics." In *Style in Language*, edited by Thomas Sebeok. Cambridge, 1960.
———. "Grammatical Parallelism and Its Russian Facet." *Language*, XLII (1966), 399–428.
———. "Poetry of Grammar and Grammar of Poetry." *Lingua*, XXI (1968), 597–609.
Jakobson, Roman, and Morris Halle. *Fundamentals of Language*. The Hague, 1956.
Jameson, Frederic. *The Prison-House of Language*. Princeton, 1972.
———. "Wyndham Lewis as a Futurist." *Hudson Review*, XXVI (1973), 295–329.
Jarrell, Randall. "Walt Whitman: He Had His Nerve." *Kenyon Review*, XIV (1952), 63–71.
Jellicorse, John. "The Poet as Persuader: A Rhetorical Explication of the Life and Writings of Walt Whitman." Ph.D. dissertation, Northwestern University, 1967.
Jespersen, Otto. *Negation in English and Other Languages*. Copenhagen, 1917.
Johnston, Kenneth, and John Rees. "Whitman and the Foo-Foos: An Experiment in Language." *Walt Whitman Review*, XVII (1971), 3–10.
Kanjo, Eugene. "Time and Eternity in 'Crossing Brooklyn Ferry.'" *Walt Whitman Review*, XVIII (1972), 82–90.
Kinkead-Weekes, Mark. "Walt Whitman Passes the Full-Stop By . . ." In *An English Miscellany: Presented to W. S. Mackie*, edited by Brian Lee. London, 1977.
Kinneavy, James. *A Theory of Discourse: The Aims of Discourse*. Englewood Cliffs, 1971.
Kiparsky, Paul. "The Role of Linguistics in a Theory of Poetry." *Daedalus*, CII (1973), 231–44.
Klein, Ernest. *A Comprehensive Etymological Dictionary of the English Language*. 2 vols. New York, 1966.
Klein, George. *Perception, Motives, and Personality*. New York, 1970.
———. "The Personal World Through Perception." In *Perception: An Approach to Personality*, edited by Robert Blake and Glenn Ramsey. New York, 1951.
Klein, George, and Herbert Schlesinger. "Where Is the Perceiver in Perceptive Theory?" In *Perception and Personality: A Symposium*, edited by Jerome Bruner and David Krech. Durham, 1949.
Klima, Edward. "Negation in English." In *The Structure of Language*, edited by Jerry Fodor and Jerrold Katz. Englewood Cliffs, 1964.
Kress, Gunther, and Robert Hodge. *Language as Ideology*. London, 1979.

BIBLIOGRAPHY

Krieger, Murray. *The Play and Place of Criticism.* Baltimore, 1967.
Kummings, Donald. "Whitman's Voice in 'Song of Myself': From Private to Public." *Walt Whitman Review,* XVII (1971), 10–15.
Kurrick, Maire. *Literature and Negation.* New York, 1979.
Laferrière, Daniel. *Sign and Subject: Semiotic and Psychoanalytic Investigations into Poetry.* Lisse, 1978.
———. "Similarity and Contiguity Processes in the Dream-Work." *Sub-stance,* III (1972), 39–52.
Lasswell, Harold. *Language of Politics.* New York, 1949.
Leach, Edmund. *Culture and Communication.* Cambridge, Eng., 1976.
Leech, Geoffrey. *English in Advertising.* London, 1966.
———. *A Linguistic Guide to English Poetry.* London, 1969.
———. "Linguistics and the Figures of Rhetoric." In *Linguistic and Critical Approaches to Literary Style.* New York, 1966.
———. *Semantics.* Penguin, 1974.
Le Guern, Michel. *Sémantique de la Métaphore et de la Métonymie.* Paris, 1972.
Lemaire, Anika. *Jacques Lacan.* Translated by David Macey. London, 1977.
Levenston, Edward. "Metaphor, Speech Act and Grammatical Form." *Poetics,* V (1976), 373–81.
———. "Speech and/or Writing: Lyric Poetry and the Media of Language." *PTL,* IV (1979), 451–74.
Levin, Samuel. "Concerning What Kind of Speech Act a Poem Is." In *Pragmatics of Language and Literature.* New York, 1976.
———. "On Meaning and Truth in the Interpretation of Poetry." *Poetics,* VII (1978), 339–50.
———. *The Semantics of Metaphor.* Baltimore, 1977.
Lodge, David. *The Modes of Modern Writing: Metaphor, Metonymy, and the Typology of Modern Literature.* Ithaca, 1977.
Lynen, John. *The Design of the Present.* New Haven, 1969.
McAuley, James. "The Rhetoric of Australian Poetry." *Southerly* (March, 1976), 3–23.
McElderry, Bruce. "Personae in Whitman (1855–1860)." In *Whitman in Our Season,* edited by B. Bernard Cohen. Hartford, 1971.
Mack, Dorothy. "Metaphoring as Speech Act: Some Happiness Conditions for Implied Similes and Simple Metaphors." *Poetics,* IV (1975), 221–56.
McWilliams, Wilson. *The Idea of Fraternity in America.* Berkeley, 1973.
Male, Roy. "Whitman's Radical Utterance." In *Style in the American Renaissance,* edited by Carl Strauch. Hartford, 1970.
Mandelstam, Osip. *Mandelstam: The Complete Critical Prose and Letters,* edited by Jane Gray Harris and Constance Link. Ann Arbor, 1979.
Marcuse, Herbert. *Negations: Essays in Critical Theory.* Boston, 1968.
———. "The New Sensibility." In *An Essay on Liberation.* Boston, 1969.

BIBLIOGRAPHY

Martinich, A. P. "Sacraments and Speech Acts." *Heythrop Journal*, XVI (1975), 289–303, 405–417.

Matthiessen, F. O. *American Renaissance*. New York, 1940.

Merrell, Floyd. "Metaphor and Metonymy: A Key to Narrative Structure." *Language and Style*, XI (1978), 146–63.

Miles, Josephine. *Style and Proportion: The Language of Prose and Poetry*. Boston, 1967.

Mill, John Stuart. "What Is Poetry?" In *Literary Essays*, edited by Edward Alexander. Indianapolis, 1967.

Miller, Edwin. *Walt Whitman's Poetry: A Psychological Journey*. New York, 1968.

Miller, F. DeWolfe. "The Partitive Studies of 'Song of Myself.'" In *Whitman in Our Season*, edited by B. Bernard Cohen. Hartford, 1971.

————. "Whitman's 16.4 Diary." *American Book Collector*, IX (May, 1961), 21–24.

Miller, J. Hillis. "The Fiction of Realism: *Sketches by Boz*, *Oliver Twist*, and Cruikshank's Illustrations." In *Dickens Centennial Essays*, edited by Ada Nisbet and Blake Nevius. Berkeley, 1971.

Miller, James, Jr. *The American Quest for a Supreme Fiction: Whitman's Legacy in the Personal Epic*. Chicago, 1979.

————. *A Critical Guide to Leaves of Grass*. Chicago, 1957.

Milosz, Czeslaw. *The Captive Mind*. New York, 1955.

Mirsky, D. "Poet of American Democracy." In *Walt Whitman Abroad*, edited by Gay Wilson Allen. Syracuse, 1955.

Mitchell, Roger. "A Prosody for Whitman?" *Publications of the Modern Language Association of America*, LXXXIV (1969), 1606–1612.

————. "Towards a System of Grammatical Scansion." *Language and Style*, III (1970), 3–28.

Molinoff, Katherine. *Some Notes on Whitman's Family*. Monograph. New York, 1941.

Mukařovsky, Jan. "Intentionality and Unintentionality in Art." In *Structure, Sign, and Function*, edited, with introduction, by Peter Steiner. New Haven, 1978.

————. "Standard Language and Poetic Language." In *Linguistics and Literary Style*, edited by Donald Freeman. New York, 1970.

————. *The World and Verbal Art*. Translated and edited by John Burbank and Peter Steiner, with foreword by René Wellek. New Haven, 1977.

Norton, Charles Eliot. "Review of *Leaves of Grass*." In *Walt Whitman: The Critical Heritage*, edited by Milton Hindus. New York, 1971.

Nöth, Winfried. "The Semiotic Framework of Textlinguistics." In *Current Trends in Textlinguistics*, edited by Wolfgang Dressler. New York, 1978.

Ohmann, Richard. "Instrumental Style: Notes on the Theory of Speech as Action." In *Current Trends in Stylistics*, edited by Braj Kachru and Herbert Stahlke. Edmonton, Can., 1972.

————. "Literature as Act." In *Approaches to Poetics*, edited by Seymour Chatman. New York, 1973.

————. *Shaw: The Style and the Man*. Middletown, 1962.

————. "Speech, Action, and Style." In *Literary Style: A Symposium*, edited by Seymour Chatman. New York, 1971.

————. "Speech Acts and the Definition of Literature." *Philosophy & Rhetoric*, IV (1971), 1–19.

————. "Speech, Literature and the Space Between." *New Literary History*, V (1974), 37–63.

Osterwalder, Hans. *T. S. Eliot: Between Metaphor and Metonymy*. Zurich, 1978.

Pelc, Jerzy. *Studies in Functional Logical Semiotics of Natural Language*. The Hague, 1971.

Perelman, Chaim, and L. Olbrechts-Tyteca. *The New Rhetoric*. Notre Dame, 1969.

Perry, Bliss. *Walt Whitman: His Life and Work*. Boston, 1906.

Peters, Robert. "Walt Whitman: Verbal Musculature and Concealed Kinetics." In *The Great American Poetry Bake-Off*. Metuchen, 1979.

Pratt, Mary Louise. "The Ideology of Speech-Act Theory." *Centrum*, New Ser., I (1981), 5–18.

————. *Toward a Speech Act Theory of Literary Discourse*. Bloomington, 1977.

Rajasekharaiah, T. R. *The Roots of Whitman's Grass*. Rutherford, 1970.

Ray, Roberta. "The Role of the Orator in the Philosophy of Ralph Waldo Emerson." *Speech Monographs*, XLI (1974), 215–25.

Read, Herbert. *The True Voice of Feeling: Studies in English Romantic Poetry*. New York, 1953.

Reid, Alfred. "Emerson's Prose Style: An Edge to Goodness." In *Style in the American Renaissance*, edited by Carl Strauch. Hartford, 1970.

Reiss, Edmund. "Whitman's Debt to Animal Magnetism." *Publications of the Modern Language Association of America*, LXXVIII (1963), 80–88.

Rice, Donald. "Catastrop(h)es: The Morphogenesis of Metaphor, Metonymy, Synecdoche, and Irony." *Sub-stance*, XXVI (1980), 3–18.

Ricoeur, Paul. *The Rule of Metaphor*. Translated by Robert Czerny, Kathleen McLaughlin, and John Costello. Toronto, 1977.

Romano, John. *Dickens and Reality*. Guilford, 1978.

Rosenberg, Bruce. *The Art of the American Folk Preacher*. New York, 1970.

Ross, Donald. "Emerson's Stylistic Influence on Whitman." *American Transcendental Quarterly*, XXV (1975), 41–51.

Rossetti, William Michael. *The Diary of W. M. Rossetti, 1870–1873*, edited by Odette Bornard. Oxford, 1977.

Rubin, Joseph Jay. *The Historic Whitman*. University Park, Pa., 1973.

BIBLIOGRAPHY

Ruegg, Maria. "Metaphor and Metonymy: The Logic of Structuralist Rhetoric." *Glyph*, VI (1979), 141–57.

Ruhl, Charles. "Pragmatic Metonymy." In *Second LACUS Forum 1975*, edited by Peter Reich. Columbia, S.C., 1976.

Sarrazin, Gabriel. "Walt Whitman." In *In Re Walt Whitman*. Philadelphia, 1893.

Schofer, Peter, and Donald Rice. "Metaphor, Metonymy, and Synecdoche Revis(it)ed." *Semiotica*, XXI (1977), 121–49.

Searle, John. *Expression and Meaning: Studies in the Theory of Speech Acts*. Cambridge, Eng., 1979.

———. *Speech Acts*. London, 1969.

See, Fred. "The Demystification of Style: Metaphoric and Metonymic Language in a Modern Instance." *Nineteenth Century Fiction*, XXVIII (1974), 379–403.

Selincourt, Basil de. *Walt Whitman: A Critical Study*. London, 1914.

Shapiro, Karl. "Is Poetry an American Art?" *College English*, XXV (1964), 395–405.

Shephard, Esther. "An Inquiry into Whitman's Method of Turning Prose into Poetry." *Modern Language Quarterly*, XIV (1953), 43–59.

———. *Walt Whitman's Pose*. New York, 1938.

Sinclair, J. McH., and R. M. Coulthard. *Toward an Analysis of Discourse*. London, 1975.

Smith, Barbara Herrnstein. *On the Margins of Discourse*. Chicago, 1978.

———. *Poetic Closure*. Chicago, 1968.

Stich, Alexandr. "Persuasive Style: Its Relation to Technical and Artistic Styles." *Journal of Literary Semantics*, II (1973), 65–77.

Stovall, Floyd. *The Foreground of Leaves of Grass*. Charlottesville, 1974.

Strom, Susan. "'Face to Face': Whitman's Biblical References in 'Crossing Brooklyn Ferry.'" *Walt Whitman Review*, XXIV (1978), 7–16.

Sutton, Walter. *American Free Verse*. New York, 1973.

Traubel, Horace. *With Walt Whitman in Camden*. Vol. I of 5 vols. Boston, 1906.

Traugott, Elizabeth. "Generative Semantics and the Concept of Literary Discourse." *Journal of Literary Semantics*, II (1973), 5–22.

Travis, Charles. *Saying and Understanding: A Generative Theory of Illocutions*. Oxford, 1975.

Tufte, Virginia. *Grammar as Style*. New York, 1971.

Tupper, Martin. *Proverbial Philosophy*. Boston, 1850.

Tyler, Stephen. *The Said and the Unsaid*. New York, 1978.

Ullmann, Stephen. *Language and Style*. New York, 1964.

———. "Style and Personality." *Review of English Literature*, VI (1965), 21–31.

BIBLIOGRAPHY

————. *Style in the French Novel.* Oxford, 1964.

Updike, John. "Walt Whitman: Ego and Art." *New York Review of Books,* February 9, 1978, pp. 33–36.

Van Egmond, Peter. "Walt Whitman's Study of Oratory and Uses of It in Leaves of Grass." Ph.D. dissertation, University of North Carolina at Chapel Hill, 1967.

Waldron, R. A. "Metonymic Transfer." In *Sense and Sense Development.* London, 1979.

Waskow, Howard. *Walt Whitman: Explorations in Form.* Chicago, 1966.

Waugh, Linda. "The Poetic Function in the Theory of Roman Jakobson." *Poetics Today,* II (1980), 57–82.

Weathers, Winston. "The Rhetoric of the Series." In *Contemporary Essays on Style,* edited by Glen Love. Glenview, Ill., 1969.

Weaver, Richard. *Language Is Sermonic.* Baton Rouge, 1970.

Wellek, René, and Austin Warren. *Theory of Literature.* 1949; rpr. New York, 1963.

Wells, Rulon. "Metonymy and Misunderstanding: An Aspect of Language Change." In *Current Issues in Linguistic Theory,* edited by Roger Cole. Bloomington, 1977.

————. "Nominal and Verbal Style." In *Linguistics and Literary Style,* edited by Donald Freeman. New York, 1970.

Werth, Paul. "Roman Jakobson's Verbal Analysis of Poetry." *Journal of Linguistics,* XII (1976), 21–73.

Whitman, Walt. *American Primer.* Edited, with introduction, by Horace Traubel. Boston, 1904.

————. *The Correspondence of Walt Whitman.* Edited, with introductions and notes, by Edwin Miller. 5 vols. New York, 1961–1969.

————. *Daybooks and Notebooks.* Edited by William White. 3 vols. New York, 1978.

————. *An 1855–56 Notebook Toward the Second Edition of Leaves of Grass.* Edited, with introduction, by Harold Blodgett. Carbondale, 1959.

————. *The Eighteenth Presidency!* Edited, with introduction, by Edward Grier. Lawrence, Kans., 1956.

————. *Faint Clews & Indirections.* Edited by Clarence Gohdes and Rollo Silver. Durham, 1949.

————. *In Re Walt Whitman.* Philadelphia, 1893.

————. *Leaves of Grass (Comprehensive Reader's Edition).* Edited, with introduction and notes, by Harold Blodgett and Scully Bradley. New York, 1965.

————. *Leaves of Grass (1855 Edition).* Edited, with introduction, by Malcolm Cowley. New York, 1959.

————. *Leaves of Grass (Facsimile Edition of the 1860 Text).* Edited, with introduction, by Roy Harvey Pearce. Ithaca, 1961.

BIBLIOGRAPHY

————. *Leaves of Grass: A Textual Variorum of the Printed Poems.* Edited by Scully Bradley *et al.* 3 vols. New York, 1980.
————. *Notes and Fragments.* Edited by R. M. Bucke. In *Complete Writings of Walt Whitman,* IX. New York, 1902.
————. *Prose Works 1892.* Edited by Floyd Stovall. 2 vols. New York, 1963–1964.
————. *The Uncollected Poetry and Prose.* Edited by Emory Holloway. 2 vols. 1921; rpr. New York, 1932.
————. "Walt Whitman and Oratory." Edited by Thomas Harned. In *Complete Writings of Walt Whitman,* VIII. New York, 1902.
————. *Walt Whitman of the New York Aurora.* Edited by J. J. Rubin and C. H. Brown. State College, Pa., 1950.
————. *Walt Whitman's Blue Book.* Vol. I: Facsimile; Vol. II: Textual Analysis by Arthur Golden. New York, 1968.
————. *Walt Whitman's Workshop.* Edited, with introduction and notes, by Clifton Furness. 1928; rpr. New York, 1964.
Whorf, Benjamin. *Language, Thought and Reality.* Edited by John Carroll. Cambridge, 1956.
Wicker, Brian. *The Story-Shaped World.* Notre Dame, 1975.
Widdowson, H. G. "On the Deviance of Literary Discourse." *Style,* VI (1972), 294–308.
Wiley, Autrey. "Re-iterative Devices in Leaves of Grass." *American Literature,* I (1929), 161–70.
Williams, William Carlos. "An Essay on Leaves of Grass." In *Leaves of Grass: One Hundred Years After,* edited by Milton Hindus. Stanford, 1955.
Wimsatt, W. K. *The Prose Style of Samuel Johnson.* New Haven, 1941.
Winterowd, W. Ross. *Rhetoric: A Synthesis.* New York, 1968.
————. "The Rhetoric of Beneficence, Authority, Ethical Commitment, and the Negative." *Philosophy & Rhetoric,* IX (1976), 65–83.
Wright, George. "The Lyric Present: Simple Present Verbs in English Poems." *Publications of the Modern Language Association of America,* LXXXIX (1974), 563–79.
Wrobel, Arthur. "Whitman and the Phrenologists: The Divine Body and Sensuous Soul." *Publications of the Modern Language Association of America,* LXXXIX (1974), 17–23.
Zirmunskij, V. M. "On Rhythmic Prose." In *To Honor Roman Jakobson,* III. The Hague, 1967.

Index

There are no entries for Walt Whitman nor for "Song of Myself," for there would be too many references to be of any service to the reader.

INDEX

INDEX